Education Studies

Written specifically for students on Education Studies degree courses, yet also relevant for students on teacher training courses, *Education Studies: A Student's Guide* introduces a wide range of topics and issues, from knowledge and learning, policy and schooling to the ways in which education is a force for change across the globe.

Specific topics include:

- The global dimension in the curriculum
- Cultural and religious plurality in education
- Education for sustainability
- The effective teacher
- Gender and educational achievement
- Special educational needs inclusion in mainstream schools
- Information and communication technology and learning for the future
- Language, power and education.

With chapter summaries, questions for discussion and reflection, and suggestions for further reading, *Education Studies: A Student's Guide* will be a valuable source for all students of Education Studies as well as BEd and PGCE students.

Stephen Ward is Head of Education and Childhood Studies at Bath Spa University where he formerly ran the undergraduate teacher training degree and now leads the Education Studies course.

Education Studies

A Student's Guide

Edited by
Stephen Ward

RoutledgeFalmer
Taylor & Francis Group

LONDON AND NEW YORK

First published 2004
by RoutledgeFalmer
11 New Fetter Lane, London EC4P 4EE

Simultaneously published in the USA and Canada
by RoutledgeFalmer
29 West 35th Street, New York, NY10001

RoutledgeFalmer is an imprint of the Taylor & Francis Group

© 2004 Selection and editorial matter Stephen Ward, individual chapters the
contributors

Typeset in Bembo by
HWA Text and Data Management, Tunbridge Wells
Printed and bound in Great Britain by
TJ International Ltd, Padstow, Cornwall

British Library Cataloguing in Publication Data
A catalogue record for this book is available from the British Library

Library of Congress Cataloging in Publication Data
A catalog record for this book has been requested

ISBN 0–415–32118–2 (hbk)
ISBN 0–415–32119–0 (pbk)

Contents

Part II: Teaching, educational settings and policy

Part III: Knowledge, learning and the curriculum

Illustrations

Figures

Tables

Contributors

All contributors lecture in Education Studies at Bath Spa University.

June Bianchi is Senior Lecturer in Art Education, art educational consultant and multimedia artist. She initially worked in community arts education and performance, fashion and costume design and ceramics. She taught art and design in primary, secondary, further and higher education, guest lecturing in art education and visual culture at British and European universities. She has published articles on art education and has extensively exhibited her artwork.

Andy Bord is Senior Lecturer in Education. He is a former primary and deputy head-teacher and taught for two years in Hong Kong. He works on the Postgraduate Certificate in Education (PGCE) course and in Education Studies modules on effective teaching and humanities education. He has published articles on the experiences of undergraduate students in a Global Futures course. His current research interest is in education for sustainable development.

David Coulby is Head of International Activities. In Education Studies he teaches a module on Education and Europe. He is the joint Series Editor for the *World Yearbooks of Education* and author and editor of many books on educational topics. His most recent books are *Beyond the National Curriculum* and (with Crispin Jones) *Education and Warfare in Europe*. He is currently working on a volume on *Globalisation, Nationalism and Education*.

Denise Cush is Professor of Religion and Education and Head of the Study of Religions. She has taught religious studies at school and university levels, and primary and secondary religious education in teacher education courses. She teaches a module on religious and cultural pluralism in education. She has published on religion and education; her best known book is *Buddhism*. She is currently co-writing a dictionary of Buddhism, co-editing an encyclopaedia of Hinduism and researching the interest of teenage girls in witchcraft.

Dan Davies is Primary PGCE Programme Leader and Senior Lecturer in Primary Science and Design and Technology Education. He has taught in primary schools in South London, worked for the Design Council as an education officer and lectured in primary science at Goldsmiths College. He is the author of numerous articles and conference papers, and joint author of *Primary Design and Technology for the Future: Creativity, Culture and Citizenship* and *Teaching Science and Design and Technology* with Alan Howe.

Christine Eden is Head of Research in the School of Education and a sociologist with a long-standing interest in inequalities in society. Her research interests are in gender, educational achievement and the workplace. She teaches modules on debates in education, gender inequalities and research. She has written on the nature of gendered subjects and the formation of gender identities within the classroom and playground.

Howard Gibson is Senior Lecturer in Education. He was formally a lecturer in political philosophy at various universities and was born again as a primary teacher. He became interested in English, acted as a Head of Department in school and then as county advisor. He returned to higher education as a specialist in language and literacy. He enjoys making connections between politics and language and teaches and writes about it.

Meg Gomersall is Senior Lecturer in History Education. Before coming to teacher education she was a primary school teacher in London. She is a professional tutor in the PGCE course and runs the Graduate Teacher Programme. In Education Studies she teaches a module on the humanities in education. Her PhD thesis was on the education of working-class girls and she has published on history education, including the book *Working-Class Girls in Nineteenth-Century England: Life, Work and Schooling*.

Malcolm Hanson is Senior Lecturer in Mathematics Education. He is a former secondary school teacher and was Head of Mathematics in a large comprehensive school. He has worked in teacher education on undergraduate and postgraduate courses at both primary and secondary levels. In Education Studies he teaches a module on learning in mathematics.

Susan Haywood teaches Information and Communication Technology (ICT) in Education. She has a background in primary education and has worked in two Local Education Authorities (LEAs) providing ICT support to teachers. She teaches a module on learning in ICT, which addresses theoretical and pedagogical aspects of the use of new technologies in education. She has co-authored books on professional issues in primary education and practice in the foundation stage.

David Hicks is Professor in the School of Education and is internationally known for his work on the need for a global and futures perspective in the curriculum. He teaches modules on education for change, citizenship education for the future, education and environment and radical education. His most recent book is *Lessons for the Future: The Missing Dimension in Education.*

Alan Howe is Senior Lecturer in Education. He taught in primary schools in Hertfordshire, Harrow, Bristol and Bath. He teaches modules on learning in science and teaching creatively with new technologies. He has published books and articles on teaching design and technology and science in primary schools, including *Teaching Science and Design and Technology in the Early Years* with Dan Davies. His current research interests are in creativity across the curriculum.

Mim Hutchings is Senior Lecturer in Education, Language and Literacy in undergraduate, PGCE and professional development courses. She draws on her experience in early years, primary, secondary and special school teaching, mainly in multilingual classrooms and as an adviser for special educational needs. She has lectured at the University of Plymouth and University of the West of England. She is currently an Education Doctorate student at the University of Bristol.

Karen McInnes is Senior Lecturer in Early Years Education. She is a qualified speech and language therapist and has worked as a nursery teacher and early years co-ordinator in London and Bristol schools. She teaches early years modules in Education Studies and the PGCE and runs the SureStart Early Years Foundation Degree. She has written on early years and is currently co-authoring a book on early childhood with Jill Williams.

Stephen Ward is Head of Education and Childhood Studies and ran the Undergraduate Teacher Training Degree. He is a former primary and secondary school teacher and taught English as an additional language in Leeds. He has edited *The Primary Core National Curriculum* and *Teaching Music in the Primary School*. His current research is in the experiences of Education Studies students in the PGCE teacher training course.

Jill Williams is Senior Lecturer in Early Years, organising and teaching courses for undergraduates, postgraduates and teachers in professional development. She has travelled widely and used her experiences and observations of children in other cultures to support her work with students. Her publications include *Promoting Independent Learning in the Primary School* and, a title in progress, *Time to be a Child* with Karen McInnes.

Heather Williamson moved into teacher training after a period as Head of Department in a secondary school. Formerly Assistant Dean of the Faculty of Education and Human Sciences, she has taught philosophy to students studying for degrees in Education, Study of Religions and Social Sciences. Her research interests are in applied philosophy. She has written on moral and political philosophy.

Kay Wood is Principal Lecturer in Education. She has taught in secondary schools and was a researcher for the Teacher Education Project at Exeter University. She currently teaches modules on education in the USA and the Pacific Rim. She is interested in education policy and is researching the diversification of secondary education in England, particularly in relation to city academies.

Acknowledgements

The ideas in these chapters were tried out with Education Studies students at Bath Spa University. The editor and contributors are grateful to them. We learned from their enthusiastic and critical responses and they were the inspiration for this book.

Figure 2.1 is reproduced with permission from G. Pike and D. Selby, *Reconnecting: From National to Global Curriculum*, Godalming: WWF–UK, 1996. Figure 12.1 is reproduced with permission from S. Askew and E. Carnell, *Transforming Learning: Individual and Global Change*, London: Cassell, 1998.

Abbreviations

ACCAC	Qualifications, Curriculum and Assessment Authority for Wales
AIDS	acquired immune deficiency syndrome
ALS	Additional Literacy Strategy
Becta	British Educational Communications and Technology Agency
CA	classroom assistant
CAP	common agricultural policy
CDA	critical discourse analysis
DE	development education
DEA	Development Education Association
DES	Department of Education and Science
DfEE	Department for Employment and Education
DfES	Department for Education and Skills
DfWP	Department for Work and Pensions
EE	environmental education
ESD	education for sustainable development
ESDGC	education for sustainable development and global citizenship
EU	European Union
GA	Geographical Association
GCE	General Certificate of Education
GCSE	General Certificate of Secondary Education
HMI	Her Majesty's Inspectorate
ICT	information and communications technology
IEA	International Association for the Evaluation of Educational Achievement
IEP	Individual Education Plan
IIGE	International Institute for Global Education
ILEA	Inner London Education Authority
ILS	Integrated Learning Systems
ITT	initial teacher training
JADE	*Journal of Art and Design Education*
LDCs	less developed countries

LEA	Local Education Authority
LMS	local management of schools
MPs	members of parliament
NACCCE	National Advisory Committee on Creative and Cultural Education
NATO	North Atlantic Treaty Organisation
NGO	non-governmental organisation
NLS	National Literacy Strategy
NNS	National Numeracy Strategy
OECD	Organisation for Economic Co-operation and Development
Ofsted	Office for Standards in Education
PGCE	Postgraduate Certificate in Education
PISA	Programme for International Student Assessment
QAA	Quality Assurance Agency
QCA	Qualifications and Curriculum Authority
RE	religious education
SACRE	Standing Advisory Council on Religious Education
SCAA	School Curriculum and Assessment Authority
SEN	special educational needs
SMSO	Survey of Mathematics and Science Opportunities
TEK	traditional ecological knowledge
TIMSS	Third International Mathematics and Science Study
TTA	Teacher Training Agency
UDHR	Universal Declaration of Human Rights
UK	United Kingdom
UN	United Nations
UNICEF	United Nations Children's Fund
USA	United States of America
WMS	western modern science
WTO	World Trade Organisation

Introduction

WHAT IS EDUCATION STUDIES?

Education Studies is an exciting subject which can help you to understand education as a powerful force for change across the globe. It is not teacher training, nor simply the *theory* of teaching, although some people choose to take it before going on to train as teachers. As future professionals they will have a critical analysis of what education is, how it works in different countries and cultures, and visions of what it might be in different futures. Teachers should be more than 'technicians' who simply know how to deliver a national curriculum in the ways prescribed by the government. The contributors to this book are committed to this deeper understanding of what education is about.

Some take Education Studies because they are thinking about teaching but haven't yet made a definite career decision. It is also for those who have a particular interest in the theory and practice of education, such as parents or school governors. Some choose to go on to other education careers such as administrators, researchers or advisers. But Education Studies can be a subject of pure academic interest without any particular vocational outcome. It has always been possible to study fine art or architecture without becoming a practising artist or an architect designing houses. You can study education simply because it is intellectually challenging and interesting.

Education has always been a part of university teacher training courses. However, the curriculum for initial teacher training (ITT) is now regulated by the Teacher Training Agency (TTA) through its *Standards for Qualified Teacher Status* (Department for Education and Skills [DfES], TTA, 2002). Some universities have chosen to separate Education Studies from teacher training in order to allow students a wider experience of educational ideas, processes and policies than those required to meet the TTA standards. It has grown to become a popular subject in undergraduate degree courses.

WHAT DO YOU LEARN AS AN EDUCATION STUDENT?

It is sometimes argued that education isn't a proper subject, or 'an academic discipline in its own right' (Davies *et al.*, 2002) and there has long been discussion about the nature of educational theory. It is not a subject with its own method like physics or history. Instead, it draws on a range of subjects and disciplines and, as an education student, you will be learning psychology, sociology, history, philosophy, ethics, politics, economics, and international and global relations. To this long list we must add knowledge of at least some of the school curriculum subjects like English, mathematics, science or art.

Education Studies might be accused of *dabbling*: pinching little bits of knowledge from other subjects and patching them together, with no in-depth study of any of them. Rather than dabbling, I want to argue that Education Studies is a synthesis – a bringing together – of different disciplines and knowledge in order to understand education as it goes on now, what it can be in different situations or what it might become in different futures.

For example, to be able to understand children's learning of mathematics in schools we need to know something of the psychology of learning, but also to know about the nature of mathematics as a subject to know *what* they are learning. We would want to know about the pupils themselves, their different experiences as boys and girls, the diverse social cultural contexts of their backgrounds as learners and their experiences of social class, perhaps poverty and racism. Of course we should look at the nature of teaching in classrooms and the ways teachers and pupils interact with each other. But mathematics teaching in primary schools in England is now determined by the government's National Numeracy Strategy, which derives from teaching methods imported from Japan and Taiwan. The methods are urged on teachers as part of government policy to increase numeracy skills so the nation's workforce can compete in the global economy. But we also need to remember that the children are being educated to live in a culturally diverse society, with a range of ideologies and beliefs, and as citizens of the European Union. They need to learn that they are living on a globe which is full of potential for the educational and technological advances and the improvement of human rights, but is simultaneously threatened by human conflict and its own self-destruction.

So what looks to be a relatively simple matter, seven-year-olds learning place value in a school in Birmingham, spiders off into a range of possibilities and issues from individual psychology to international economics and global futures. A good education student is an expert in diversity, able to capture all that is involved in the rich picture. A good educator needs not just to be able to 'do it in the classroom', but to understand what is being done and why, see beyond it and know about alternatives futures.

ABOUT THIS BOOK

The book was written by a team of Education Studies tutors at Bath Spa University who have each taught a course module on the topic of their chapter. Our job is to guide and support students' thinking and learning and we hope to introduce, in a single volume, a broad range of topics that will stimulate your ideas and your reading, so each chapter gives questions for discussion, as well as further reading.

A job for teachers is to organise knowledge so that it makes sense to the learner. It's like arranging books in a library and it doesn't always work because one book may demand to go on two or three different shelves. Education Studies is diverse and difficult to manage, but we have arranged the content of this book into three parts:

I   International and global perspectives
II   Teaching, educational settings and policy
III   Knowledge, learning and the curriculum

If you think we've got a chapter on the wrong shelf, you're probably right and that shows that you're developing your own understanding of the subject. The following is a brief summary of the sections and contents by chapter numbers.

Part I: International and global perspectives

It is easy to think of education simply as the schooling that goes on where we live. However, we now live in an interconnected world and education can be a global force for good. To understand this we need to appreciate the effects which education has on global politics, cultures and economies. The book starts by trying to expand your thinking about the exciting possibilities education holds for humanity and the world and by examining contrasts and alternatives in different countries and cultures.

1   There has been a great deal of interest in the UK and the USA in education in the Pacific Rim countries. Kay Wood begins by looking at reasons for this and examines the links between education and the economy. She raises the question of what education really is for: individual development or to produce a work-force for the global economy?
2   David Hicks explains the different ways of understanding global and international education. He argues the case for a global perspective in the curriculum and suggests the kind of skills and knowledge pupils will need to live in a globally connected future.
3   By examining the environmental issues, David goes on to explain the role of education in creating a sustainable future for the planet.
4   The international theme continues with David Coulby's analysis of the similarities and contrasts between education systems in different countries of Europe.
5   Human rights are high on the world's political agenda now, and Heather Williamson engages you in some moral philosophy to understand the ethical issues in the education of minority groups in different countries and cultures.
6   Denise Cush explores cultural diversity in education by examining different views of religious education in different countries and the issue of faith-based schools in the UK.

Part II: Teaching, educational settings and policy

Part II looks at what education *does* to pupils through teaching in educational settings and through education policy. This time the focus is mainly on the UK, but still with some international references.

7   Stephen Ward explains the party politics of education policy in England and how the 'new right' and 'New Labour' have developed market forces in education.

8   Andy Bord looks at what it means to be a teacher, the skills of active listening and communication, and asks you to think about your ideas of yourself as a possible future teacher.

9   The special nature of early years care and education is explored by Jill Williams and Karen McInnes. They examine different views of childhood and how these affect professional practice with young children.

10   The UK government's policy is for children with special educational needs to be part of mainstream education in *inclusive* schools. Mim Hutchings guides you on how to go into a school setting and carry out a case study on a child or on a classroom situation. There is an introduction to some of the research methods that you will need as an education student.

11   Christine Eden examines the research on gender and attainment. She shows why the focus of concern has moved from disadvantaged girls to underachieving boys.

12   The last chapter in this part challenges the whole concept of traditional school settings. David Hicks explains why radical educators want to take alternative initiatives, and outlines the different ideologies that underpin these ideas.

Part III: Knowledge, learning and the curriculum

Any book with an overview of Education Studies must include the curriculum and how it is learned. This is the last part, not because it is the least important, but because we want you to view learning within the global and international contexts set out in the first part. There are six chapters on different curriculum subject areas. But they are not the usual teacher-training guidance on how to teach the subject. Instead we look at the nature of each subject – its *epistemology* – what it means to learn and to know the subject. Knowledge is not just inert 'stuff' in books and CD-ROMs to be taken off the shelf, taught and learned. Knowledge is contested and dangerous with continuing debates about what should count, what is relevant, who should learn it and how. While the chapters are not about pedagogy (how to teach), they are relevant to teachers. Good teachers know the subject, but they are better teachers if they understand the nature of the subject, how it is learned, the underlying issues and debates and why some learners may find it difficult.

13   Alan Howe and Dan Davies challenge the traditional science curriculum which has been treated as simply a quantity of facts to be learned and tested. They explain a postmodern view of scientific knowledge and argue that pupils should learn to ask scientific questions and engage in proper scientific activities related to life in the real world.

14   Susan Haywood and Mim Hutchings show that information and communications technology (ICT) has powerful effects on the way we learn and on the whole nature of knowledge. They show the potential for computers in the hands of learners and how we need to prepare pupils for 'the unforeseeable future' of fast-moving technology.

15   Why are so many people nervous about mathematics when it is one of the subjects which gets the most teaching in schools? Malcolm Hanson explains the origins of these anxieties and the myths about the subject. He takes up the comparative points about mathematics teaching in the Pacific Rim in Chapter 1 by looking at some of the international research on the teaching of mathematics.

16   Howard Gibson introduces us to some of the ways in which language works. He suggests it is not just a neutral conduit for communication: our language choices convey all kinds of meanings and he shows how de-naturalizing it reveals the power relations between teachers and pupils.

17   Art encompasses a whole range of creative forms in different cultures and June Bianchi demonstrates the importance of the visual arts in our lives. She argues for a *postmodern* art and design curriculum which enables pupils to understand the role of art in offering an enquiring approach to the world.

18   The final chapter returns to the topic of education for a sustainable future through the humanities curriculum. Meg Gomersall introduces debates about history and geography teaching, arguing that pupils should not just be remembering the story of the gunpowder plot, but engaging as historians examining evidence. Rather than remembering facts about different countries, geography should help pupils to understand the nature of society. In this way they are equipped to challenge the distorted versions of history and other cultures and to formulate their own view of the world: its past, its present and its future.

Of course, we do not have space to cover the whole of the knowledge on, or even the subjects of, the school curriculum. However, it is hoped that the selection of subjects offered here will give examples of the kind of thinking about the curriculum and learning in Education Studies.

Stephen Ward

QUESTIONS FOR DISCUSSION

- Is Education Studies a proper degree subject?
- Are global and international issues really important?
- What are your reasons for studying education?
- How is Education Studies relevant if you are not going to teach?

RECOMMENDED READING

Other books on Education Studies:

Bartlett, S. and Burton, D. (2003) *Education Studies*, London: Sage.

Bartlett, S., Burton, D. and Peim, N. (2001) *An Introduction to Education Studies*, London: Paul Chapman.

Davies, I., Gregory, I. and McGuinn, N. (2002) *Key Debates in Education*, London: Continuum.

Mattheson, D. and Grosvenor, I. (1999) *An Introduction to the Study of Education*, London: David Fulton.

For the Quality Assurance Agency (QAA) view of what should be included in Education Studies and the skills to be learned by undergraduates see:

Quality Assurance Agency for Higher Education (2000) *Education Studies*, Gloucester: QAA. www.qaa.ac.uk.

On the relationship between Education Studies and teacher training, see:

Crook, D. (2002) 'Educational Studies and Teacher Education', *British Journal of Educational Studies*, 50(1), March: 57–75.

REFERENCES

Davies, I., Gregory, I. and McGuinn, N. (2002) *Key Debates in Education*, London: Continuum.

DfES/TTA (2002) *Qualifying to Teach: Professional Standards for Qualified Teacher Status and Requirements for Initial Teacher Training*, London: Teacher Training Agency.

Part I

Global and international perspectives

1 International Perspectives: The USA and the Pacific Rim

Kay Wood

Looking at education in other countries and in other cultures can change our ideas about how education works and what education ultimately is *for*. In this chapter you will learn about:

- education in the United States of America (USA) and in the Pacific Rim countries of Japan, China and South Korea
- the global economy and why western governments are so interested in education in the Pacific Rim
- importing methods from other educational systems
- what we can learn from cultures with a different world view.

EDUCATION, THE ECONOMY AND TEACHING METHODS

There is a belief in western societies and in some developing countries that there is a strong link between the national level of educational achievement and the health of the economy. The expectation is that education increases economic prosperity, advances technological development and thereby contributes to national wealth. These are not new ideas. The 1870 Education Act in England and Wales was intended to produce skilled workers who could compete in an era of growing industrial productivity. For the same reasons the USA, early in the twentieth century, introduced vocational elements into the curriculum. Schooling was seen as a way of not only giving the young the necessary skills, but preparing them psychologically for work (Bowles and Gintis, 1976). Debate about the relationship between school and work has intensified since the end of the twentieth century as capitalism has spread and globalisation has made demands on countries to compete with each other for industrial markets (see also Chapter 7).

The debate about the relationship between education and the economy has been fuelled in recent times by international comparisons which measure, amongst other things, pupil performance at different ages, particularly in relation to 'key skills' in mathematics, science and language. Publications in the 1990s such as Office for Standards in Education (Ofsted) (1996) suggested that children in the United Kingdom (UK) were doing less well than children from Pacific Rim countries, in particular China, Japan and South Korea. The debate intensified when 'Asian tiger' economies seemed to be thriving. It led to a western interest in the education systems of the Pacific Rim and linked with a flurry of reports (Her Majesty's Inspectorate [HMI], 1992) indicating the need to learn from the school organisation and teaching methods in these countries (see also Chapter 14).

In developing countries there has been a strong focus on the development of basic skills of literacy and numeracy. South Korea has been cited as a prime example. It has moved from being a peasant economy to a world power in just 30 years. In the 1960s it was at the end of a devastating civil war with 80 per cent of its buildings destroyed and with few natural resources, little capital for investment and hardly any technology. Between 1985 and 1995 it became one of the world's leading steel producers and subsequently moved spectacularly into the 'sunrise' electronics industries. Although a number of economic and social factors contributed to this success, its education system has been singled out for particular praise. In 1945, 78 per cent of the population was illiterate; 96 per cent is now literate. Enrolment in primary schools has trebled and nearly everyone stays on at school until they are eighteen. More than 60 per cent of high school graduates go on to higher education compared with about 40 per cent in the UK.

Singapore has taken further steps towards developing its economy and education. It gained independence from Britain in 1959 and was then faced with a political and economic challenge: how to move from an underdeveloped third-world country to a developed country at the cutting edge of economic performance. It did this initially by focusing on key skills in elementary education and developing a labour-intensive economy. It moved on in the 1970s, extending secondary and vocational education by progressing to a more technological economy. Finally in the 1980s it expanded higher education and upgraded technical skills which would feed directly into key industries, such as financial services. This has produced a high standard of living in Singapore. The state has taken a strong role in directing economic development; nevertheless, education has undoubtedly played its part.

Skills in literacy, numeracy and science are seen as a prerequisite for successful economies in a global market place. Pacific Rim countries seem to have based their stronger economic performance on robust improvements in primary, and increasingly secondary, education. But precise connections between the two are elusive. Lewin (1997) queries the extent to which the perceived improvements are directly transportable between cultures, while Adnett and Davies (2002) and Wolf (2002) dispute that the two are connected at all. The perceived imperatives of literacy and numeracy have, nonetheless, impacted upon education in the USA and in England and Wales.

In the USA the National Commission on Excellence in Education (1983) suggested that public education was heading for cataclysmic disaster. It identified performance in science and mathematics as being very low compared with Japan and Germany. It also pointed to a 'rising tide of mediocrity', suggesting that American students had low expectations and spent less time studying than did students in other industrialised countries (Kazamias, 2000). This echoed concerns about standards in the UK in the 1970s and 1990s. One of the solutions in the USA was the Goals 2000 legislation, signed by Bill Clinton in 1994, which suggested that every American state should develop rigorous standards, clearly indicating what children should know and be able to do. In the USA, however, individual states are responsible for their own educational policies and the federal government can only make recommendations as to what should happen in schools.

The significantly better performance of students in some Pacific Rim countries led to an interest in what Pacific Rim countries were actually doing in education. English educationalists and researchers went to South Korea, Taiwan and Japan to see what was going on. Teaching methods became a key focus. Investigations in South Korea, for example (Ofsted, 1996), suggested that what contributed to pupil progress was a combination of whole-class teaching, a clear curriculum, checking that pupils had fully understood what they had been taught and ensuring that the whole class was marching forward together.

These findings were supported by an HMI report (1992) on teaching in Japanese primary schools which suggested that whole-class teaching enhances primary pupils' learning. All pupils in a typical Japanese elementary class work on a single subject, moving towards the same goal, but there is also some group and individual work. Lessons have a three-part structure:

1   the teacher explains things clearly using the blackboard
2   pupils do a task together and then some work on their own
3   the teacher takes up the lesson again with the whole class.

Lower ability children are expected to do much more than would be expected of them in the UK, but bright children tend to coast more and are not so fully stretched. Pupils mostly sit in rows facing the teacher and the teacher only moves around to check pupils' work. Work is organised so as to be manageable for the majority of the class and sometimes quick learners are encouraged to help slow learners. This three-part lesson became the basis of the National Literacy and Numeracy Strategies in England and Wales, which focus on whole-class teaching with strong pupil involvement (see Chapter 7).

Problems with importing ideas from other education systems

It is important to compare education systems with a view to learning from the practice of others. It challenges assumptions and stops people from being ethnocentric. Nevertheless, what appears simple at first glance becomes remarkably complex on closer inspection. Education is a social process deeply embedded in national culture and it is difficult to detach elements of the process, such as teaching methods, from their cultural background. Global economic pressures are leading governments around the world to construct their education systems in similar ways, but there may not be a system that fits all situations and cultures: what works in Kyoto may not work in Manchester.

Many Pacific Rim cultures are influenced by Confucian traditions. This is true of China, Japan and South Korea. Confucius was a philosopher and teacher who set up the first primary schools in China around 500 BC. He initiated a philosophy for living which emphasised the importance of being virtuous and showing compassion. This is summed up in the Chinese word *jen*, which roughly translated means 'duty to your neighbour'. Confucius also believed that respect should be shown for authority and tradition, both within the family and in wider society. These beliefs formed the foundation of a world view which sees society as a hierarchy stretching from the lowliest person through his/her superiors and ultimately to the emperor himself. Individual happiness comes from showing proper respect to one's superiors and by subordinating one's own needs to those of the wider group. Ultimately one might reach elder status oneself.

Despite the massive changes in China and Japan during the twentieth century, the importance of Confucian ideas are still strong. They permeate all areas of life, including education. Pupils in Japanese primary schools are taught from their earliest moments that the *sempai-kohai* relationship of senior to junior is important in all aspects of life. This relationship begins as early as three when children learn the difference between the polite and plain styles of speech in Japanese. If you are talking to someone older than yourself, or someone you do not know well, your style of speech changes. Humility and deference to superiors is of the utmost importance. Teachers traditionally have been treated with respect as part of this tradition and their pupils are unlikely to question what they are taught (HMI, 1992). This may well contribute to the Japanese success in teaching basic skills.

Confucian traditions support living and working in a group-orientated society, but in Japan this does not involve mindless following of the group. Children from a very young age are encouraged to take responsibility for themselves. This is seen in the education of pre-school children. Lewis (1995: 7) maintains that Japanese education creates a sense of community amongst its younger pupils by minimising competition, involving children in leadership roles and 'focusing discipline on what it means to be a kind, responsive member of the school community – not on rewards and punishments'. This sits well with the Confucian tradition.

Belief systems such as these are likely to have a profound effect on education. Japanese education encourages persistence (Blinco, 1993). Pupils are encouraged to believe that all can succeed with constant effort. So it is the duty of the pupil to try hard. There is a pervasive belief in Japanese society that all children are infinitely malleable and that children can be imbued with qualities which will last into adulthood. For Japanese teachers, therefore, all children are capable of success and they have strong expectations that their pupils will perform well. These beliefs are communicated to the pupils themselves (Lewis, 1995).

On the other hand, the western world view stresses the importance of the development of the individual over and above the needs of the group. Performance is seen as determined by inherited intelligence and social class. Some children, it is claimed, will be bound to succeed and others to fail. Personal success is paramount. Persistence is not a valued quality in education in the UK and the lack of perseverance has been highlighted recently by employers as a major failing in graduates. This raises questions as to the degree to which importing teaching methods from one culture to another can succeed without attitude change in the receiving country. Ofsted (1996) argue that teachers in England and Wales can learn from other countries and that by changing teaching methods we are likely to increase pupils' literacy and numeracy skills.

However, whilst we might regard increased persistence and concern for others as values worth encouraging, there are other aspects of education in the Pacific Rim countries which we may not be so keen to import. One of the factors in Japanese success at primary level has been a tightly controlled curriculum. Monbusho, the Japanese Ministry of Education, produces graded textbooks for each subject. The texts, which are well produced and colourful, are provided for all subjects except physical education and all teachers in public and private education must use them. There are strict controls on the publication of the textbooks, which are carefully scrutinised by senior government officials to check that they are correct. There has been recent controversy in Japan over plans to introduce a more nationalist slant to the teaching of history and current affairs. Indeed the teaching of history in Japan has been contentious for a number of years with claims that major atrocities, such as the so-called 'rape of Nanking', have been systematically excluded from textbooks (Paris, 2000). In China, the reform of the curriculum and some attempts to allow city schools to produce their own textbooks has not diminished the strong political education which is nationally inspired (Lewin *et al.*, 1994).

The introduction of the National Curriculum in England and Wales produced a similar furore over the content of the history syllabus (Coulby and Bash, 1991), but the worry about what pupils are being taught in school is substantially increased when governments have control over both the curriculum and the accompanying text books. This is further exacerbated when teachers are encouraged to follow the textbook carefully and there is no material from other sources. If one of the criteria for successful pupils' learning is a tightly controlled curriculum, a consequence is likely to be a limited perspective for the student.

Recent worries have been expressed in both China and Japan about the rigidity of pupils' thinking and the lack of creativity and spontaneity in classroom life. The 1984 National Council on Educational Reform in Japan identified the need for the cultivation of creativity and the encouragement of thinking ability. This has been further supported recently by calls for greater inventiveness in classroom teaching, echoing requests in China for the encouragement of more creative pedagogies (Lewin *et al.*, 1994). The heavy emphasis on competition in secondary schooling in Japan, and increased selection for key schools in China, has highlighted the effects that extreme pressure may have on schoolchildren. It may be that well-disciplined children, working to a clearly defined curriculum in a competitive system, present evidence that they are reaching high standards in basic skills. But it is important to ask questions about the potential cost of such standards both for pupils individually and for society as a whole. The fostering of creativity and inventiveness may well lie at the heart of creating a sustainable world.

INFLUENCES ON EDUCATION IN THE USA AND ENGLAND

In the last 30 years, education in England and Wales and the USA has largely been driven by the demands for economic competitiveness. The increasing stress on the development of basic skills and their accompanying tests has led to a narrowing of the curriculum, particularly at primary level. Subjects such as art, music and drama which were previously considered to be important at elementary level have gradually been pushed to the margins. This has been part of a changing discourse in education itself. Neo-liberals in England and the USA have argued that schools are part of a monolithic state system which is grossly inefficient and which has had no incentive to innovate or respond to consumer preferences. Schools, they suggest, need to answer to the demands of the market place. This has led to powerful voices in the USA arguing that business should take a stronger hand in reforming education. Having provided the critique of schools in 1989, the National Business Roundtable in the USA began a nationwide campaign to reform public schools. Heads of multinationals like Procter and Gamble and Rank Xerox were called in to help schools become more 'in tune' with the business world. The arrangement is made even stronger in the USA by the system of school government that exists. There is a preponderance of business people on school boards; they have links at a local level and ultimately at a state level with corporate leaders who have access to government.

It is not just the treating of schools as businesses in England and the USA, or the closer ties in the USA between business and education, which have been a cause for concern. Increasingly the conflation of pupil and consumer has impacted upon life in schools. Multinationals in the USA have been allowed directly to influence the curriculum through the provision of set books, such as the General Motors economics course. Companies have been allowed to sell directly to pupils through franchise arrangements with schools allowing children to buy and consume only one soft drink, such as Coca Cola, and to drink it in class, so increasing consumption. They may offer monthly prizes for achievement, with success being rewarded with free meals at Pizza Hut. There are similar initiatives occurring in the UK with Cadbury's sponsoring sports equipment, curriculum materials being provided by multinationals and some schools offering rewards in the form of meals from fast food chains.

We are becoming so used to these developments that they often pass without notice. Apple (2001) has suggested that neo-liberal policies for education and the economy have become so pervasive that they appear as an established fact. People no longer ask what education is for; it is understood to be beyond debate. These forces are strong, but there is a formidable tradition in the USA and in the UK which has questioned the degree to which education should be linked to the demands of the economy. The earliest schooling in the USA championed by Horace Mann, the father of American education, consisted of common schools which would have a common curriculum, be free of religion and which all children would attend irrespective of wealth or social status. Mann championed Pestalozzi's ideas of innovative teaching styles and respect for the needs of the child. Initially schools were not there to provide basic skills. Mann thought the attitudes taught in schools would help industry but this was not a prime aim of schooling. These ideas were later furthered by William T. Harris who believed that schools should teach skills for work, such as self-reliance or ability to work hard, but that the curriculum should be largely humanistic with a stress on arts and literature, language, maths, history and geography (Cuban and Shipps, 2000). He thought that vocational training would separate children by class and rule out the working class from many occupations. Vocational training should therefore have a lower priority.

Likewise in England and Wales, a strong tradition in primary education has drawn on the progressive European philosophers and educationalists such as Rousseau, Pestalozzi, Froebel and Montessori with these theories finding public acknowledgement in the Plowden Report of 1967. The orthodoxy of the 1960s and 1970s put the child at the centre of the learning process, with play being an integral part of the primary experience. Children were encouraged to be active learners, taking respon-sibility for their own learning, and formal testing was frowned upon as being unsuitable for properly assessing pupils. These ideas permeated primary schools, and educators came, mainly from the USA, to view these ideas in action, particularly in schools in Oxfordshire and Leicestershire.

The progressive tradition was further developed by John Dewey (1961), an American philosopher and educator, who argued that the prime role of education was to produce citizens able to participate actively in a 'reasonable society'. He suggested that an aim for most people would be to live in a society which is on the whole caring, equitable and just and that schooling has an important role to play in achieving this. He argued that learning how to talk and compromise with others is as important an educational goal as achieving high academic standards.

A potent strand in education based on the writings of Dewey has argued that, far from supporting the economy, education should be the main vehicle for counteracting the private interests of the economy. The purpose of education should not be to service the economy. It should not be the means to ensure that pupils become 'happy' workers and team players, each one doing his or her part to maximise production. Rather, education should be seen as a good in itself and not solely as a means to an end (Carlson, 1997).

Education, for Dewey, is the cornerstone in the maintenance of a strong democracy. He believed that education has an important role in the creation of a more democratic society and in helping to reduce society's inequalities. It should help pupils to envisage a more humane future. Apple and Beane (1999) argue that schools have a duty to introduce pupils to a democratic way of thinking. This involves designing democratic curricula and schools which are fundamentally democratic in structure. Education is a process which can help pupils to understand and demystify the everyday world so that they can see the power structures in society and the common-sense beliefs that underpin them. In this sense education is about empowerment: giving an individual the ability to take control of his/her life. It is not sufficient to do this just at a personal level. Apple and Beane suggest that the development of the individual needs to be linked to the local community and to the political and cultural empowerment of marginalised groups such as ethnic minorities and pupils living in poverty. Education is seen as having the potential to be transformative: to change society at large through the actions of individual teachers, schools and groups of pupils developing opposite discourses (Freire, 1970) (see Chapter 12).

LEARNING FROM OTHER CULTURES

Initial interest in the Pacific Rim economies opened up a rich world for educators. Teaching methods were fascinating, but more so were the cultural backgrounds which supported educational practices. Cross-cultural research offers measurable inter-national comparisons, but also, in its most discerning aspects, asks questions about the function and role of education in an increasingly globalised and inter-connected world. What can different societies learn from each other at a deeper level of cultural understanding and what role does education play in this? How do profoundly different world views offer insights that others can benefit from?

Sullivan (1998: 32) has called attention to the fact that the growth of capitalism and the 'free' market are having a major global effect on education. The doctrine of competition and choice as exemplified in the English and American education systems is now affecting the Pacific Rim and, in the course of doing this, sacrifices 'equal opportunity, social justice and education for democracy'. It tends to ride roughshod over cultural differences and is essentially 'anti-humanistic'. On the other hand he recognises that there has also been a counter-development in the recognition of the rights of indigenous peoples for an education that is grounded in their own culture. Around the Pacific Rim, from aboriginal people in Australia, native Americans in the USA to the People of Tonga, there has been a growing awareness of the possibility of indigenous peoples co-operating in the furtherance of their own educational systems (see Chapter 4). The recognition of the rights of indigenous peoples may have arisen from a belated sense of social justice on the part of dominating cultures. However, as in the case of Japan and China, further investigation demonstrates that different educational approaches can be grounded in different world views.

A consideration of Australian Aboriginal and Native American beliefs and values reveals a startlingly different approach to the physical world in which we live. Aborigines have a close symbiotic relationship with the land, of which they see themselves as caretakers and guardians (Swain, 1993). In a similar way Native Americans have a sense of kinship with other life forms. These views are at odds with those of western societies which see the world as a place for exploitation and production (Kawagley and Barnhardt, 1999). Aboriginal and Native American education are informed by a particular understanding of the world and by a strong spirituality. They involve personal transformation through knowledge of history, ritual and myth, often encoded in dance, art and song (Peat, 1996). This contrasts with a western approach which has focused on education in terms of facts and figures which can be passed on in books and programmes of study. While it is easy to romanticise such approaches and use information out of context, a study of other world views and educational systems undoubtedly poses a challenge to the neo-liberal assumptions of western capitalism and the associated education systems.

CONCLUSION

We live in a fluid world where global trends are evident. However, strong cultural influences produce particular environments between which the exchange of innovations must be handled with care and sensitivity. The core of education can be a critical dialogue which challenges and enlivens debate in and about our dominant institutions and their cultural perspective, especially education. The dialogue should involve and engage all stakeholders, including teachers and their pupils, and could provide robust solutions to local needs which are also flexible, responsive and adaptive.

QUESTIONS FOR DISCUSSION

- How far should education serve the needs of the economy?
- Should education help pupils to think critically about the society in which they live?
- Do western societies put too much emphasis on the individual at the expense of the group?
- What would be the effect of teachers believing that all pupils can succeed?
- Is it a good idea to encourage persistence in pupils and, if so, how would we do it?
- Should governments have tight control of the curriculum and teaching materials?
- Is creativity and inventiveness desirable in pupils and how do we foster it?
- What can we learn from the world views of indigenous peoples?

REFERENCES

Adnett, N. and Davies, P. (2002) *Markets for Schooling*, London and New York: Routledge.

Apple, M. (2001) *Educating the 'Right' Way*, New York: RoutledgeFalmer.

Apple, M. and Beane, J.A. (eds) (1999) *Democratic Schools: Lessons from the Chalk Face*, Milton Keynes: Open University Press.

Blinco, P.M.A. (1993) 'Persistence and education: a formula for Japan's economic success', *Comparative Education*, 29(2): 171–83.

Bowles, S. and Gintis, H. (1976) *Schooling in Capitalist America*, London: Routledge and Kegan Paul.

Carlson, D. (1997) *Making Progress*, New York: Teachers' College Press.

Coulby, D. and Bash, L. (1991) *Contradiction and Conflict: The 1988 Education Act in Action*, London: Cassell.

Cuban, L. and Shipps, D. (2000) *Reconstructing the Common Good in Education*, Stanford, CA: Stanford University Press.

Dewey, J. (1961) *Democracy and Education*, London: Macmillan.

Freire, P. (1970) *Pedagogy of the Oppressed*, New York: Herder and Herder.

HMI (1992) *Teaching and Learning in Japanese Elementary Schools*, London: HMSO.

Kawagley, A.O. and Barnhardt, R. (1999) 'Education indigenous to place', in G. Smith and D. Williams (eds) *Ecological Education: On Weaving Education, Culture and the Environment*, New York: State University of New York Press.

Kazamias, A.M. (2000) 'Crisis and reform in US education', in D. Coulby, R. Cowen and C. Jones (eds) *Education in Times of Transition: World Yearbook of Education*, London: Kogan Page.

Lewin, K.M., Hui, X., Little, A.W. and Jiwei, Z. (1994) *Educational Innovation in China*, Harlow: Longman.

Lewin, K.M. (1997) 'Education in emerging Asia: patterns, policies and the futures into the 21st century'. Paper prepared for the Oxford International Conference on Education and Development.

Lewis, C.C. (1995) *Education, Hearts and Minds: Reflections on Japanese Pre-school and Elementary Education*, Cambridge: Cambridge University Press.

National Commission on Excellence in Education (1983) *A Nation at Risk: The Imperative for Educational Reform*, Washington, DC: US Government Printing Office.

Ofsted (1996) *Worlds Apart: A Review of International Surveys of Educational Achievement Involving England*, London: The Stationery Office.

Paris, E. (2000) *Long Shadows: Truth, Lies and History*, London: Bloomsbury.

Peat, D. (1996) *Blackfoot Physics: A Journey into the Native American Universe*, London: Fourth Estate.

Sullivan, K. (ed.) (1998) *Education and Change in the Pacific Rim*, Wallingford: Triangle Books.

Swain, T. (1993) *A Place for Strangers: Towards a History of Australian Aboriginal Being*, Cambridge: Cambridge University Press.

Wolf, A. (2002) *Does Education Matter?* London: Penguin.

RECOMMENDED READING

Apple, M. (2000) *Educating the 'Right' Way*, New York: RoutledgeFalmer. Gives a clear account of the nature of the New Right, its partnership with the religious right and their current effects on education in the USA.

Apple, M. and Beane, J.A. (eds) (1999) *Democratic Schools: Lessons from the Chalk Face*, Milton Keynes: Open University Press. Has good accounts of particular schools which have tried to adopt democratic principles and practices.

Carlson, D. (1997) *Making Progress*, New York: Teachers' College Press. Gives a history of progressive ideas in education and demonstrates how these are currently challenging neo-liberal ideas for schools.

Cuban, L. and Shipps, D. (2000) *Reconstructing the Common Good in Education*, Stanford, CA: Stanford University Press. Traces the history of education in the USA indicating its early engagement with the importance of communal values.

HMI (1992) *Teaching and Learning in Japanese Elementary Schools*, London: HMSO. Gives a clear and easily accessible account of Japanese elementary education.

Lewis, C.C. (1995) *Education, Hearts and Minds: Reflections on Japanese Pre-school and Elementary Education*, Cambridge: Cambridge University Press. An interesting and lively read on early years education in Japan.

Ofsted (1996) *Worlds Apart: A Review of International Surveys of Educational Achievement Involving England*, London: The Stationery Office. Provides a critical review of international comparisons in education.

Paris, E. (2000) *Long Shadows: Truth, Lies and History*, London: Bloomsbury. Draws on a range of examples from France to America and Japan to indicate how governments rewrite national histories to suit their own ends.

Sullivan, K. (ed.) (1998) *Education and Change in the Pacific Rim*, Wallingford: Triangle Books. A key text in understanding the effects of globalisation on education in the Pacific Rim and in developments in the education of indigenous people.

2 The Global Dimension in the Curriculum

David Hicks

Why do teachers need to know about global issues, events and trends? How can we help young people understand the rapidly changing world in which they live? What resources are available to assist in teaching about such matters? This chapter explores:

- the rationale for a global dimension in the curriculum
- two frameworks for implementing such a dimension
- how they relate to selected areas of the curriculum.

GLOBAL TRENDS

We can only understand life today in our own communities if it is set in the wider global context. What happens elsewhere in the world constantly impacts on our daily lives even if we may not be aware of it. We need to know something about the 'state of the world'. Some current global trends (World Watch Institute, 2002) include:

- a steady increase in global surface temperatures over the last 50 years
- a surge in the use of renewable energy sources such as solar and wind power
- the most widespread slowdown in economic growth since the 1980s
- the persistence of widespread poverty and an increasing rich–poor gap
- the number of wars and armed conflicts continues to decrease.

Climate change, energy use, economic growth, wealth and poverty, and violent conflict affect our local communities and day-to-day living. Many risks that society faces in the early twenty-first century are now global in nature. Once science was seen as having all the answers. Now science and technology are seen as contributing to contemporary problems, from the storage of nuclear waste to carbon emissions as a factor in global warming. The forces of globalisation, engineered by the rich world, are binding the world more closely together, but are also being more fiercely resisted than ever before (Roddick, 2001).

These issues are sometimes uncomfortable to look at and people often prefer to act as if they do not exist. This is the *psychology of denial* – if I pretend something isn't happening it may just go away. In reality, of course, problems we choose to ignore may only get worse. Every person who chooses to act for change does make a difference, especially if they join with others. 'But,' you may say, 'I still don't really see what this has got to do with education.' Well, it is something that educators in the UK have been concerned about since the 1920s. Progressive teachers at that time felt that education needed to be both more child-centred and more *world-minded*: not only knowing more about the world but showing greater tolerance and respect between both groups and countries.

Richardson (1990) captures the contemporary importance of two long-standing educational traditions:

> The one tradition is concerned with learner-centred education, and the development and fulfilment of individuals. This tradition is humanistic and optimistic, and has a basic trust in the capacity and will of human beings to create healthy and empowering systems and structures ... The second tradition is concerned with building equality, and with resisting the trend for education merely to reflect and replicate inequalities in wider society of race, gender and class; it is broadly pessimistic in its assumption that inequalities are the norm wherever and whenever they are not consciously and strenuously resisted.
>
> Both traditions are concerned with wholeness and holistic thinking, but neither, arguably, is complete without the other. There cannot be wholeness in individuals independently of strenuous attempts to heal rifts and contradictions in wider society and in the education system. Conversely, political struggle to create wholeness in society – that is, equality and justice in dealings and relationships between social classes, between countries, between ethnic groups, between women and men – is doomed to no more than a partial success and hollow victories, at best, if it is not accompanied by, and if it does not in its turn strengthen and sustain, the search for wholeness and integration in individuals.
>
> (Richardson, 1990: 6–7)

Recently there has been renewed interest in a global dimension in the school curriculum. Eight out of ten 11–16-year-olds feel that it is important to learn about global issues at school in order to make better choices about how they might lead their lives (MORI, 1998). The Department for Education and Skills (DfEE) (2000) document *Developing a Global Dimension in the School Curriculum* and non-governmental organisations (NGOs) such as Oxfam (1997) call for an emphasis on 'global citizenship' in both primary and secondary schools. The Development Education Association (DEA) (2001) stresses the importance of 'global perspectives in education' and the Department for International Development is making funding available to support schools in teaching about global issues (www.dfid.gov.uk).

Clarifying 'global' terminology

A number of different terms may be used when referring to the global dimension in the curriculum, but they do not all mean the same thing. Here the meanings are clarified:

Global education   The term used internationally to designate the academic field concerned with teaching and learning about global issues, events and perspectives. During the 1970s–1980s in the United Kingdom (UK) this field was known as 'world studies'.

Development education   Originated with the work of NGOs that were concerned about issues of development and north–south global relations. Focus of concern has widened to embrace other global issues but *development* remains the core concept.

Global dimension   Refers to the curriculum as a whole and the ethos of a school: those subject elements and cross-curricular concerns that focus on global interdependence, issues and events.

Global perspective(s)   What we want students to achieve as a result of having a global dimension in the curriculum; in the plural it refers to the fact that there are different cultural and political perspectives on global matters.

International dimension   Literally 'between countries', as in international relationships; also refers to the study of a particular concern, e.g. education, as it manifests in different countries (see Chapters 1 and 4). So 'international' refers to the *parts* and 'global' to the *whole*.

Global citizenship   That part of the citizenship curriculum which refers to global issues, events and perspectives; also being or feeling a citizen of the global community (as well as cultural or national communities).

Globalisation   The innumerable interconnections – economic, cultural, technological, political – which bind the local and national into a global community; the consequence of *neo-liberal* economic policies which see everything, including education, as a commodity to be sold in the global market place.

I use the term 'global education' as shorthand for the concerns of this chapter. Sometimes the terms above get used as if they were interchangeable, and if we are not careful this can lead to a general fuzziness about global education. Having a link with a school elsewhere in the world or taking a school trip abroad is not necessarily good practice in global education. Neither necessarily is teaching about global warming or the war in Iraq. A number of key components *have* to be present before one can properly use the term 'global education' or argue that there is a global dimension in the curriculum.

PLANNING THE CURRICULUM

The place to begin is with the global issues, trends and events that young people need to understand in order to make sense of their lives today. These may be selected from the news because they are topical and pressing or they may relate to what is already present in curriculum subjects, such as geography, history, religious education or English. Most global issues fall into four broad areas:

- wealth and poverty
- human rights
- peace and conflict
- the environment.

These issues are present in our own countries and communities: they are both local *and* global in nature.

It is important not to overwhelm pupils with the extent of particular *problems*, as it may lead to disengagement and feelings of disempowerment (Hicks, 2002). Whilst they need to become more knowledgeable about the nature of particular problems, they equally need to learn about the practical *solutions* that can contribute to resolving them. It is exploring case studies of action for change and the experience of being able to contribute to this that actually empowers young people.

Global education has a long history in the UK and as a result has developed a range of tried and tested principles for introducing a global dimension into the curriculum (Hicks, 2003). Two of the best-known frameworks for planning such a dimension will be considered. The first comes from the International Institute for Global Education (IIGE) (Pike and Selby, 1999) and the second from Oxfam (1997). Both have been successfully used by teachers in a number of schools.

Framework 1: The International Institute for Global Education

Figure 2.1 is taken from Pike and Selby (1996, 1999) and the model has four components. This is the 'irreducible minimum' that needs to be present in order for the curriculum to have a global dimension. The four components are briefly described below and in Table 2.1.

The four components of global education

The issues dimension   There are four broad problem areas that need to be explored: wealth and poverty, human rights, peace and conflict, and the environment. Pupils need to understand specific examples from each of the problem areas and a range of *solutions* to such problems.

The spatial dimension   This involves exploration of the interconnections that exist between the local and the global. It focuses on the concept of interdependence between issues, people, places and countries, whilst also exploring the nature of dependency, i.e. the fact that many such connections are inequitable ones.

Figure 2.1 The four dimensions of global education
Source: Pike and Selby, 1996, 1999

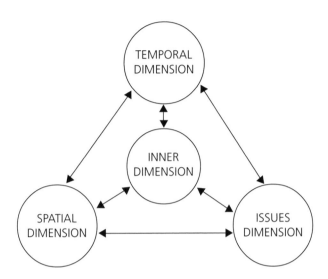

The temporal dimension   This involves exploration of the connections that exist between past, present and future. It focuses on the need to think critically and creatively about the future impact of local–global issues and investigates the nature of possible, probable and preferable futures.

The inner dimension   This relates to one's own personal growth and development. It is about the personal and interpersonal skills needed to work co-operatively with others. It is also about the forms of teaching and learning that are most appropriate for the exploration of global issues, events and trends. In particular, it requires a holistic and participatory approach that focuses on differing values, perspectives and political literacy.

Table 2.1 shows in more detail what Pike and Selby see as essential within each of the four components. The key ideas for each component are listed in the second column followed by a familiar subdivision for teachers, a breakdown into knowledge, skills and attitudes. Detailed examples of classroom activities can be found in Pike and Selby (1996, 1999, 2000; Fountain, 1995).

Framework 2: A curriculum for global citizenship – the Oxfam Model

Many NGOs in Britain, such as Oxfam, Greenpeace and Amnesty International, are concerned about the state of the world. Some have long-established education programmes run by staff with considerable experience of schools. The resources they produce for teachers are often directly tailored to the needs of the National Curriculum

Table 2.1 The four dimensions of global education

	Key ideas	Knowledge	Skills	Attitudes
Spatial dimension	• interdependence • local–global systems	• of local/global connections and dependencies • of global systems • of the nature and function of a system • of communication between areas of knowledge • of the common needs of all humans and other species • of oneself as a whole person	• relational thinking (seeing patterns and connections) • systems thinking (understanding the impact of change in a system) • interpersonal relationships • co-operation	• flexibility in adaptation to change • willingness to learn from and teach others • willingness to work as a team member • consideration of the common good • sense of solidarity with other people and their problems
Issues dimension	• local–global issues • interconnection between issues • perspectives	• of critical issues at inter-personal through global levels • of interconnections between issues, events and trends • of a range of perspectives on issues • of how perspectives are shaped	• research and enquiry • evaluating, organizing and presenting information • analysing trends • personal judgement and decision making	• curiosity about issues, trends and the global condition • receptivity to, and critical examination of, other perspectives and points of view • empathy with/respect for other people and cultures
Temporal dimension	• phases of time as interactive • alternative futures • action	• of the relationship between past, present and future • of a range of futures, including possible, probable and preferred • of sustainable development • of potential for action, at personal to global levels	• coping with change and uncertainty • extrapolation and prediction • creative and lateral thinking • problem solving • taking personal action	• tolerance of ambiguity and uncertainty • preparedness to consider long-term consequences • preparedness to utilize imagination and intuition • commitment to personal and social action
Inner dimension	• journey inwards • teaching/learning processes • medium and message	• of oneself – identity, strengths, weaknesses and potential • of one's perspectives, values and worldview • of incongruities between professed beliefs and personal actions	• personal reflection and analysis • personal growth – emotional, intellectual, physical, spiritual • learning flexibility (learning within a variety of contexts and in a variety of ways)	• belief in own abilities and potential • recognizing learning as a life-long process • genuineness – presenting the real person • preparedness to take risks • trust

Source: Pike and Selby, 2000

and are often of a very high quality. Oxfam's (1997) *A Curriculum for Global Citizenship* has been widely used by educators in the UK. There is, of course, no separate National Curriculum subject called 'global citizenship', but a key element of citizenship at primary and secondary levels is the wider global scene.

The main features of the Oxfam framework for planning are listed below as knowledge and understanding, skills, values and attitudes. Tables 2.2, 2.3 and 2.4 show how each relates to key stages in England and Scotland. Examples of classroom activities can be found in Young and Commins (2002) and at www.oxfam.org.uk/coolplanet.

Key elements for global citizenship

Knowledge and understanding

Social justice and equity   Understanding of inequality and injustice within and between societies. Knowledge of basic human needs and rights and our responsibilities as global citizens.

Globalisation and interdependence   Knowledge about the world and its affairs: the links between countries, power relationships and different political systems. An understanding of the complexities of global issues.

Peace and conflict   Understanding of historical and present-day conflicts and conflict mediation and prevention.

Sustainable development   Knowledge of how to take care of things. A recognition that the earth's resources are finite, precious and unequally used. An understanding of the global imperative of sustainable development.

Diversity   Understanding of cultural and other diversity within societies and how the lives of others can enrich our own. Knowledge of the nature of prejudice towards diversity and how it can be combated.

Skills

Critical thinking   Ability to assess viewpoints and information in an open-minded and critical way and to be able to change one's opinions, challenge one's own assumptions and make ethical judgements as a result.

Ability to challenge injustice and inequalities   Ability to recognise injustice and inequality in whatever form it is met and to select appropriate action.

Ability to argue effectively   Ability to find out information and to present an informed, persuasive argument based on reason.

Co-operation and conflict resolution   Ability to share and to work with others effectively, to analyse conflicts objectively and to find resolutions acceptable to all sides.

Values and attitudes

Empathy   Sensitivity to the feelings, needs and lives of others in the world; a sense of common humanity and common needs and rights; a capacity for compassion.

Sense of identity and self-esteem   A feeling of one's own value and individuality.

Belief that people can make a difference   A realisation that individuals can act to improve situations, and a desire to participate and take action.

Value and respect for diversity   Appreciation that everyone is different but equal and that we can learn from each other.

Concern for the environment and commitment to sustainable development   Respect and concern for the environment and all life within it. A willingness to consider the needs of future generations and act responsibly.

Commitment to social justice and equity   An interest in and concern about global issues; commitment to fairness and readiness to work for a more just world.

Table 2.2 Global citizenship: knowledge and understanding

Knowledge and understanding	Pre Key Stage 1 Pre stages P1–P3	Key Stage 1 Stages P1–P3	Key Stage 2 Stages P4–P6	Key Stage 3 Stages P7–S2	Key Stage 4 S3–standard grade	16–19
Social justice and equity	• what is fair/unfair • what is right and wrong	• awareness of rich and poor	• fairness between groups • causes and effects of inequality	• inequalities within and between societies • basic rights and responsibilities	• causes of poverty • different views on the eradication of poverty • role as global citizen	• understanding of global debates
Diversity	• awareness of others in relation to self • awareness of similarities and differences between people	• greater awareness of similarities and differences between people	• contribution of different cultures, values and beliefs to our lives • nature of prejudice and ways to combat it	• understanding of issues of diversity	• deeper understanding of different cultures and societies →	
Globalisation and interdependence	• sense of immediate and local environment • awareness of different places	• sense of the wider world • links and connections between different places	• trade between countries • fair trade	• awareness of interdependence • our political system and others	• power relationships north/south • world economic and political systems • ethical consumerism	• complexity of global issues
Sustainable development	• living things and their needs • how to take care of things • sense of the future	• our impact on the environment • awareness of the past and the future	• relationship between people and environment • awareness of finite resources • our potential to change things	• different views of economic and social development, locally and globally • understanding the concepts of probable and preferable futures	• global imperative of sustainable development • lifestyles for a sustainable world →	• understanding of key issues of Agenda 21
Peace and conflict	• our actions have consequences	• conflicts past and present in our society and others • causes of conflict and conflict resolution – personal level	• causes of conflict • impact of conflict • strategies for tackling conflict and for conflict prevention	• causes and effects of conflict, locally and globally • relationship between conflict and peace	• conditions conducive to peace	• complexity of conflict issues and conflict resolution

Source: Oxfam, 1997.

Table 2.3 Global citizenship: skills

Skills	Pre Key Stage 1 Pre stages P1–P3	Key Stage 1 Stages P1–P3	Key Stage 2 Stages P4–P6	Key Stage 3 Stages P7–S2	Key Stage 4 S3–standard grade	16–19
Critical thinking	• listening to others asking questions	• looking at different viewpoints • developing an enquiring mind	• detecting bias, opinion and stereotypes • assessing different viewpoints	• media literacy • making informed decisions	• critically analysing information • making ethical judgement	• handling contentious and complex issues
Ability to argue effectively	• expressing a view	• beginning to state an opinion based on evidence	• finding and selecting evidence • beginning to present a reasoned case	• learning to develop/change position through reasoned argument	• arguing rationally and persuasively from an informed position	• political literacy • participating in relevant political processes
Ability to challenge injustice and inequalities	• beginning to identify unfairness and take appropriate action		• recognising and starting to challenge unfairness	• starting to challenge view-points which perpetuate inequality	• selecting appropriate action to take against inequality	• campaigning for a more just and equitable world
Respect for people and things	• starting to take care of things – animate and inanimate • starting to think of others	• empathising and responding to the needs of others • making links between our lives and the lives of others	• making choices and recognising the consequences of choices	• growing ability to take care of things – animate and inanimate	• following a personal lifestyle for a sustainable world	
Co-operation and conflict resolution	• co-operating • sharing • starting to look at resolving arguments peacefully • starting to participate	• tact and diplomacy involving/including society and others	• accepting and acting on group decisions • compromising	• negotiation	• mediation	• conflict resolution

Source: Oxfam, 1997.

Table 2.4 Global citizenship: values and attitudes

Values and attitudes	Pre Key Stage 1 Pre stages P1–P3	Key Stage 1 Stages P1–P3	Key Stage 2 Stages P4–P6	Key Stage 3 Stages P7–S2	Key Stage 4 S3–standard grade	16–19
Sense of identity and self esteem	• sense of identity and self worth	• awareness of and pride in individuality	• sense of importance of individual worth	• open-mindedness		
Empathy and sense of common humanity	• concern for others in immediate circle	• interest and concern for others in wider sphere	• empathy towards others locally and globally	• compassion • sensitivity to the needs and rights of others	• sense of common humanity and common needs	• sense of individual and collective responsibility • commitment to the eradication of poverty
Commitment to social justice and equity	• sense of fair play	• sense of personal indignation • willingness to speak up for others	• growing interest in world events • sense of justice	• concern for injustice and inequality • willingness to take action against inequity	• commitment to social justice and equity	
Valuing and respecting diversity	• positive attitude towards difference and diversity	• valuing others as equal and different • willingness to learn from the experiences of others	• growing respect for difference and diversity	• respecting rights of all to have a point of view	• valuing all people as equal and different	
Concern for the environment and commitment to sustainable development	• appreciation of own environment and living things • sense of wonder and curiosity	• concern for the wider environment • beginning to value resources • willingness to care for the environment	• sense of responsibility for the environment and the use of resources	• concern about the effects of our lifestyles on people and the environment	• concern for the future of the planet and future generations • commitment to a lifestyle for a sustainable world	• commitment to sustainable development
Belief that people can make a difference	• willingness to admit to and learn from mistakes	• awareness that our actions have consequences • willingness to co-operate and participate	• belief that things can be better and that individuals can make a difference	• willingness to take a stand on global issues	• willingness to work towards a more equitable future	

Source: Oxfam, 1997.

These two frameworks for planning come from different sources but have much in common. Either provides a sound template for auditing what goes on in school and for planning detailed lessons across the curriculum. One difference between them is that Pike and Selby are explicit about the need to help children to think critically and creatively about the future, whilst this is merely implicit in the Oxfam framework. Detailed examples of how to develop a futures perspective can be found in Hicks and Holden (1995) and Hicks (2001; 2002).

PRACTICE

All subjects can contribute to a global dimension and a wide range of resources exists to support this endeavour. Here are some possibilities for early years, science and citizenship.

Early years

There is a common and erroneous belief that younger children are unaware of the wider world and that it should be left to Key Stage 2. However, young children are aware of the world in their own way. Fountain (1990) points out that nursery and infant children regularly (and also see Chapter 9):

- call each other names (prejudice)
- arbitrarily exclude others from their play (discrimination)
- argue over materials (resource discrimination)
- protest that rules are not fair (human rights)
- quarrel and fight (peace and conflict)
- waste consumable materials (environmental awareness)
- find that more can be accomplished by working together (interdependence).

So some of the key concerns of global education are there in the classroom from the beginning and how the teacher deals with these is important. For younger children, 'the world' is not be construed in the same way as for older children, but it is still the world, *their* world. This may relate to the family, the street, the park, the shops, going to town, going on holiday, places seen on television. Their sense of the world is generally very immediate and often local. At the same time:

> Children come into contact with people and places beyond their direct experience on a regular basis. This indirect contact includes television, holidays, books, toys, food … Children are therefore gaining knowledge about, and forming attitudes towards other people, places and cultures from an early age … In studying distant places, therefore, teachers should be concerned with challenging certain attitudes, as well as fostering others.
>
> (Martin, 1995: 4)

So developing children's self-esteem – their empathy for others, respect for diversity, concern for the environment and ability to resolve conflicts fairly – needs to begin at an early age. Page (2000) has also shown that younger children, in their own way, are quite capable of thinking about the future. In their playful mix of fact and fantasy, she argues, they are developing positive feelings about their place in the future and their role in its creation.

Citizenship

Citizenship in the curriculum offers a variety of contexts for children to think about their place in the *local* and *global* communities, two sides of the same coin and thus inextricably bound together. The nature of good citizenship is being discussed in a number of countries. In their nine-country study, Cogan and Derricott (1998) found that the following qualities were seen as vital for 'effective citizenship' in the twenty-first century:

- seeing problems in a global context
- working co-operatively and responsibly
- accepting cultural differences
- critical and systemic thinking
- solving problems non-violently
- following an environmental lifestyle
- defending human rights
- participating in politics.

This list was not drawn up by teachers, but by people with an interest in the nature of good citizenship. Teachers, however, readily recognise most of these characteristics as behaviours which they actively seek to promote in the classroom. It should be noted that the term 'politics' is used here in its widest sense of questions to do with the distribution of power in local and global society and how people gain it and use it. One can talk about the politics of the family, a relationship or an institution. Understanding the difference between 'power over' and 'power with' is one of the most valuable distinctions that can be made in citizenship.

One of the most interesting aspects of citizenship is that it seeks to develop skills of participation and responsible action. It is legitimate not only to learn about the world but also to act to change it. This involves identifying possible 'projects for change', whether in the school, local or global community, and working with others to achieve particular positive goals. It is just such active involvement in daily life that gives young people a sense of purpose and hope. Both pupils and teachers are often surprised to find just how many local and national groups there are working for change. The focus ranges from the environment, homelessness and human rights to globalisation, animal rights and transport. There are many classroom resources that look at different aspects of global citizenship. Three in particular are Clough and Holden (2002), Young and Commins (2002), and Hicks (2001).

Science

An excellent example of the possibilities in science are set out in *Science: The Global Dimension*, one of a series of subject booklets published by the DEA. The rationale is that it 'offers pupils opportunities to explore real issues with real solutions where there are clear social, moral and ethical choices made by scientists and all those involved in the journey from scientific principle and research to practical application' (Brownlie, 2003: 4). Amongst the issues that could be discussed in science at Key Stages 3 and 4 are the following statements:

- Fast food shops in our high streets are to blame for deforestation in Latin America.
- It is easier to get funding for research into obesity and slimming treatments than it is for malaria.
- Poverty is the most environmentally destructive force on the planet.
- The promotion of baby formula milks has improved infant survival and health.
- Terminator gene technologies benefit farmers in India.
- Nuclear power is clean, safe and easy to use.

(Brownlie 2003: 7)

Such an approach to science education has many benefits for pupils. It makes it easier for them to appreciate the relevance of science to their own lives, to find science more interesting and motivating, to develop informed opinions and take appropriate action about scientific matters, and to understand their own role in global society (see Chapter 13).

CONCLUSION

This chapter has set out the rationale for a global dimension in the curriculum by referring to current global trends and also to official DfEE requirements. It offers two different models for planning such a global dimension – from the International Institute for Global Education and from Oxfam – both of which offer practical ideas for curriculum implementation. All curriculum subjects can contribute in different ways to a global dimension and three examples have been used to illustrate this from early years, citizenship, and science,

QUESTIONS FOR DISCUSSION

- Which of the two frameworks for planning do you prefer and why?
- How can your main subject contribute to the global dimension?
- Which of the classroom resources listed do you find valuable and why?

REFERENCES

Brownlie, A. (2003) *Science: The Global Dimension*, London: DEA.

Clough, N. and Holden, C. (2002) *Education for Citizenship: Ideas into Action*, London: Routledge Falmer.

Cogan, C. and Derricott, R. (1998) *Citizenship for the 21st Century*, London: Kogan Page.

DEA (2001) *Global Perspectives in Education: The Contribution of Development Education*, London: DEA.

Fountain, S. (1990) *Learning Together: Global Education 4–7*, Cheltenham: Stanley Thornes.

Fountain, S. (1995) 'Change and the future', in S. Fountain (ed.) *Education for Development: A Teacher's Resource for Global Learning*, London: Hodder and Stoughton.

Hicks, D. (2001) *Citizenship for the Future: A Practical Classroom Guide*, Godalming: Worldwide Fund for Nature UK.

Hicks, D. (2002) *Lessons for the Future: The Missing Dimension in Education*, London: RoutledgeFalmer.

Hicks, D. (2003) 'Thirty years of global education: a reminder of key principles and practices', *Educational Review* 55(3): 265–75.

Hicks, D. and Holden, C. (1995) *Visions of the Future: Why We Need to Teach for Tomorrow*, Stoke-on-Trent: Trentham Books.

Martin, F. (1995) *Early Years Geography*, Cambridge: Chris Kington.

MORI (1998) *Children's Knowledge of Global Issues: A Research Study Among 11–16 Year Olds*, London: MORI.

Oxfam (1997) *A Curriculum for Global Citizenship*, Oxford: Oxfam's Development Education Programme.

Page, J. (2000) *Reframing the Early Childhood Curriculum: Educational Imperatives for the Future*, London: RoutledgeFalmer.

Pike, G. and Selby, D. (1996) *Reconnecting: From National to Global Curriculum*, Guildford: World Wide Fund for Nature UK.

Pike, G. and Selby, D. (1999) *In the Global Classroom*, Vol. 1, Toronto: Pippin Publishing.

Pike, G. and Selby, D. (2000) *In the Global Classroom*, Vol. 2, Toronto: Pippin Publishing.

Richardson, R. (1990) *Daring to be a Teacher*, Stoke-on-Trent: Trentham Books.

Roddick, A. (2001) *Take It Personally: How Globalization Affects You and Powerful Ways to Challenge it*, London: Thorsons.

World Watch Institute (2002) *Vital Signs: The Trends that are Shaping our Future 2002–2003*, London: Earthscan.

Young, M. and Commins, E. (2002) *Global Citizenship: The Handbook for Primary Teaching*, Cambridge: Chris Kington/Oxford: Oxfam.

RECOMMENDED READING

For a global perspective

ACCAC (2002) *Education for Sustainable Development and Global Citizenship*, Qualifications, Curriculum and Assessment Authority for Wales, Birmingham: ACCAC Publications.

DfEE (2000) *Developing a Global Dimension in the School Curriculum*, London: DfEE.

Goldstein, T. and Selby, D. (2000) *Weaving Connections: Educating for Peace, Social and Environmental Justice*, Toronto: Sumach Press.

Osler, A. and Vincent, K. (2002) *Citizenship and the Challenge of Global Education*, Stoke-on-Trent: Trentham Books.

Pike, G. and Selby, D. (1999) *In the Global Classroom*, Vol. 1, Toronto: Pippin Publishing.

Pike, G. and Selby, D. (2000) *In the Global Classroom*, Vol. 2, Toronto: Pippin Publishing.

Richardson, R. and Miles, B. (2003) *Equality Stories: Recognition, Respect and Raising Achievement*, Stoke-on-Trent: Trentham Books.

For a futures perspective

Fien, J. (2002) *Teaching and Learning for a Sustainable Future*, Paris: UNESCO, CD-ROM and at www.unesco.org/educational/tlsf.

Fountain, S. (1995) Change and the future, in: *Education for Development: A Teacher's Resource for Global Learning*, London: Hodder and Stoughton.

Hicks, D. (2001) *Citizenship for the Future: A Practical Classroom Guide*, Godalming: World Wide Fund for Nature UK.

Hicks, D. and Holden, C. (1995) *Visions of the Future: Why We Need to Teach for Tomorrow*, Stoke-on-Trent: Trentham Books.

Hutchinson, F. (1996) *Educating Beyond Violent Futures*, London: Routledge.

Page, J. (2000) *Reframing the Early Childhood Curriculum: Educational Imperatives for the Future*, London: RoutledgeFalmer.

USEFUL ORGANISATIONS AND WEBSITES

Centre for Global and Futures Education: www.bathspa.ac.uk/school-of-education.

Department for International Development: www.dfid.gov.uk.

Development Education Association: www.dea.org.uk.

International Institute for Global Education: www.oise.toronto.ca.

Oxfam: www.oxfam.org.uk/coolplanet.

3 Education and Environment

David Hicks

Why do teachers need to know about environmental events and trends? How can we help young people to understand the current crisis of sustainability? What resources are available to assist in teaching about such matters? This chapter sets out to answer questions such as these and, in particular, explores:

- the rationale for an environmental component in the curriculum
- the origins, nature and purposes of environmental education
- why this has been replaced by education for sustainable development.

RATIONALE

In 1992 and 2002 two of the most important events of the last 50 years took place in Brazil and South Africa: the Earth Summits, attended by leaders from most countries of the world and activists from numerous international non-governmental organisations (NGOs). Why did so many people come together and what did they discuss? They came because since the early 1970s it has been recognised that human activity is increasingly threatening the environment or biosphere – that narrow zone of earth, air and water on which all life (plants, creatures, humans) depends. They also came because since the early 1970s it has increasingly been recognised that issues of development, i.e. global wealth and poverty, are threatening people's life chances in both rich and poor countries of the world. The welfare of planet and people, issues of environment and development, are now seen as inextricably related. The term 'sustainable development' is used both to describe these joint concerns and to highlight what needs to be achieved.

Environmental issues

Many environmental issues have been in the news over the last few years: the impact of global warming; genetically modified crops; sources of energy – nuclear or renewable; food safety and the nature of farming; transport problems in our cities. In different ways each of these is already affecting daily life in our own communities. Whilst environmental issues as such are not the focus of this chapter, the way in which education responds to them is. This reflects increasing public awareness of the major environmental dilemmas that we face and which we need creatively to resolve (see, for example, the periodical *Green Futures*).

People respond in a variety of ways. Many individuals and local authorities are aware of the need to use resources wisely so they recycle paper, glass and plastics and try not to waste water or electricity. In relation to transport, many people try to use bus, train and bike as well as car; they may be interested in countryside/urban conservation and in diet and healthy eating. Going a step further we find people who profess a particular interest in environmental matters; they may belong to Friends of the Earth or Greenpeace and perhaps belong to a local wildlife or woodland trust. They are prepared to write to members of parliament (MPs) and newspapers to make their views known and to argue an environmental case.

The most committed and concerned will be expert on specific issues, interested in supporting particular campaigns. They will see connections between issues and espouse a deeper green lifestyle: using renewable energy, sharing a car, living more sustainably. They are prepared to attend protests and demonstrations and, if necessary, to take direct action in support of chosen causes. What people see as the problem, the causes of the problem and solutions to the problem will vary, of course, depending on their ideological perspective (see, for example, *The Ecologist* and Pepper, 1996).

Development issues

Many crucial development issues have been in the news over the last few years. These include the impact of World Bank and International Monetary Fund restructuring policies on the economies of less developed countries (LDCs); proposals to cancel LDC debt; the impact of acquired immune deficiency syndrome (AIDS) in Africa; refugees and migrants; patenting of seeds by agribusiness transnational corporations; concerns about the impact of globalisation. Many of these issues impact on our own communities too. Development issues as such are not the focus of this chapter but the way in which education responds to them is. This reflects increased public awareness of issues relating to global wealth and poverty and the need for their successful resolution (see, for example, the periodical *The New Internationalist*).

People tend to be more aware of environmental issues than development issues. However, there are still different levels of response and concern. Many people take part in occasional donations to NGOs when particular disasters occur and are reported on the news. This may be to do with floods, famine, lack of water or homelessness. Others take a particular interest in development issues and may belong to NGOs such as Oxfam, Christian Aid or Amnesty International. They will be prepared to write to MPs and newspapers to make their views known about appropriate development.

Like those most committed to environmental issues, those committed to action on development will be knowledgeable and support campaigns. They will see connections between issues and espouse a less material lifestyle by becoming an ethical consumer and investor and living more sustainably. They may attend demonstrations such as anti-globalisation and take direct action in support of chosen causes. What people see as the problem will again vary depending on their ideological perspective.

Education for sustainable development

Education for sustainable development (ESD), sometimes known as 'education for sustainability', is a post-Rio phenomenon of the 1990s that focuses on these two major concerns in order to prepare young people more effectively for life in the twenty-first century. The importance of ESD is referred to in the revised 2000 version of the National Curriculum:

> Education for sustainable development enables pupils to develop the knowledge, skills, understanding and values to participate in decisions about the way we do things individually and collectively, both locally and globally, that will improve the quality of life now without damaging the planet for the future. There are opportunities for pupils to develop their understanding of sustainable development within the school curriculum, in particular in their work in geography, science, PSHE and citizenship.
>
> (Department for Employment and Education [DfEE] 1999: 23)

This chapter looks at how this important educational shift came about. To do so we need to know something about the origins and purpose of environmental education (Palmer, 1998).

ENVIRONMENTAL EDUCATION

Environment literally means surroundings: this room, this city, this landscape. It embraces rural and urban, natural and human-made, people and planet. It cannot be treated as separate from other areas of human experience since all life is interconnected. The natural environment is a proper focus of human and educational concern for several important reasons, including the following:

Source of all life   The biosphere consists of a thin film of matter around the planet which supports life – soils, water, atmosphere and plants – which, together with solar insolation make earth a habitable place. This living layer, the biosphere, can be likened in thickness to the skin on an apple. All life on earth depends on these natural systems for its health and well-being. Humans are no exception. Whatever the state of our science and technology at present we cannot live without drawing on the natural resources of the earth. Educators therefore need to know about the nature of the biosphere and the ways in which it works.

Awe and wonder   The rising and setting of the sun, the turning of the year, volcanic eruptions, storms at sea, the ability of the land to bring forth water and food in abundance, our companion creatures, all have long been a source of awe and wonder. Some argue that the sense of loss people feel today around community/purpose/

meaning, together with the anxiety and stress of modern living, arise primarily because we are suffering from a deep historical trauma – the removal of our lives from the cycles of the natural world. Educators need to appreciate the natural world because it is a source of beauty, awe, wonder and healing, all prerequisites to human well-being.

Human impact   Humans have always had an impact on the natural environment, although only significantly in the last few thousand years. Even the wildest British landscapes have been created by human impact: the Lake District or the Somerset levels. The last 300 years (the Scientific Revolution, the Industrial Revolution and urbanisation) have seen the greatest impact. Worldwide we find soil erosion, desertification, endangered species, damage to habitats, toxic waste, depletion of ozone layer and global warming. Human activity threatens the well-being of the biosphere itself. Educators should be concerned about human impact because it affects quality of life now and in the future.

A long tradition

Sterling (1993: 8) has noted that: 'In a little over a quarter of a century, environmental education has progressed from relative obscurity to being discussed as instrumental to achieving a sustainable world.' Over this period the emphasis in environmental education has shifted, from conservation of the countryside in the 1960s and 1970s (plants, trees, hedgerows, wildlife), to national and global problems in the 1970s and 1980s (pollution, resource depletion, global warming) and issues of sustainability in the 1990s. International developments in environmental education over this period were very much influenced by NGO activity on the environment, such as the United Nations Conference on Environment in 1972. In particular, the United Nations Educational, Scientific and Cultural Organisation and the United Nations Environment Programme (UNEP) promoted environmental education at milestone international conferences in the 1970s and 1980s and gradually agreed definitions of its nature and scope.

Prior to the National Curriculum, environmental education depended on school and Local Education Authority policy. Its importance was officially signalled by *Environmental Education from 5 to 16* (Department of Education and Science [DES], 1989). More recent recognition came with *Teaching Environmental Matters Through the National Curriculum* (School Curriculum and Assessment Authority [SCAA], 1996). This shows how all subjects in the National Curriculum can help contribute to an environmental perspective.

The greatest body of experience in environmental education lies with NGOs such as the World Wide Fund for Nature, the Council for Environmental Education, and the National Association for Environmental Education. Each of these offers invaluable advice and support for teachers and has its own publications and website. Amongst subject associations the Geographical Association (GA) has a lot to offer, see for example, *Awareness into Action: Environmental Education in the Primary Curriculum* (1995).

Aims of environmental education

The SCAA document on environmental education suggests that:

> Environmental education aims to: i) provide all pupils with opportunities to acquire the knowledge, understanding and skills required to engage effectively with environmental issues, including those of sustainable development; ii) encourage pupils to examine and interpret the environment from a variety of perspectives – physical, geographical, biological, sociological, economic, political, technological, historical, aesthetic, ethical and spiritual; iii) arouse pupils' awareness and curiosity about the environment and encourage active participation in resolving environmental problems.
>
> (SCAA 1996: 2)

Three different but interrelated forms of environmental education have frequently been noted, as follows:

Education about the environment   The most common form of this emphasises knowledge and facts about natural systems, focuses on ecological concepts and technical solutions to problems, and generally neglects human causes and changes needed in social and political systems to resolve problems.

Education through the environment   Students' experiences in the environment are used as a medium for education; direct contact adds reality and relevance, and experiential learning awakes the affect/feelings. Taking place in school grounds and on field visits, the aim of this method is to develop environmental concern, based on the idea that you can't protect what you don't love.

Education for the environment   This form of education engages students in exploration and resolution of real issues. It promotes awareness of human agency and politics of the environment, environmentally conscious lifestyles, and engagement in responsible and active citizenship locally, nationally and globally.

Anecdotal evidence suggests that the most common form of environmental education in schools in the United Kingdom is *about* the environment. Good practice is based on education *through* the environment, but education *for* the environment is less often to be found. In fact all three should be seen as vital interrelated perspectives. David Orr (1994) argues that if education does not help students become environmentally aware it becomes part of the problem.

> Education is not widely regarded as a problem, although the lack of it is. The conventional wisdom holds that all education is good, and the more of it one has, the better ... The truth is that without significant precautions, education can equip people merely to be more effective vandals of the earth. If one listens carefully, it may even be possible to hear the Creation groan every year in late May when another batch of smart, degree-holding, but ecologically illiterate, *Homo sapiens* who are eager to succeed are launched into the biosphere.
>
> (Orr, 1996: 5)

Without a detailed knowledge of environmental issues, Orr argues, people are likely to continue damaging the earth. Unless education specifically addresses this matter it will be part of the problem rather than part of the answer.

So what impact has environmental education had on children? Morris and Schagen (1996) report on research with 15–16 year olds. Their main findings were that young people who were found to be both informed and had developed positive attitudes towards the environment showed that they were more predisposed to action than those with factual information alone. The extent to which schools can play a role in this seems greater than that which had been previously identified or assumed in other studies. Whilst being significantly more concerned about the global environment, pupils are more likely to feel ownership, and therefore motivation about problems, if emphasis is put on the local manifestation of that issue and its relationship to their daily lives.

Parry and Scott (1997) report the following findings: environmental education has a key role to play in encouraging children and their families to adopt environmentally responsible lifestyles, but influences other than formal education are also critical. An over-concentration in schools on global issues such as ozone depletion and deforestation can result in a sense of powerlessness about effectiveness of individual action. Pupils are often not helped to see that global problems are the result of cumulative individual actions and that environmental action must tackle the causes (human behaviours), not merely the symptoms. Girls are more likely than boys to have high levels of environmental awareness and be involved in environmental action. A valuable overview of the research on learning in environmental education has been provided by Rickinson (2001).

EDUCATION FOR SUSTAINABLE DEVELOPMENT (ESD)

In the revised National Curriculum of 2000, ESD has a place in both the primary and secondary orders. This came about as a result of recommendations made by the government's Sustainable Development Education Panel (1998). As well as being a response to international and public concern, ESD also draws on three long-standing educational traditions in the UK.

Influences on ESD

The first, of course, is the long and rich tradition of environmental education which provides one of the main building blocks for ESD. Remember, however, the distinction made between education *about*, *through* and *for* the environment – and the fact that it is the first two which seem to be the more common in schools. Historically, environmental education (EE) has not necessarily been about sustainability, so the question arises as to whether ESD is something different from EE?

Development education (DE) is the second main building block for ESD. It had its origin 30 years ago in the educational work of NGOs concerned about issues of inequality and injustice. Over that period it has had considerable influence on mainstream good practice. The Development Education Association (DEA), with its publication *The Development Education Journal*, is one of the key organisations in this field. The DEA (www.dea.org.uk) sees development education as encompassing the following principles:

- enabling people to understand the links between their own lives and those of people throughout the world
- increasing understanding of the economic, cultural, political and environmental influences which shape our lives
- developing the skills, attitudes and values which enable people to work together to bring about change and take control of their own lives
- working towards achieving a more just and sustainable world in which power and resources are more equitably shared.

The third broad influence on ESD is the field of global education already described in Chapter 2. Various development organisations came together with DfEE (2000) to produce the influential document *Developing a Global Dimension in the School Curriculum*.

Practitioners and advocates of ESD still often betray their EE or DE origins by the way in which they discuss the field. Some may place more emphasis on environment and others on development. ESD *is* different, however, because it gives equal weight to the welfare of both people (social) and the planet (environmental) and the inter-relationships between the two. However, it is likely that the meanings of sustainability will always be contested as a result of people's differing beliefs and values about the nature of society (Davison, 2001).

Meanings of sustainability

What teachers initially think the term ESD means will thus be bound up with their prior notions (if any) of what the term 'sustainability' means. Fien (1998) and others have made an important distinction between 'sustainable growth' and 'sustainable development'. The former refers to a technocentric and reformist view of the world, i.e. a sustainable future can be attained through development of existing technology and some minor changes to the global economic system. Sustainable development, on the other hand, argues that science and technology can also be part of the problem and that fundamental changes are needed in the global economic system (especially in rich-world lifestyles) before a sustainable future can be achieved. This also relates to what environmentalists call 'light green' and 'dark green' perspectives on action for change. It is also important to note that views of the environment may differ radically in different cultures. An excellent example of this in relation to indigenous peoples can be found in Smith and Williams (1999).

We have also noted that traditional mainstream education, i.e. education as developed under modernity, is seen by radical ecologists as part of the problem rather than solution to environmental dilemmas. As Orr (1994) argues, much of schooling has actually been about 'education for *un*sustainability'. This is because the dominant social and political forces in capitalist society favour technocentric 'sustainable growth' rather than ecocentric 'sustainable development' and this perspective is, in turn, reflected in mainstream education.

As a result we can identify different forms of ESD. Huckle (1995) argues that:

> Education for sustainability has to question dominant forms of knowledge and values, rediscover lost histories, knowledge and values, and encourage pupils to envision and realise desirable futures. Above all, it has to deconstruct and reconstruct culture since cultural issues are the starting point for understanding the issue of who has power and how it is reproduced and manifested in the social relations of everyday life.
>
> (Huckle 1995: 3)

Compare this with the Sustainable Development Education Panel (1998):

> Education for sustainable development is about the learning needed to maintain and improve our quality of life and the quality of life of generations to come. It is about equipping individuals, communities, groups, businesses and government to live and act sustainably, as well as giving them an understanding of the environmental, social and economic issues involved. It is about preparing for the world in which we will live in the next century and making sure that we are not found wanting.
>
> (Sustainable Development Education Panel (1998: 30)

These two definitions represent different forms of ESD. The Panel definition can be described as 'weak' ESD, i.e. it is non-critical of existing the social/economic order, and has a non-problematised and non-political view of sustainable development. It is also the most common form of ESD. Huckle's definition is a 'strong' form of ESD, more radical, critical and concerned about suggesting fundamental socio-political changes. The Panel definition is also 'narrow' ESD, since it stays within the existing theory and practice of DE and EE, whereas Huckle's 'broad' ESD seeks to create a new educational paradigm, or play a key part in forming one (Huckle and Sterling, 1996; Sterling, 2001). It is more far-reaching in its social, environmental, economic and educational implications.

Support and guidance

To find out more about how issues of sustainable development can be explored at different key stages and subject areas, consult the QCA website (www.nc.uk.net/esd). Recent curriculum developments in Wales are particularly interesting because education for sustainable development and global citizenship (ESDGC) have been brought together to create a single cross-curricular dimension. Education for sustainable development and global citizenship (Qualifactions, Curriculum and Assessment Authority for Wales [ACCAC], 2002) is described as being about:

- the links between society, economy and environment and between our own lives and those of people throughout the world
- the needs and rights of both present and future generations
- the relationships between power, resources and human rights
- the local and global implications of everything we do and the actions that individuals and organizations can take in response to local and global issues.

Nine key concepts have been identified to help explore appropriate knowledge and understanding, attitudes, values and skills for ESDGC:

1   *Interdependence:* understanding how people, the environment and the economy are inextricably linked at all levels from local to global;
2   *Citizenship and stewardship:* recognising the importance of taking individual responsibility and action to make the world a better place;
3   *Needs and rights:* understanding our own basic needs and about human rights and the implications for the needs of future generations of actions taken today;
4   *Diversity:* understanding, respecting and valuing both human diversity (cultural, social, economic) and biodiversity;
5   *Sustainable change:* understanding that resources are finite and that this has implications for people's lifestyles and for commerce and industry;
6   *Quality of life:* acknowledging that global equity and justice are essential elements of sustainability and that basic needs must be met universally;
7   *Uncertainty and precaution:* acknowledging that there is a range of possible approaches to sustainability and global citizenship and that situations are constantly changing, indicating a need for flexibility and lifelong learning;
8   *Values and perceptions:* developing a critical evaluation of images of, and information about, the less and more economically developed parts of the world and an appreciation of the effect these have on people's attitudes and values;
9   *Conflict resolution:* understanding how conflicts are a barrier to development and a risk to us all and why there is a need for their resolution and the promotion of harmony.

Envisioning the future

In order to work towards a sustainable future we need to be able to envision some of the features of such a society. The importance of this has been stressed by Jones (1998) and different scenarios of sustainability have been described by Dauncey (1999). The exploration of preferred futures is a crucial element in the model of global education described in Chapter 2. I want to conclude by sharing the findings of a small research study into students' preferred futures (Hicks, 2002). The question it was concerned with was 'How do students envision their preferable futures for society?' As a result of drawing future timelines, using visualisation and drawing posters, a sample of some 90 students, drawn from three different universities, identified the key features of their desirable future. This led to the identification of 12 key themes and their indicators, shown in rank order below.

1   *Green:* clean air and water, trees, wildlife, flowers;
2   *Convivial:* co-operative, relaxed, happy, caring, laughter;
3   *Transport:* no cars, no pollution, public transport, bikes;
4   *Peaceful:* absence of violent conflict, security, global harmony;
5   *Equality:* no poverty, a fair share for all, no hunger;
6   *Justice:* equal rights of people and planet, no discrimination;
7   *Community:* local, small, friendly, simpler, sense of community;
8   *Education:* for all, ongoing for life, holistic, community;

9   *Energy:* lower consumption, renewable and clean sources;
10   *Work:* for all, satisfying, shared, shorter hours;
11   *Health:* better health care, alternative, longer life;
12   *Food:* organic farming, locally grown, balanced diet.

Primarily these students want a future characterised by environmental concern, citing respect and reverence for the biosphere as their highest priority. They also referred to clean air, land and water, together with a richness and diversity of species, and an abundance of trees and flowers. Secondly, they want a more convivial future, one which stresses quality of life and human interaction. Reference was made to a sense of social well-being, to a co-operative atmosphere, to less stress and more shared laughter. An awareness and celebration of interconnectedness with the planet and with each other are thus the primary features of their preferred futures. They also want to live in a future which is more peaceful, both locally and in the world as a whole. It involves a greater sense of security and harmony as a result of living in a less violent society. Transportation is one of the issues and in their preferred future the emphasis is on cheap and efficient public transport, particularly trams and cycles.

What is particularly striking about this vision of the future is that it is based on many of the key features that a sustainable society should exhibit. Such a society would thus embody principles that respond to some of the deepest human needs in relation to self, society and environment. As a result education for sustainable development may be one of the most timely innovations of the late twentieth century.

CONCLUSION

This chapter has set out the rationale for education for sustainable development within the school curriculum. Such a rationale is based on the need to address environmental and development issues in the local-global community and on the DfEE requirement for this to occur in schools. A distinction is made between the long tradition of environmental education and the more holistic notion of ESD which embraces the welfare of both people and planet. It is noted that when students envision their preferred futures many want a society which is characterised by more sustainable lifestyles.

QUESTIONS FOR DISCUSSION

- What makes ESD different from traditional EE?
- How can other degree subjects contribute to ESD?
- Which of the resources listed do you find valuable and why?

REFERENCES

Dauncey, G. (1999) *Earthfutures: Stories from a Sustainable World*, Gabriola Island, BC: New Society Publishers.

Davison, A. (2001) *Technology and the Contested Meanings of Sustainability*, Albany: State University of New York Press.

DES (1989) *Environmental Education from 5 to 16*, London: DES.

DfEE (1999) *The National Curriculum: Handbook for Primary Teachers in England*, London: DfEE.

DfEE (2000) *Developing a Global Dimension in the School Curriculum*, London: DfEE.

Fien, J. (1998) 'Environmental education for a new century', in D. Hicks and R. Slaughter (eds) *Futures Education: The World Yearbook of Education 1998*, London, Kogan Page.

Geographical Association (GA) (1995) *Awareness into Action: Environmental Education in the Primary Curriculum*, Sheffield: GA.

Huckle, J. (1995) 'Greening educational studies', paper presented to Green Academic Network.

Jones, C. (1998) 'The need to envision sustainable futures', in D. Hicks and R. Slaughter (eds) *Futures Education: The World Yearbook of Education 1998*, London: Kogan Page.

Morris, M. and Schagen, I. (1996) *Green Attitudes or Learned Responses?* Slough: National Foundation for Educational Research.

Orr, D. (1994) *Earth in Mind: On Education, Environment and the Human Prospect*, Washington, DC: Island Press.

Palmer, J. (1998) *Environmental Education in the 21st Century*, London: Routledge.

Parry, J. and Scott, A. (1997) *Learning to be Green: The Future of Environmental Education*, Brighton: ESRC Global Environmental Change Programme, University of Sussex.

Rickinson, M. (2001) 'Learners and learning in environmental education: a critical review of the evidence', *Environmental Education Research*, 7(3), special issue.

Smith, G. and Williams, D. (eds) (1999) *Ecological Education in Action: On Weaving Education, Culture, and the Environment*, Albany: State University of New York Press.

Sterling, S. (1993) '25 years in a nutshell', *Annual Review of Environmental Education*, 6: 8.

Sustainable Development Education Panel (1998) *First Annual Report 1998*, London: Department of Environment, Transport and Regions.

RECOMMENDED READING

ACCAC (2002) *Education for Sustainable Development and Global Citizenship*, Qualifications, Curriculum and Assessment Authority for Wales, Birmingham: ACCAC Publications.

Fien, J. (ed.) (2001) *Teaching and Learning for a Sustainable Future*, Paris: UNESCO (CD-ROM).

Hicks, D. (2001) *Citizenship for the Future: A Practical Classroom Guide*, Godalming: World Wide Fund for Nature UK

Hicks, D. (2002) *Lessons for the Future: The Missing Dimension in Education*, London: RoutledgeFalmer.

Huckle, J. and Sterling, S. (eds) (1996) *Education for Sustainability*, London: Earthscan.

Orr, D. (1994) *Earth in Mind: On Education, Environment and the Human Prospect*, Washington, DC: Island Press.

Pepper, D. (1996) *Modern Environmentalism: An Introduction*, London: Routledge

Roddick, A. (2001) *Taking it Personally: How Globalization Affects You and Powerful Ways to Challenge It*, London: Thorsons.

SCAA (1996) *Teaching Environmental Matters Through the National Curriculum*, London: SCAA.

Sterling, S. (2001) *Sustainable Education: Re-visioning Learning and Change*, Dartington: Green Books.

USEFUL ORGANISATIONS AND WEBSITES

Council for Environmental Education: www.cee.org.uk.

Department for Education and Skills: www.dfes.gov.uk.

Development Education Association: www.dea.org.uk.

The Ecologist: www.theecologist.org.

Education for sustainable development in the national curriculum: www.nc.uk/esd.

National Association for Environmental Education: www.naee.co.uk.

Qualifications and Curriculum Authority: www.nc.uk.net/esd/index.htm.

World Wide Fund for Nature: www.wwf.org.uk.

4   Education in Europe

David Coulby

Pupils in the United kingdom (UK) are growing up in Europe and an understanding of Europe's place in the world is important to them and their teachers. It is also interesting to examine the similarities and differences between schooling and education in some of the countries of Europe. This chapter describes and explains three trends:

- the trend towards European unification
- the move towards conversion in matters of educational policy and practice
- areas of radical difference between education systems in Europe.

Europe as a whole is tending to come together politically, economically and culturally. Within the social sciences, not least in Education Studies, Europe is increasingly being used as the unit of analysis and description, rather than that of individual states. Europe, in the current lexicon, is seen and analysed as an educational space (Novoa and Lawn, 2002). Unfortunately this coming together of Europe is happening in an exceedingly complex and conflicted way. Furthermore, any convergence in matters of education is at least matched by areas of stubborn isolationism as states and more local administrative levels seek to retain control over educational institutions and practices.

THE TREND TOWARDS EUROPEAN UNIFICATION

The trend towards European unification is complex because it involves two main international bodies – the European Union (EU) and the North Atlantic Treaty Organisation (NATO) – as well as many less important organisations. The nature of these two bodies in terms of membership and policy is also complex and fractured, raising the vexed question of which states actually belong to Europe. This section examines these issues by considering firstly the EU and then NATO.

The European Union at the time of writing consists of 15 member states: Belgium, the Netherlands, Luxembourg, Germany, France, Italy, Ireland, Denmark, the UK, Spain, Portugal, Greece, Finland, Sweden and Austria. A further tranche of 10 states have negotiated entry (accession) for 2004: Latvia, Lithuania, Estonia, Poland, Hungary, the Czech Republic, Slovakia, Slovenia, Malta and Cyprus. This will dramatically increase the number of members and thereby the political complexity of the Union and the possibilities for conflict. However, it will not make such a large impact on the number of people in the Union as most of these states have small populations and only Poland has a large number of people. Two more countries, Romania and Bulgaria, have agreed a timetable to accession. A further country, Turkey, has been accepted for accession in principle, but controversially no timetable has yet been agreed. Other countries, including those of former Yugoslavia and of the southern Mediterranean littoral, have expressed interest in eventual membership.

EU membership then does not include the whole of Europe. Norway, perhaps on the basis of confidence in its own oil wealth, and Switzerland, on the basis of banking wealth and the tangible gains of the policy of neutrality during the twentieth century, have consciously opted not to be members. Some of the European mini-states with advantageous tax and banking regimes remain beyond EU control: Liechtenstein, Monaco. The movement of the EU to the east, following the fall of communism in eastern Europe in 1989 and the break-up of the Soviet Union in 1991, has been painfully slow. The EU could hardly be said to have raced to embrace and assist the new democracies. The more impoverished and politically suspect states of former Yugoslavia remain beyond the pale. The question of the eventual entry of other former Soviet states (apart from the three Baltic countries) remains to be addressed: Ukraine, Belarus and indeed Russia itself.

Even within itself the EU is divided with some states subscribing to some policies, for example on immigration, and some states not (Budge and Newton, 1997). This is referred to as the multi-track Europe. Critically, there is no unified policy on foreign affairs and defence (considered in the discussion of NATO below) or on the common currency. Possibly the most potent symbol of European unification and the greatest achievement of the EU and Sweden, the euro, will probably be the currency of all the member states except the UK at the end of 2003. The accession countries have targets and a timetable to provide for their eventual membership of the euro zone. Already the euro has become a preferred international currency for those states which for economic or often political reasons wish to avoid using the dollar. It is not unreasonable to predict that the euro will soon replace the dollar as the international trading currency of choice. The UK's reluctance to join the euro zone remains, however, significant. After Germany, the UK has the second largest population and the second largest gross domestic product (wealth) of any of the EU countries. In London it has by far Europe's largest financial sector. It is a nuclear power and a highly significant member of NATO. Opinion polls continually suggest an overwhelming majority against euro membership. This presents a major political struggle for both main parties within the UK and also an apparent vote of no confidence in the euro project and perhaps even the European project as a whole.

Beyond the euro the successes of the EU are very much open to question. It has signally failed to achieve a unified foreign policy. Most recently this was evident in the split that emerged over the desirability of the 2003 invasion of Iraq. An even more fatal division occurred over policy with regard to the break-up of former Yugoslavia. Here, historically conditioned policies by Germany over the early recognition of Croatia and, most fatally, by the UK's inability, under the Conservatives, to take a critical stance against Serbia, played a significant part in the initiation and prolongation of the bloodshed. It was only decisive action by the United States of America (USA) over Bosnia and, with the UK, over Kosovo, that averted the strong threat of genocide in Europe (Simms, 2001). The role of education in these conflicts has been significant. The treatment of minorities by states throughout Europe can test the boundaries between education and warfare (Coulby and Jones, 2001).

The EU's main policy and the one that absorbs nearly half of its large budget is the common agricultural policy (CAP). This policy provides subsidies for inefficient (in terms of world competition) farmers, especially in France and the other Mediterranean countries. One of its effects is to make it impossible for non-subsidised farmers in the majority world to compete to export food to the lucrative European market. It is one of the major areas of the EU's non-compliance with the terms of the World Trade Organisation (WTO). There has been strong pressure from both the European Commission (EC) itself and from the states of northern Europe to reduce or abolish the CAP. An important deal between France and Germany in 2002 guaranteed the continuation of the CAP at close to current levels as well as probably presaging the wider breach in the EU that subsequently emerged over Iraq. Whether the CAP can survive in the face of international hostility, the opposition of the UK and the pressure of the new member states, where agriculture is an important economic dimension, remains to be seen.

To cavil at waste, ineffectiveness and divisiveness within the EU is to miss the point. The EU emerged as part of the post-World War II settlement in Europe. It provided a mechanism for the peaceful coexistence of France and Germany. The alliance between these two states remains the key cornerstone of the EU to this day. The EU has undoubtedly played a major role in preserving peace between states in Europe for nearly 60 years. The other major international organisation in Europe, NATO, has played an even more active role in the preservation of European peace.

NATO does not have the same membership as the EU. The USA, the world's only superpower, is a member of NATO, as is Canada. Many of the EU countries and the accession countries belong to NATO, but not all. Ireland and Austria are not part of NATO. Norway belongs to NATO but not the EU. France, Europe's second nuclear power, although currently a full member of NATO, has had an uneasy relationship with the organisation, especially with its perceived Anglo-American leadership. Turkey, persistently kept at arm's length by the EU, is a full member of NATO. The organisation has borders with Iraq and the former Soviet Union and significant American military bases in eastern Anatolia.

Turkey has a rapidly expanding population which is already at the same level as Germany's. It has two mega cities, Ankara and Istanbul. The latter is one of the most important cities in the development of Europe as a whole, controlling the entrance to the Black Sea. Turkey is a democracy, though with a looming military presence. It is a secular state, though the influence of Islam seems to be on the increase, not least in politics and education. It has a rapidly developing and vibrant economy based in part on trade with Eastern Europe and the Turkic states of the former Soviet Union (the now independent countries of Kazakhstan, Turkmenistan, Uzbekistan, Tajikistan and Kyrgyzstan). It has a significant Kurdish population in eastern Anatolia which it has so far preferred to deal with militarily rather than politically. It has an uneasy relationship with Greece, its neighbour and co-member of NATO, which periodically flames up into military standoffs. It is in military occupation of the northern part of soon-to-be EU member Cyprus. There are significant Turkish minorities in many cities of the EU, in Belgium as well as Germany. Geographically, Turkey is perceived to be split between two continents with Istanbul (formerly Constantinople, Byzantium, I Polis) on the European side of the straights and the vast bulk of Anatolia on the Asian side. It is not hard to see that Turkey presents the EU with a sequence of challenges. The crude rejection of a timetable for Turkish membership by France's Chirac in 2002 represented perhaps an inability to come to terms with Islam and even a Francocentric racism rather than a sustained political evaluation. Whether the EU and Turkey can come to an accommodation will be a severe test of the commitment to internationalism, democracy and interculturalism on the part of both parties.

Many states in the European Union, especially France, see NATO as an organisation whose time has passed. The Cold War between Russia and the west is over and the UK and USA have pulled back from their camps in Germany. They would like to see it gradually superseded by a European Defence Force. Given the commitment of the UK to NATO and given the partiality of many states, not least those of Eastern Europe, to having their integrity guaranteed by the military might of the USA, this is unlikely to happen in the near future. It is within this framework then that progress towards European unification remains complex and contested.

CONVERGENCE IN POLICY AND PRACTICE

It is the explicit policy of the EU, as well as less powerful organisations such as the Council of Europe, to shift to greater educational convergence between the European states (EC, 1996; 2002). An example of this in action would be the inclusion of a 'European theme' in school and university curricula at all levels. The EU has enthusiastically advocated and financed this policy. It has been adopted by states with varying degrees of enthusiasm. It conflicts with the nationalist versions of history and culture so often promoted by European curricular systems. Germany and Poland still cannot agree a school version of their shared history. The states of Spain cannot even agree a school version of national history, between Castile and Catalonia to take but one example. In Cyprus the Turkish invasion of 1974 and its aftermath remains an important and separate curriculum subject. In this context it is likely to take a considerable time for states to accept a version of European history and culture which matches the EU's agenda of progress towards civilisation, harmony and unity.

Actual areas of convergence have occurred more as a common response to changes in the wider political and economic climate than as a result of centralist EU policy. An important example here would be the shift towards English as the first foreign language for all education systems in Europe. There are minor reservations on this generalisation, not least with regard to France, but it conveys the wider picture. Spain and Portugal abandoned French in favour of English as part of their liberalisation in the 1970s. The Eastern European and former Soviet Baltic States enthusiastically relegated Russian and adopted English in 1989 and 1991 respectively. The adoption of English in many states has been wholesale and successful. English is effectively the second language of the Netherlands. Courses at university level taught in English are to be found in Finland, Denmark and Spain. In most European countries there is a vigorous industry providing supplementary, evening and vacation courses in English. The EU has not advocated this trend, preferring to stress an official three-language policy – English, German and French – and to advocate the lesser-spoken languages of the Union: Danish, Finish, Swedish, Greek, Dutch and Portuguese. Nor has the EU yet acknowledged English as its common language. Meanwhile much of the Union's diabolised bureaucracy is actually a translation factory, ensuring that documentation is available in all 11 recognised languages.

The spread of English throughout European education systems is far from a matter for Anglo-Saxon self-satisfaction. The spread of English represents one component of cultural imperialism which is accompanying globalisation. In educational terms it may put in jeopardy, not the lesser official languages of the Union which will be well protected by their states, but rather the minority languages of the European nations: Catalan, Friesian, Breton, Vlach, Welsh and Sami. Fortunately many states, including France, Spain and the UK, have belatedly come to see the importance of their national languages. Nevertheless, some European languages such as Gaelic, Sami and Livonian are on the brink of extinction.

Another area of convergence has been the increase in the number of years of compulsory schooling. In some states this results from continuing schooling to an older age. In others it results from an earlier start with schooling gradually replacing kindergarten. The emerging pattern is for schooling to continue to the age of 18 either as a result of state compulsion or economic necessity. This leads to the key school examination at or around this age: *licencio*, *abitur*, *baccalaureate*, *licence*, A-levels. The key characteristic of this exam is that, by simply passing or by achieving a specific grade, it allows entrance to a place at university. In most states, though not really in Germany, the better the performance in this exam, the higher the status of the university and the degree programme which the student can access.

It is at university level that there is the greatest amount of actual and potential convergence. Across Europe before and after 1991 there has been a great increase in higher education both in terms of student numbers and in terms of the range of subjects which can be studied to degree level. New universities and other higher educational institutions (*hogescholen*) have been opened. Older universities have expanded. New courses in social and technical sciences have proliferated and more areas of vocational work have been brought to university level, not least the education of teachers. Research and higher degrees have also flourished with universities developing specialist areas of knowledge which they then go on to teach at undergraduate level. In this way universities are key players in the emerging knowledge economy. They tend to be prioritised by the state to the extent to which it is engaged in that economy, both Finland and the UK being well advanced in this respect. University education, from being the exception of the elite 60 years ago, is becoming the expectation of the majority. The UK is leading the way in this respect as it intends to shift the percentage of the age cohort in higher education from 36 per cent to 50 per cent by 2010.

The final area of convergence also concerns higher education, in this case with regard to the duration and pattern of study. Given the expenditure necessitated by university expansion, it is not surprising that the far-reaching changes being advocated by the proponents of harmonisation concern particularly the length and level of the first and second degrees. These were the key structural policies accepted by the signatories of the Bologna Declaration (European Ministers in Charge of Higher Education, 1999). In this Declaration the Ministers accepted a model of higher education which involves a three-year undergraduate degree, followed by a two-year masters degree. This is sometimes referred to as the BA–MA model and is to some extent derived from the structure of degrees in England and the USA. However, the attractiveness of this model for the Ministers of Education was not some fond positive view of English universities. Far from it. English universities offer the shortest and therefore the cheapest undergraduate degrees in Europe. Some European countries, such as the Netherlands, had already been looking for ways to shorten the amount of time students spent on their first degrees. The Bologna Declaration facilitates and legitimates this process. As well as harmonisation, the process is driven by the much less lofty ideal of reducing the cost to the state of each graduate.

Obviously the implementation of these changes is happening differentially within the 15 countries. The UK Secretary of State signed the Declaration knowing that very little change would be needed in universities in the UK. Italy initially appeared to have found the changes to the structure of the degree courses unproblematic. A law of 1999 specified that a three-year *laurea* be followed by a two-year *laurea specialistica*. The implementation of this scheme has, however, proved problematic. In the Netherlands politicians would have welcomed the Declaration because it allowed them to push through the shortening of the first degree which had proved a far from popular policy. Unlike the UK, which transformed all its polytechnics into universities in the 1992 Education Act, the Netherlands have so far not addressed the issue of the bipartite education system. Despite changes in title, the *hogescholen* have not become universities. The bipartite system remains also in Scandinavia, Belgium, Greece and Germany.

In Finland reforms initiated in the 1990s have resulted in the universities shifting to a three-plus-two model in most subjects. However, a first degree taken in a poly-technic can still need a minimum of three-and-a-half to four-and-a-half years of full-time study to complete. In Germany the shift to the three-plus-two model has been facilitated by legislation. But the adoption of the new model is at the discretion of the individual institutions. There is thus a dual system with some higher education institutions offering Bologna-style degrees and some preferring the traditional pattern. German universities, like the rest of the education system, are decentralised and con-trolled at the level of the *Land*, the administrative region. They also enjoy considerable autonomy. In order to meet the requirements of Bologna, and thereby reduce unit costs, the central state is playing a more active role in higher education reform. In Greece, despite popular opposition and the resistance of the universities, the bipartite system is being eroded. A new law (in 2001) has made the Technological Institutes part of the higher education system but without giving them the full status of universities. Again Bologna has been used as a pretext to justify politically desirable or expedient changes.

The continuation of bipartite higher education in so many European states could be seen to represent both the strength of entrenched university interests and the persistence of an elitist structure. To this extent the post-1992 changes in the UK may be seen as egalitarian as well as widening participation. But this is not the case. In practice the universities in the UK are organised in a highly hierarchical way with Oxbridge and London at the top and the large urban ex-polytechnics at the bottom.

This is reflected in both student choice and arcane funding arrangements which favour the elite universities. Although it is possible that other states will gradually abolish the bipartite divide in higher education, the focus of the chapter has now shifted from convergence to differences in European education.

DIFFERENCES BETWEEN EUROPEAN EDUCATION SYSTEMS

The first section of this chapter highlighted some of the ways in which the UK is an anomaly in Europe. This is also the case with regard to education. The UK has far more private schooling than other European countries, over 8% of the cohort attending such schools. Fee-paying schooling has a status which is unusual in other countries and it is linked to the elite universities (about half of all Oxford and Cambridge students come from private schools) in a way which would be unthinkable elsewhere. In the UK, as far as the rich and the powerful are concerned, the publicly provided school system is for other people's children. This partly explains its chronic lack of funding and the way that it has been treated by all sides as the guinea pig for the wilder side of policy studies experimentation by both political parties since at least 1987 (see Chapter 7).

The extent to which religious institutions are involved in the control and curricular content of schools and universities differs widely across Europe. In France there are a few private, religious schools, but that is the total extent of religious involvement in the education system of a state that prides itself on the integrity of its laity. By contrast, in the Netherlands, Belgium and the UK there are distinct religious schooling systems up to and including university level. These systems also differentiate in terms of the actual religions and denominations. In the UK there are state schools; there are also Church of England (Protestant) and Roman Catholic schools. Both these denominations are represented in sufficient numbers to constitute a separate system. There are also a few Jewish, Islamic and Greek Orthodox schools. Gloucestershire University, as well as many smaller higher education institutions, is a Church of England university. The extent to which religion penetrates the school curriculum also differs between countries. Not all systems have a daily act of collective worship, though this is compulsory in the UK which also boasts at least one school which teaches biblical rather than Darwinian theories of evolution. In Greece, not only is Greek Orthodox religion a compulsory subject, but all teachers in public schools are meant to be followers of this religion (see Chapter 6).

It is probably in terms of curricular content that the greatest differences exist between European systems at school level. This results from the historical role that states have played in 'nation-building' through education. In all states in Europe, though much more in Greece, Latvia, Romania and the UK and much less in Norway and Finland, the teaching of history, national language and social and cultural subjects is infused with nationalism (Coulby, 2000). History in the school curriculum is all too often the story (legend, myth) of the heroic struggle of the nation to escape foreign oppression; of the glorious unifications of all parts of the nation under one monarch/republic; of the spread of the nation's civilisation to all other parts of a benighted world. The teaching of literature and culture can be equally triumphalistic as schools celebrate the richness of the nation's cultural products and activities and either ignore or denigrate those of other nations. Schools in Norway teach children to be citizens of Norway and the world, schools in England teach children to be citizens of England, confident that that means citizens of the world; schools in Latvia teach children to be citizens of Latvia in contradistinction to the world. These are fundamental differences and contribute hugely to the contrasting national identities that are found in Europe. National and nationalist curricular systems at school level remain the most intractable divergence in education between states.

Selection of pupils at secondary level according to their perceived abilities is a practice which is perhaps dying out in Europe, but only very slowly. Bipartite and tripartite secondary education systems remain in some regions and some states. In most of the German *Länder*, selection at secondary level continues to be the largely uncontested norm with middle-class children attending the *Gymnasium* and progressing via the *Abitur* to university. There are usually two further types of school in subservience to the *Gymnasium*. In Transylvania there are grammar schools and non-grammar. Here the pattern is complicated by the fact that both tiers exist as Romanian-speaking and Hungarian-speaking (in some cities German-speaking also). In the UK some local education authorities like Kent and Wiltshire retain secondary selection despite the fact that the evidence has been incontestable for decades that school performance overall is better in non-selective systems. In the Netherlands secondary stratification is more by curriculum than institutions. There, in secondary schools, pupils may be following three absolutely distinct curricula, each with its own exam and destination in higher education or the workplace. Progress towards the common school, taken for granted in France as well as the USA, remains slow, reflecting the vested political interests of middle-class parents wishing to continue elite and socially exclusive secondary schooling for their children.

One of the benevolent effects of looking at education from an international or even a comparative perspective may be that it provides a shock with regard to anomalous practice in one's own system. This may well be the case for students in the UK with regard to the education of children and young people perceived to have special needs (Daniels and Garner, 1999). The whole industry of detailed categorisation (labelling) and separate, special provision (segregation) is absent in countries such as Italy and Norway. All children are educated together in the least restrictive environment with the maximum of social and curricular integration. The glacial progress towards inclusion in the UK reflects a society which too readily rejects and segregates children on the basis of perceived difference (see Chapter 10). The process tends to be self-perpetuating as those educated in non-special schools fail to develop the attitudes and skills which would allow them to integrate with those whom they perceive to be needy.

CONCLUSION

The differential access to higher education resulting from the extent of provision of university places was highlighted earlier. Given the increasing scope of the knowledge economy, the appetite of young people and their parents for university education and wider international trends (the USA and South Korea already exceed the UK target of 50 per cent of the age cohort), this is likely to be an area of educational provision where differences will gradually reduce over time.

In conclusion, it may be that convergence within European education systems, as perhaps at the political level of the continent as a whole, is largely illusory. Where it does occur, as in the spread of English as a second language, it is the result of wider economic and political forces, rather than of centralist dictat.

QUESTIONS FOR DISCUSSION

- In what areas of the school and university curriculum is convergence between European countries actually desirable?
- Is the unification of Europe a desirable policy objective? If so, how can it be assisted by educational policies?
- Churchill once advised De Gaulle never to put the UK in a position where it had to choose between Europe and the sea. Is the UK now in this position? Which way should it choose?

REFERENCES

Budge, I. and Newton, K. (1997) *The Politics of the New Europe: Atlantic to Urals*, London: Longman.

Coulby, D. (2000) *Beyond the National Curriculum: Curricular Centralism and Cultural Diversity in Europe and the USA*, London: RoutledgeFalmer.

Coulby, D. and Jones, C. (2001) *Education and Warfare in Europe*, Aldershot: Ashgate.

Daniels, H. and Garner, P. (eds) (1999) *World Yearbook of Education 1999: Inclusive Education*, Series edited by D. Coulby and C. Jones, London: Kogan Page.

EC (1996) *Teaching and Learning: Towards the Learning Society*, Brussels: EC.

EC (2002) *A new impetus for European youth. White Paper*, Luxembourg: Office for Official Publications of the European Communities, Brussels: EC.

European Ministers in Charge of Higher Education (1999) *The Bologna Declaration: The European Higher Education Area*, Bologna: European Ministers in Charge of Higher Education.

Novoa, A. and Lawn, M. (eds) (2002) *Fabricating Europe: The Formation of an Education Space*, Series, London: Kluwer Academic Publishers.

Simms, B. (2001) *Unfinest Hour: Britain and the Destruction of Bosnia*, Harmondsworth: Penguin.

RECOMMENDED READING

The World Yearbook of Education series, edited by D. Coulby and C. Jones, provides good coverage of current issues in international education. There is usually a good deal of material on Europe. The titles listed below are relevant to the topics of this volume.

Bourne, J. and Reid, E. (eds) (2003) *The World Yearbook of Education 2003: Language Education*, London: Kogan Page.

Coulby, D., Cowen, R. and Jones, C. (eds) (2000) *The World Yearbook of Education 2000: Education in Times of Transition*, London: Kogan Page.

Coulby, D., Gundara, J. and Jones, C. (eds) (1997) *The World Yearbook of Education 1997: Intercultural Education*, London: Kogan Page.

Daniels, H. and Garner, P. (eds) (1999) *The World Yearbook of Education 1999: Inclusive Education*, London: Kogan Page.

Thomas, E. (ed) (2002) *The World Yearbook of Education 2002. Teacher Education: Dilemmas and Prospects*, London: Kogan Page.

5 Human Rights and Education

Heather Williamson

This chapter is intended to help you to:

- understand the relationship between moral philosophy and human rights
- recognise your own assumptions, and those of others, about morality and human rights
- apply an understanding of human rights theory to education policy.

A PHILOSOPHICAL APPROACH

Many young people are concerned about human rights issues such as poverty and the spread of acquired immune deficiency syndrome (AIDS). The expression of interest demonstrated in the protests by young people against the outbreak of war in Iraq in 2003 was evidence of this. Despite the cynic's view that attending rallies was a means of skipping lessons (Bloom, 2003), the sincerity of many of the young people taking part in these rallies must be acknowledged. Young people should have the opportunity to discuss some of these issues within the curriculum, but for education policy makers and future teachers there are some fundamental questions about the relationship between education and human rights that need to be addressed. This chapter is designed to encourage you to use the insights of philosophy to assist you in addressing these questions. Philosophy invites you to clarify concepts by looking closely at the way in which words are being used. It also invites you to unearth your own assumptions and those of other people and to examine arguments and formulate new ones.

We have a habit of thinking of human rights problems as other people's problems. AIDS in Africa is seen as a problem for Africans, not for us. We may sympathise with Ethiopia in its attempt to cope with famine, or even telephone our credit card number to alleviate our own conscience, but rarely do we see starvation as *our* problem. If we do recognise that in some ways we are responsible for such problems we tend to feel helpless given the quantity and scale of them.

In reality it is the industrial countries of the west that hold the power to prolong or alleviate these problems and ought to own the problems. It is estimated that 1 per cent of the world's population has the benefit of a higher education and we (you and I) are numbered in that 1 per cent. Approximately 1 per cent of the world's population has a computer and thus access to unlimited information. We are the ones with the computers. What do we do with the information available to us? Approximately two-thirds of the world's population suffer from malnutrition while the other third wastes enormous quantities of food. Can we justify this? Frequently, instead of the 'west' acknowledging its share of the responsibility for hunger, disease and conflict, it seems to abuse its power by continuing to work to its own advantage. If we believe in education we need to acknowledge that it has a role to play in helping us to understand our part in both the creation of these problems, and their resolution.

MORAL THEORIES

Before we look at the role of education we need to understand a little moral philosophy. Hudson (1980) argued that for a century philosophers had been torn between two overarching views of morality: a *utilitarian* one, now generally recognised as a consequentialist theory because it is rooted in the idea that we can only come to understand what is the morally right thing to do by assessing the consequences of our action; and an *intuitionist* one, which claims that there are at least some moral principles that cannot be subordinated to the principle of utility. Most moral philosophy is broadly either utilitarian or intuitionist.

In its simplest form, the principle of utility suggests that the morally right action is the one that provides for the 'greatest happiness of the greatest number of people' regardless of the consequences for individuals (John Stuart Mill, 1861). In contrast, the intuitionist claims that there are some actions which should be forbidden however beneficial the consequences of such action might seem.

Determinists argue that both intuitionists and utilitarians are wrong in assuming that human beings have free will and can choose what to do. They argue that all of our choices and actions are the result of factors beyond our control. Although the success of the sciences has led many people to accept determinism, there remain arguments for believing that human beings can initiate change. The most common of these rests on an appeal to our subjective experience. It claims that as individuals we are constantly aware of being in a position where we must choose between alternatives. Our experience is reflected in our language. We talk of having *intentions* and failing to act in accordance with them. We experience *regret* because we believe we could have behaved differently. If our choices are so predetermined that we cannot initiate change then it would be logical to give up trying to overcome the problems we identify within society. Many people therefore prefer to hold on to the belief that they can make decisions to act to bring about change. They argue that people such as William Wilberforce who campaigned against slavery succeed in initiating change.

Let us assume that we have at least some measure of free will and accept Hudson's broad distinction between utilitarians and intuitionists. How then should we judge the morality of an action? Should we judge it by its consequences or do we claim that some actions are always morally wrong, whether or not they appear to result in beneficial consequences? There are problems with both suggestions. A committed utilitarian might want to argue that the Al Qaeda suspects imprisoned on Cuba in 2002 should have been tortured to release information. They might want to claim that access to this information would have resulted in the greatest happiness for the greatest number of people. The information collected could have been used to save many more lives than those lost when the twin towers were destroyed on 11 September 2001. The intuitionist would regard torture as morally wrong because the perpetrators would have been violating the *rights* of the prisoners. To put it in the terms of Immanuel Kant (1785), the prisoners would have been treated as a 'means to someone else's end' and not as 'ends in themselves'. The intuitionist would argue that we should not use other people for our own ends, however beneficial the consequences may seem. Vlastos (1984) argues that we need to distinguish between merit and worth. Human beings, he claims, have worth regardless of how depraved their behaviour may be and society should not violate their fundamental rights to suit its own ends. Critics of this view who take an extreme utilitarian position would argue that the suggestion that human beings have rights, just because they are human beings, is an illusion. Rights can only be claimed in the context of a contract, which depends on the will of the majority. Whichever position we prefer to take up it is now common for people to assume they have rights and to seek recognition of these in the legal system.

What do we mean by rights?

In the seventeenth and eighteenth centuries the common people found it increasingly necessary to free themselves from the tyrannical power of dynastic monarchies exercised by virtue of belief in the divine right of kings. The English revolution (1642–9) led to the execution of Charles I, so destroying the king and his absolute power. The philosopher John Locke (1690) argued that human beings should respect what he called the law of nature by recognising the rights of all individuals to their own life, liberty and property. Almost a century later in America, the colony sought to exert its independence from George III. In 1776, Thomas Jefferson wrote in his preamble to the complaints of the colony against the King, 'We hold these truths self-evident that all men are created equal; that they are endowed by their creator with certain inalienable rights; that amongst these are life, liberty and the pursuit of happiness' (Boyd, 1958: 436). In France, the revolution of 1789 aimed at establishing that all human beings had the right to liberty, equality and fraternity. Thomas Paine (1791) is often credited with fermenting many of the ideas that led to the movements asserting the liberty of the individual. He claims in *The Rights of Man* that sovereignty resides in human beings and is not bestowed by members of a class or nation.

Although in our own time many different prefixes to rights are used – fundamental rights, universal rights – the term 'human rights' remains appropriate because it draws attention to the essential point that rights are possessed by people by virtue of the fact that they are *human* beings. These rights are perceived as *universal*, because all human beings have them, and *natural*, because they do not depend on institutions created by human societies. This allows them to be regarded as independent of governments and as a standard by which governments can be judged.

The rights to life, liberty and property are often regarded as *negative* rights. This is because these rights originate in the claim for freedom from interference by others. Some people believe that these are fundamental rights and the only ones with which we should concern ourselves. Even the claim to these rights is challenged in different ways and debates within society reflect these challenges. Whether any individual or group of individuals should own land is an example of such a debate. It can be argued that the earth should belong to all creatures and no human being should claim dominion over a portion of it. *Positive* rights are those associated with maintaining a reasonable standard of living and are sometimes referred to as welfare, economic or social rights. These are rights that depend on society or institutions within society to assert and maintain. They include the right to work, healthcare and education.

Following World War II in 1948 the Universal Declaration of Human Rights (UDHR) was drawn up. Since then there has been a proliferation of declarations and conventions, clarifying and elaborating the clauses in the UDHR. These declarations may be nothing more than moral prescriptions. Their power as a moral force depends on who is prepared to sign them. Some sets of rights are accepted by governments and incorporated into law. Those that are become *legal* rights. The European Convention of Human Rights (ECHR) was signed in Rome in 1950 and the United Kingdom was the first nation state to ratify the convention on 18 March 1951. The Convention was finally incorporated into English Law when the Human Rights Act came into force in 1998. These various instruments rest on the appeal to a rights-based morality, which assumes that all human beings have rights and it is therefore the responsibility of all human beings to respect the rights of all other human beings.

The use of human rights language is now common and has been used in the struggles for equal opportunities for women and against colonialism, apartheid and oppression in the Soviet Bloc. Globalisation may now be increasing a shared sense of the inevitable interrelationship and interdependence between peoples across the world, which makes the language of rights even more attractive. There has been a developing recognition that a rights-based morality, rather than one based on the principle of utility, may be necessary if we are to resolve some of the major problems in the world. Only by accepting that all human beings have rights are we able to engage appropriately with these problems. The work of the United Nations (UN) is based on the premise of a rights-based morality.

In practice this rights-based morality seeks to ensure that the global community of human beings actively works to secure the rights of *all* human beings. The right to life implies that the world community, represented currently by the UN, has a responsibility to intervene wherever life is in danger. This danger may come from active attempts to destroy the life of others, as in ethnic cleansing and genocide, or in passive cases where people are dying from starvation or disease.

Is it possible to justify a rights-based morality?

Some people would claim that it is self-evident that human beings have these rights and therefore the claim to rights needs no justification. Nevertheless a number of justifications are possible. The most significant of these is that provided by John Rawls (1972). He suggests that we should imagine ourselves behind a 'veil of ignorance' where we know nothing about our own position or prospects. In this 'original position' we are invited as individuals to come together to decide on the principles of the society in which we would like to live. Rawls argues that we would agree on two principles. The first would be to allow for everyone to have as much liberty as possible consistent with equal liberty for everyone else, and the second would allow for liberties, powers, opportunities and wealth to be distributed equally, unless an unequal distribution works to the advantage of society in general and particularly to the advantage of the most vulnerable groups in society. Rawls believes we would be aware that we might be born into a vulnerable group in society where, for example, we were disabled or had no source of clean water. Given this, we would wish to develop a society which would take the responsibility for alleviating these difficulties for us, a fair society in which we knew we would be cared for.

Rawls's views are contentious. He has been accused of assuming that other people would share his instincts and take up the same cautious position. It is suggested that some of us may choose to gamble in the hope that we might be born lucky! A much more significant challenge to Rawls comes from Nozick (1975). He argues that Rawls's position ignores the concept of entitlement and suggests that we are entitled to keep what we earn. He accuses Rawls of asking us to imagine that goods are just 'there', not worked for or earned. It is clear that some people are capable of, and do make, a more significant contribution to society than other people. We might suggest a brain surgeon deserves more, should be paid more and should be entitled to keep it. However this argument ignores the circumstances of our birth, our genetic inheritance and our upbringing and access to education.

What Rawls really shows us is that if we wish to claim rights for ourselves we need a new kind of social contract. We need to take seriously our obligations to work towards a fairer society. We need to be willing to sacrifice our own interests for the interests of others. Whether we accept the arguments of Rawls or reject them, we need to recognise that his work has been appropriated in the defence of liberal democracy. Liberal democracies have begun to use Rawls's position to empower them to take action in a way that allows them to set aside one of the key precepts associated with the Peace of Westphalia (1648). According to this key precept nation states were inviolable. In other words, one nation state agreed not to interfere with another's internal affairs. However, by claiming that all human beings have rights, we are claiming that human rights are universal. If human beings have rights then inevitably someone has a corresponding responsibility. Having a responsibility implies a duty to act. This means that we have the responsibility and duty to protect the rights – at least the right to life and liberty – of all other human beings, not just those in our own nation state. Liberal democracies now use this argument to justify the claim that it is morally right to intervene in another country where human rights are being abused.

Cultural rights

There are those who argue that the UDHR and the rights claimed within it are just another expression of western imperialism. The values embodied in it are the values of the western powers and we are wrong to project these as universal. The argument here is that the west may not like the values it sees in operation in other countries, but within the context of the culture of that nation state they have a validity of their own by ensuring a society that is socially cohesive. We may be in sympathy with this, but we have to ask ourselves whether it was any of our business that the Taliban should deny women access to education in Afghanistan. The counter-claim by the west is that there are some values that transcend culture. Of these the most generally held ones remain the right to life and liberty. If any of the customs or practices of other cultures conflict with the right to life or liberty, then life and liberty must take priority. This allows those who accept a rights-based morality, not merely the right to challenge cultural practices they believe conflict with the right to life or liberty, but the *responsibility* to do so wherever such practices are found.

HUMAN RIGHTS AND EDUCATION

What does the claim that 'human beings have rights' mean for the future of education? In England we see at least some successes: primary and secondary education is provided for all children free at the point of delivery and the current government is striving towards providing higher education for up to 50 per cent of young people. Progress has also been made in the fight against racial prejudice, working towards gender equality, providing for pupils with special needs and promoting religious freedom.

While there are successes we are still left with a number of questions:

- Should we also be aiming at educating children to work towards a fairer world, a more just world?
- What should we expect of the English education system if we made an explicit acknowledgment of a rights-based morality which not only encouraged us to recognise our own rights but also our obligations to all other human beings across the globe?
- How should we design our education system so that young people come to understand the need to carry the responsibility that is implied by the claim that 'rights are universal'?

The Convention of the Rights of the Child

If we believe we should be educating young people to work towards a fairer and more just world, one in which the rights of all human beings are taken seriously, then we must look first to respecting the rights of young people themselves. The Convention of the Rights of the Child came into force as international law in 1990 (UN, 1989). This is the UN convention that has been signed by more countries than any other – 191 states are parties to the Convention. A superficial examination of it would lead you to believe that the English education system is compliant with it. The clauses on education are not in question and largely implemented, but a more thorough analysis demonstrates that the clauses fall into three main areas: participation, provision and protection. In general there is acceptance of the need to comply with the clauses on provision and protection, but little understanding or commitment to the prior requirements of participation. Article 12 of the Convention reads:

1   States Parties shall assure to the child who is capable of forming his or her own views the right to express those views freely in all matters affecting the child, the views of the child being given due weight in accordance with the age and maturity of the child.

2   For this purpose, the child shall in particular be provided the opportunity to be heard in any judicial and administrative proceedings affecting the child, either directly, or through a representative or an appropriate body, in a manner consistent with the procedural rules of national law.

(UN, 1989: 4)

The Convention makes it clear that a child has the same rights as an adult. The role of the adult is not to exercise the rights of the child *for* the child but to provide appropriate direction to the child in the exercise *by the child* of the rights recognised within the Convention.

There is a case to be made for the liberation of children, just as there is for women and for black people. There is a case for the empowerment of all pupils, just as there is for the empowerment of the disabled so they can fight for the recognition of themselves as human beings. 'Inclusivity' has become a buzzword in education, but if it is to mean anything then we must recognise that approximately 50 per cent of the world's population is under 25 and the majority of these young people are excluded from decisions affecting their own future. Before movements demanding the liberation of women or of black people, men claimed that they knew what was in the best interests of women; white people believed that they knew what was in the best interests of black people. As adults we believe that we know what is in the best interests of children. We believe our major responsibility is to protect children and provide for them. The Convention on the Rights of the Child makes it clear that our priority should be to ensure that the rights of participation are fully respected.

The Education Reform Act (Her Majesty's Stationery Office [HMSO], 1988) does not address the role of the child in its own education. The Children Act (HMSO, 1989), in marked contrast, does require the child's voice to be heard. When a court is discharging its duties in respect of a particular child the court is required to have particular regard for the 'ascertainable wishes and feelings' of the child concerned. If an infant's views are expected to be taken seriously in the case of divorce or adoption, why not in its education?

Harris (1982) argued that the distinction between adults and children based on the supposed incapacity of children cannot be sustained. Were we to use the criterion of competence to decide who should have full political status then many adults would need to be excluded and many children included in the numbers of those granted such status. Lindley (1986) argued that we deny children the opportunity to exercise an autonomous choice. A genuine respect for young people would generate educational programmes which would lead young people to claim control over their own lives and ultimately to seek the power to vote.

The aim of education

Stephen Ward suggests in Chapter 7 that the main aim of government policy over the last 30 years has been the maintenance and development of economic strength, to gear the economy to having an ever-greater competitive edge in a global economy. Is this what the aim of our education system should be? Or should it be more radical? Should education be aimed at revolutionising western attitudes? If we take the rights of others seriously then perhaps one of the aims of the English education system should be to help the next generation to work towards providing a reasonable standard of living for all other human beings before protecting a high standard of living for themselves.

The presence of poverty, disease and conflict, which often reflects the violation of human rights, provides a strong argument for suggesting that young people should be empowered to create a fairer, more just world. Young people need to be helped to understand the causes of poverty, disease and conflict and the role of human beings in causing such problems as well as finding ways of eliminating them. The next generation needs to understand, not just the achievements of the past and present generations, but much more their failures. It may not be an exaggeration to claim that the current generation, in presiding over world poverty, has been as guilty of as great a crime against humanity as those who prolonged the slave trade. We may not like sacrificing an ever-higher standard of living for ourselves, but if we accept the principle that all human beings have rights and we claim these rights for ourselves then it is our responsibility to act in accordance with this principle and seek to secure the rights of others.

The curriculum

In Chapter 4 David Coulby argues that we celebrate our own nation's achievements and ignore our weaknesses and our global responsibilities. As members of the European Union our fortress mentality and the Common Agricultural Policy prevent economic development in the third world. If the rights of others are to be taken seriously then the school curriculum needs to help young people to recognise the interrelationships within the world economy and the interdependence of all human beings. Young people need to understand how the trade barriers which the west sets up to protect their citizens are in many cases the very causes of the problems young people sympathise with.

The Hague recommendations regarding The Educational Rights of National Minorities (1996) include the right of children to be educated in the 'histories, cultures and traditions' of their own culture. It might be preferable for all children to have the right to an education which includes a range of cultures systematically selected for their variety. Were these taught from the perspectives of those cultures children might gain a deeper understanding of the strengths and weaknesses of their own culture and that of others. This strategy might also help young people to understand the interrelationship and interdependence of people belonging to different cultures. The Hague Convention also includes the right of children to be educated in their mother tongue, but since all children will normally become fluent in their mother tongue it might be more beneficial for all children to have the curriculum taught to them in a foreign language. Given that the European Union has a policy that all children should learn three languages, and that the learning of another language can be a means of providing an insight into another culture, perhaps consideration should be given to delivering the curriculum in Arabic or Mandarin.

The hope must be that such a curriculum would lead to understanding, empathy, compassion and action, not towards a continuing competition to gain economic supremacy but towards a world in which a real effort is made to create a fairer society where the rights of others to life and liberty are respected.

CONCLUSION

Warnock (1971) suggested that the object of morality is to 'countervail limited sympathies and their most damaging effects'. Our limited sympathies manifest themselves in our selfish attitudes which lead us to prioritise our concern for ourselves, the economy of our nation state and that of Europe. These limited sympathies have damaging effects on the rest of the human beings in the world. Perhaps our education system should be helping the next generation overcome these limited sympathies and take seriously their responsibilities.

QUESTIONS FOR DISCUSSION

- Should human beings claim rights without acting on their corresponding responsibilities?
- Should young people be at liberty to choose to earn their own living instead of, or as well as, attending formal schooling?
- What structures might be put in place in the education system to allow young people the liberty to participate in the selection of the aim and content of their own education?
- How would the school curriculum need to change to allow young people to develop an understanding of the responsibility the west has for human rights problems and their own responsibility for assisting in resolving them?

REFERENCES

Bloom, A. (2003) 'Protests over war seen as truancy', *Times Educational Supplement*, 21 March 2003.

Boyd, J. (ed.) (1958) *The Papers of Thomas Jefferson*, Princeton, NJ: Princeton University Press.

The Hague recommendations regarding the Educational Rights of National Minorities (1996/7) *International Journal on Minority and Group Rights*, 4(2).

Harris, J.(1982) 'The political status of children', in K. Graham (ed.) *Contemporary Political Philosophy*, Cambridge: Cambridge University Press.

HMSO (1988) *Education Reform Act*, London: HMSO.

HMSO (1989) *The Children Act*, London: HMSO.

Hudson, W.D. (1980) *A Century of Moral Philosophy*, London: Lutterworth.

Kant, I. (1785) *Grundlegung zur Metaphysik der Sitten*, trans. Paton, H.J. (1948) *Groundwork of the Metaphysic of Morals*, London: Hutchinson.

Lindley, R. (1986) *Autonomy*, London: Macmillan.

Locke, J. (1690) *Two Treatises of Government*, P. Laslett (ed.) Cambridge: Cambridge University Press 1967.

Mill, J.S. (1861) *Utilitarianism*, M. Warnock (ed.) (1962), London: Collins/Fontana.

Nozick, R. (1975) *Anarchy, State and Utopia*, Oxford: Blackwell.

Paine, T. (1791) *The Rights of Man*, Harmondsworth: Penguin (1969).

Rawls, J.A. (1972) *A Theory of Justice*, Oxford: Oxford University Press.

UN (1989) *Convention of the Rights of the Child*, London: HMSO.

Vlastos, G. (1984) 'Justice and equality', in J. Waldron (ed.) *Theories of Rights*, Oxford: Oxford University Press.

Warnock, G.J. (1971) *The Object of Morality*, London: Methuen.

FURTHER READING

Falk, A. (2000) *Human Rights Horizons*, London: Routledge. An in-depth study of the pursuit of justice through the development of human rights in a globalised world.

Harrison-Barbet, A. (1990) *Mastering Philosophy*, New York: Palgrave. Sections 6 and 7 (pp. 185–275) provide a useful introduction to moral and political philosophy.

Richardson, R. (1990) *Daring to be a Teacher*, Staffordshire: Trentham Books. Chapter 4 (pp. 29–44) 'Learning towards Justice' argues that the purpose of education is to transform society to make it less unequal and less unjust.

Symonides, J. (2000) *Human Rights: Concepts and Standards*, Aldershot, England: UNESCO. A comprehensive treatment of both the concept of rights and the whole range of rights that are now embodied in human rights instruments.

USEFUL ORGANISATIONS AND WEBSITES

Amnesty International www.amnesty.org.

Oxfam www.oxfam.org.

Save the Children www.savethechildren.org.

United Nations Children's Fund www.unicef.org.

United Nations www.unitednations.org.

6 Cultural and Religious Plurality in Education

Denise Cush

In this chapter the following main points will be covered:

- the meaning of 'cultural and religious plurality'
- the relationship between culture and religion and the problems with these labels
- international diversity of educational response to religious plurality
- positive pluralism
- religious education
- 'faith-based' schools.

CULTURAL AND RELIGIOUS PLURALITY

Human beings do not agree on fundamental issues concerned with the meaning and purpose of our lives and how we should live them. We differ in our views of human nature and destiny, the nature of reality, reliable authorities and sources of knowledge, and the purpose of education. We also disagree on ethical issues from war to abortion. Our customs and practices, values and priorities differ from culture to culture, family to family, individual to individual. This has always been the case, but now global communications make us much more aware of it. The traditional plurality of groups with different beliefs and customs has been extended with plurality of function. Countless sub-worlds of types of employment and leisure pursuits have developed. Geir Skeie (1995: 84) has usefully distinguished between 'plurality' as a descriptive term for this and 'pluralism', which is used to refer to a prescriptive or evaluative position or ideology (usually positive) on the fact of plurality. This chapter will concentrate on religious and cultural plurality and discuss how education systems can respond.

CULTURE AND RELIGION

Although the terms 'culture' and 'religion' are in common use, there is no agreement as to what these words mean, whether they refer to the same dimension of human experience or to two distinct areas, or whether they are useful terms at all. 'Culture' tends to be defined as the learned aspects of being human, as opposed to 'nature', the biological heritage we are born with. It includes language, customs, and beliefs, and is passed on from one generation to the next by means of socialisation and education. The way in which we use the word 'culture' can suggest that there are distinct 'sets' of language/customs/beliefs to which an individual 'belongs'. It also assumes an individual can be 'torn between' two of them. 'Cultures' can be seen as essentially different and therefore having different educational needs. A right-wing extreme is apartheid and one left-wing version is communitarianism. In education, either of these could (and did, in South Africa under apartheid) lead to separate provision for the different categories of pupils. It might also suggest that a person from one 'culture' cannot make judgements about the beliefs and practices of another. On the other hand, 'cultures' can be viewed as fluid, internally diverse and contested, influenced by and influencing other cultural streams (Jackson, 1997). An individual therefore does not so much 'belong' to 'a culture', but is influenced by and engaged with a number of cultural streams. Cultures are not only challenged and changed by interactions with other cultures, but may be criticised from within (the concept of 'counter-culture'). Jackson's (1997: 83) research with young Hindus in Britain reveals them, not as negatively 'caught between two cultures', but as having the 'multiple cultural competence' to navigate multiple cultural streams successfully.

'Religion' is notoriously difficult to define. Although dictionaries might attempt it, academics in the study of religions have more or less given up trying. Definitions focusing on belief in God only suit theistic religions and leave Buddhism out. Those which focus on the supernatural rule out those worldviews that see no natural–supernatural distinction. If defined as 'beliefs', religion is seen as a western post-enlightenment view, inappropriately imposed on non-western traditions, which tend to be more about 'doing'. Similarly the division of the beliefs and practices of peoples into clearly distinguished 'isms' – Buddhism, Hinduism, Christianity, Islam – is seen as an artificial construct of nineteenth-century thinking (Jackson, 1997). In reality, 'religions' are internally diverse, and the dividing lines between them are not clear, particularly in non-western (e.g. Indian) traditions or postmodern manifestations of religion such as 'new age'. In many non-European languages (e.g. African languages such as Setswana), there is no word that translates into the English 'religion', or way of distinguishing between 'religious' and 'non-religious'; there is just how people live their lives. Thus the current trend in academic circles is to take what is called a 'non-essentialist' view of the term religion: 'religion' tends to be viewed as an artefact of the academy (Smith, 1998: 281), a tool for analysis, rather than having any relationship to reality 'out there'.

In the light of dissatisfaction with the term 'religion', there are scholars who suggest we should ditch it altogether and stick to 'culture' (Fitzgerald, 1995). The definition of culture found in Abercrombie *et al.* (1994: 98), 'the total set of beliefs, customs, or way of life of particular groups', could easily be acceptable as a definition of religion. However, this would seem to be begging the question of whether 'religions' are human creations or divine revelations, because 'cultures' are human constructs. From a believer's point of view, a clear distinction can be made between 'religion' (the eternal truths) and 'culture' (the changeable social context in which eternal truths are expressed). It does make sense to talk of 'religions' adapting to different 'cultures' or making changes in what is merely 'cultural'. What counts as 'religion' is seen as unchangeable; what counts as 'culture' is seen as changeable. In practice there is often no agreement on what is religious and what is cultural. Ordaining women as priests, monogamy, not cutting one's hair, honouring ancestor spirits and local gods, and female circumcision all may be viewed as religion or as culture by different people, or the distinction may not make sense to them. In any case, 'culture' as a label suffers from the same artificiality as the term 'religion'. Perhaps we should find another term to encompass the beliefs, values and customs of everyone, whether 'religious' or not.

RESPONSES TO CULTURAL AND RELIGIOUS PLURALITY: MULTICULTURAL/INTERCULTURAL EDUCATION

'Multicultural education' can refer to any attempt on the part of education to respond to cultural plurality, or particular approaches which can then be contrasted with other approaches such as 'anti-racist'. The basic idea behind 'multicultural education' is that cultural diversity should be appreciated and reflected in the school curriculum. Music, art and literature should include examples of African, Indian and Chinese origin, as well as European; history, geography and religious studies should be worldwide, not just national; mathematics and science should emphasise the contributions of non-western peoples such as 'Arabic' numerals. 'Multicultural education' has been criticised for being superficial and for failing to address the real roots of racism and discrimination, and sometimes for making relationships between different groups worse by stressing differences and reinforcing stereotypes. The term 'multicultural society' might suggest that several discrete cultures exist in competition. Instead the term 'intercultural' has become popular, to reflect the fact that 'cultures' are fluid, changing and interacting, with exciting new 'hybrids' emerging all the time. The debates about 'multiculturalism' which so characterised the 1980s have been overshadowed in the United Kingdom (UK) by the priorities of the National Curriculum, literacy, numeracy, and information and communication technology (ICT). Nevertheless, in some classrooms, teachers are making valiant efforts to ensure that children's views of the world are not restricted to a nationalist or Eurocentric outlook.

INTERNATIONAL DIVERSITY OF RELIGION IN EDUCATION

The response by state-funded education systems worldwide to the plurality of 'religious' and 'non-religious' beliefs, values and customs is varied, but can be summarised into three basic options – the secular, the confessional and the non-confessional. Simply put, this means either having no religious education, having religious education with the primary aim of nurturing children in the religion of their heritage, and religious education that aims to be open, multifaith and unbiased.

The word 'secular' has many different meanings, but is used here to mean that the education system does not officially include consideration of religions. It is not a subject on the timetable. This does not imply that pupils, teachers and parents are not themselves religious. The most powerful country in the world, the United States of America (USA), takes this secular option in state-funded schools, in spite of being one of the most 'religious' countries in the world in terms of people's self identity in surveys (roughly 80 per cent 'religious'). Other countries that currently take the 'secular' option in state-funded schools include France (except Alsace and part of Lorraine), Russia, Albania, China and Japan. Some of the most common arguments given for excluding religion from the curriculum are:

- it is too personal and private and should be left to the family and community
- it is impossible for teachers to be impartial in such a contested area
- any study risks highlighting areas of difference and conflict between people
- academic evaluation might seem to criticise pupils' religious and cultural heritage
- any presentation in school is bound to be so simplified that it misrepresents and stereotypes the tradition in question.

In the USA the major consideration is that the First Amendment to the 1787 Constitution sought to protect religious freedom by instituting a complete separation between 'church' and 'state' so that there was 'no establishment' of religion. This has been interpreted as meaning that no public funds can be used for teaching about religions in schools, and thus no religious education. However, this clause was interpreted differently in different eras, and in different states. An important ruling in 1963 (the 'Schempp decision') made it clear that it is only promoting a particular religion that is ruled out, rather than teaching about religion. The increasing awareness of plurality has led several states, such as California, to include teaching about religions in the history syllabus. However, lacking a separate subject means that there are no teachers specially qualified to teach religious studies, and the controversial nature of the subject means that many teachers would leave religion out. Nevertheless, there is a lobby which argues that the much-vaunted religious freedom of the USA is only really guaranteed by education which included learning about religions, rather than leaving pupils in ignorance. In France, similar suggestions are being made. Pupils need to understand Islam to understand world affairs. So 'religion' finds some place in a general humanities curriculum, though not as a discrete subject. A further example is Taiwan where the subject of 'life education', introduced in 1997, includes consideration of the different religious perspectives current in that country.

In communist China (and in Eastern European countries before 1989), religion is not included in the curriculum because it is deemed simply wrong, untrue and as having a negative influence on human development. However, an examination of children's textbooks could lead one to the conclusion, not that no religion was taught, but that the beliefs, values and customs (i.e. the 'religion' of Marxism) was taught to children in a 'confessional' way, in order that they might share those beliefs, values and customs.

Most of the countries of Europe take the confessional approach to religious education. This means that schools contribute to the nurturing of children within the particular faith tradition of their family, or what is deemed to be the heritage of the country. There are many variations. Religious education can be compulsory or optional, the syllabus can be decided by the state or the churches/groups concerned or a partnership of both. There may or may not be an alternative subject, such as 'ethics', for the 'non-religious'. It can be taught by the ordinary class teacher or by paid or unpaid church workers coming into school. Where one particular tradition forms part of the dominant construction of national identity – Catholicism in Poland, Orthodoxy in Romania or Greece – that tradition forms the basis of the syllabus. Where there is more awareness of diversity, separate religious education classes may be offered for the main groups represented. For example, in the majority of German *Länder* there is choice between Protestant and Catholic religious education, and in Finland until recently there was a choice between Lutheran or Orthodox religious education and 'ethics' for the non-religious.

A growing minority of countries take the non-confessional approach and attempt to provide a religious education that is open, balanced and impartial, and is seeking to educate children *about* religion rather than promote a particular religion or religion in general. These include England and Wales, Scotland, Sweden, Norway, South Africa and Namibia, and upper secondary years in Denmark and Finland. The countries with the longest experience of this are Sweden, England, Wales and Scotland, which have pioneered non-confessional multifaith religious education since the late 1960s. South Africa, which made the decision to take the non-confessional route in 2000, has decided to call the subject 'religion education' to emphasise that it does not have the aim of 'making people religious'.

It is possible to construct arguments in favour of the secular, the confessional and the non-confessional approaches to education as being the best way to ensure freedom of religious belief and to promote harmony rather than conflict in a religiously and culturally plural world. However, ignorance is a dangerous option. An increasingly plural world calls for a positive approach to plurality of beliefs and values.

POSITIVE PLURALISM

'Positive pluralism' is a term coined in 1991 to describe an approach which sees the plurality of religious and non-religious beliefs, values and customs as a positive resource for the human race rather than a problem to be solved. It is outlined in Cush and Francis (2001) and was developed from practical experience in an English context. The positive pluralist approach is based on 'epistemological humility' – in other words, you may have your own sincerely and deeply held views, beliefs, values and customs, but are not arrogant enough to think that you have nothing to learn from others, even when their views differ greatly. Plurality is to be welcomed and respected. Schools should respect the religious and cultural backgrounds of all pupils, whether religious or not, but also accept that these perspectives are open to debate and critical evaluation in the *public* forum that is education. This is not to maintain that all views/beliefs/traditions are equally valid, a position that no one really holds when pressed, nor does it suggest the teaching of universalism – the belief that all religions fundamentally are the same, just different paths to the same goal, as these are themselves confessional positions.

Religious education should take a non-confessional, multifaith (and non-faith) approach, which attempts to be as far as is humanly possible impartial and empathetic, where all children are taught together, and where no one tradition is privileged in terms of its truth claims. Plurality within the so-called 'religions', and interactions and hybridity between them, need to be recognised. The non-confessional approach means learning *about* religions and non-religious views rather than learning *to be* 'religious'. It does not rule out students exploring and developing their own perspectives on religious issues and questions, whether or not these perspectives turn out to be the same as their family/community heritage or any previously recognised worldview.

RELIGIOUS EDUCATION IN ENGLAND AND WALES

In England and Wales, non-confessional religious education is well established, and was an early advocate and location for multicultural education. Religious education has been a compulsory subject in the school curriculum since 1944. It was established as non-confessional in 1971 (Schools Council, 1971), and reinforced as part of the 'basic curriculum' in 1988. The 1988 Education Reform Act, repeated in the 1996 Education Act, requires religious education to 'reflect the fact that the religious traditions in Great Britain are in the main Christian, while taking account of the other principal religions represented in Great Britain' (1996 Education Act, section 375.3). It is an uneasy compromise between two lobbies and is open to a variety of interpretations as to which religions are included and what proportion of the syllabus is spent on each. Religious education is not part of the National Curriculum, as each Local Education Authority (LEA) must produce an 'agreed syllabus' for use in its schools. The parties agreeing the syllabus are the Church of England, other faiths and other Christian denominations, teachers' representatives and elected members of the LEA. The *local* nature of the syllabus allows for considerable 'grassroots' involvement, and the local Standing Advisory Council on Religious Education (SACRE) has been a forum for different faith communities to meet and get to know each other. In Bradford, a student version of the SACRE has allowed young people from different faith communities to meet and get to know each other in an area where demographic patterns tend to make some schools mono-religious or mono-cultural.

The syllabus has been locally determined since 1944, but the Qualifications and Curriculum Authority (QCA) has produced some non-statutory guidance at national level which has led to some uniformity. These include the Model Syllabuses for Religious Education (SCAA, 1994) and the National Expectations for Attainment in Religious Education (QCA, 2000). Moves to introduce a national syllabus met with opposition from the local SACREs, but this was resolved in November 2003 when the Secretary of State, Charles Clarke, directed the QCA to develop a non-statutory national framework for religious education. Religious education is a subject from which parents can withdraw their children on grounds of conscience, a right which is seen by some as anachronistic, and does not apply to other subjects to which parents may have conscientious objections, such as ICT (see Chapter 15).

The situation in England and Wales is complicated by the presence of state-funded 'schools with a religious character', one category of which is allowed to provide its own *confessional* religious education. This is an example of the complexities which arise in the area of religion, culture and education.

THE 'FAITH SCHOOLS' DEBATE

Internationally, Christian churches and religious organisations such as Buddhist monasteries pioneered education for the poor as well as the rich. Many countries, including England and Wales, have private schools independently funded by religious groups. However the history of education in England and Wales has given rise to the existence of state-funded 'faith-based' schools. In 1870, when state education was introduced, it supplemented rather than replaced the voluntary provision by religious groups, and some state assistance was given to allow the voluntary schools to survive and meet basic standards. This is known as the 'dual system'. The 1944 Education Act established two categories of state-funded voluntary schools, a distinction which still persists today, with the addition of a third numerically small category of 'foundation schools'. The two important categories are the voluntary controlled and voluntary aided schools. The former is controlled by the LEA from which it receives all its funding. These schools must follow the non-confessional Locally Agreed Syllabus for religious education, but as a reflection of their original foundation may conduct denominational worship. The voluntary aided category receives the majority of its funding from the LEA, but in return for providing some of the funding itself, the religious body is allowed to provide religious education of a confessional, denomi-national nature, as well as worship in the tradition to which it belongs.

'Faith-based' schools have become controversial in recent years for a number of reasons. Both the Church of England and the current government are in favour of increasing the number of such schools, partly because they are popular with parents and perceived as obtaining good academic results. In addition, since 1998, a few schools with a foundation in religions other than Christianity or Judaism have gained voluntary aided status, including four Muslim and two Sikh schools. Reading the debate in the educational and general media throughout 2001 and 2002 revealed that racism, and in particular Islamophobia, coloured the discussions. Far more people opposed separate Muslim schools than separate 'Church' schools (43 per cent to 27 per cent in a 2001 MORI poll), and both editorials and letter writers expressed fears that separate Muslim schools might be 'training grounds for terrorists'.

Department for Education and Skills figures for the year 2000 show that state-funded voluntary schools account for roughly one-third of primary schools (6,384 of 18,158) and one-sixth of secondary schools (589 of 3,550). Of the total, 4,716 are Church of England and 2,110 Roman Catholic, the rest being counted in single figures or tens and the next largest group being Jewish schools at 32. Arguments for and against state-funded faith-based schools can be found in Cush (2003) and Jackson (2003).

If the system was started from scratch, perhaps the fully comprehensive pluralist community school would work best. However, as a substantial faith-based school system exists, and appears to be working, what matters is not so much who runs and pays for the schools, but the values and attitudes of the school, and the way it approaches religious and cultural plurality, whatever its foundation. Many faith-based schools are trying to make up for the disadvantages of segregation by making links with schools of another character, and following multifaith and multicultural curricula. The voluntary controlled option, where the school can have a faith foundation but must follow a non-confessional syllabus for religious education 'agreed' by all the local faith communities, is one that could perhaps be explored further.

PEDAGOGIES: AIMS, CONTENT AND METHODS

As well as the general issue of confessional or non-confessional education, there are debates about the aims, content, and learning and teaching methods for religious and cultural diversity in the classroom. As for aims, some would stress the role of education in the personal development of the pupils in beliefs, values and cultural identity whether within the tradition of the family or community, or as an individual. Others stress learning about the rich diversity of religions and cultures in order to better understand other people with whom one will be increasingly mixing in society. Yet others prioritise the philosophical and ethical insights which religious and non-religious thinking can apply to the crucial issues facing humanity today.

Religious education has often been the vehicle for issues-based education as described by David Hicks in Chapter 2 (the global dimension) and Chapter 3 (the environment). It is also a locus for the discussion of human rights (Chapter 5), development education, war and peace, injustices such as racism and sexism, and the work of groups such as Oxfam, Amnesty International and their equivalents from non-western cultures. Interestingly, at several European conferences where teachers from both confessional and non-confessional systems met, all tended to agree that religious education is about all three of these aims: personal development, religious and cultural understanding, and engagement with crucial issues.

Content generally depends on the approach and aims. Different countries study different religious traditions. Some, but not all, include non-religious beliefs, values and customs, or the human issues mentioned above. In England and Wales, Christianity, Buddhism, Hinduism, Islam, Judaism and Sikhism have become traditional, and philosophy and ethics are increasingly popular in the upper secondary schools. The Taiwanese 'life education' syllabus includes Taoism, Buddhism, Islam, Catholic and Protestant Christianity, Shinto, Mormonism, the Unification Church (Moonies) and Kwan Tao. Interestingly for our topic, 'Confucianism' does not feature as it is not considered a 'religion', as it is by the west, rather the underlying culture shared by all (see Chapter 1).

With regard to the 'how' of teaching religion, many influential pedagogies have been developed. These can be explored in Grimmitt (2000). Some stress the importance of the experience and interests of the pupils as setting the agenda, some the importance of authentic encounters with the religious communities studied. Some emphasise the importance of engaging with and evaluating the truth claims of traditions, and others allowing space for pupils to explore their own spirituality. However all, in one way or another, are attempting to build bridges between the experience of the student and the religious material being studied.

MORAL EDUCATION, CITIZENSHIP, WORSHIP

Other areas of school provision which need to take account of cultural and religious plurality are spiritual development, moral education, personal and social education, health education, and citizenship education. Often these are attempted without thinking through the full implications of cultural and religious diversity and the real disagreements on fundamental issues. There is also the issue of the practice of prayer and worship in school. This has been a matter of controversy in the USA. In England and Wales, the attempt to provide non-confessional religious education is compromised by the legal requirement for community schools to provide daily 'collective worship' which is 'wholly or mainly of a broadly Christian character.' There is the possibility of parental withdrawal and schools can be exempted from the requirement, but it remains a tricky area. In Norway, non-confessional religious education is compulsory, but any activity which might stray into practice, such as visiting a place of worship or learning a hymn, is optional.

CONCLUSION

There are many ways in which religious and cultural plurality impact upon education and there needs to be a subject in the school curriculum to deal directly with this area of human experience. It should allow students to learn about and respect the beliefs, values and customs of others and to develop their own, either within a heritage tradition or in critical opposition to it. It is currently called 'religious education', but it possibly needs a new name. The purpose is unlikely to be achieved if religious education is a small part of another subject such as history, social studies or citizenship; it needs to be taught by specialist teachers who are knowledgeable about the traditions and skilled in appropriate pedagogies. In the words of Peter Schreiner (2001), talking about Europe, but applicable to the world,

> RE [religious education] can elaborate a critical potential in a civil society through its international, ecumenical and inter-religious dimension. This would contribute to a sustainable Europe in which the diversity of religions and cultures is not a burden but an enrichment to co-habitation.
>
> (Schreiner 2000: 266)

QUESTIONS FOR DISCUSSION

- How can education most effectively respond to the increasing plurality of beliefs, values and practices in contemporary societies?
- What is 'multicultural education' and how does it relate to 'intercultural' and 'anti-racist' education?
- What is the relationship between religion and culture? Can religious education contribute to intercultural education?
- What is the place of faith-based schools in a plural democracy? Should the state fund such schools?

- How can schools ensure that pupils from all religious/non-religious/cultural backgrounds feel included?
- Should religious education be included in the school curriculum? If so, what should be its aims, content and methods?
- Who should decide the content of syllabuses for religious education? Is it best planned locally, nationally or internationally?

REFERENCES

Abercrombie, N., Hill, S. and Turner, B. (1994) *The Penguin Dictionary of Sociology*, 3rd edition, London: Penguin.

Chidester, D., Stonier, J. and Tobler, J. (eds) (1999) *Diversity as Ethos: Challenges for Interreligious and Intercultural Education*, Cape Town: ICRSA, University of Cape Town.

Copley, T. (1997) *Teaching Religion: Fifty Years of Religious Education in England and Wales*, Exeter: University of Exeter Press.

Cush, D. (2003) 'Should the state fund "schools with a religious character"?' *Resource*, 25: 10–15.

Cush, D. and Francis, D. (2001) 'Positive pluralism to awareness, mystery and value: a case study in RE curriculum development', *British Journal of Religious Education*, 24: 52–67.

Fitzgerald, T. (1995) 'Religious studies as cultural studies: a philosophical and anthropological critique of the concept of Religion', *Diskus*, 3(1), available online at http://www.uni.marburg.de/religionswissenschaft/journal/diskus/.

Grimmitt, M. (ed.) (2000) *Pedagogies of Religious Education*, London: McCrimmons.

Jackson, R. (1995) 'Religious education's representation of "religions" and "cultures"', *British Journal of Educational Studies*, 43: 272–89.

Jackson R. (1997) *Religious Education: An Interpretive Approach*, London: Hodder.

Jackson, R. (2003) 'The faith-based schools debate', *British Journal of Religious Education*, 25(2), special edition.

QCA (2000) *Religious Education: Non-statutory Guidance on RE*, London: QCA.

SCAA (1994) *Religious Education: Model Syllabuses*, London: SCAA.

Schools Council (1971) *Religious Education in Secondary Schools (Working Paper 36)*, London: Evans.

Schreiner, P. (2000) *Religious Education in Europe: A Collection of Basic Information about RE in European Countries*, Münster: ICCS/Comenius Institute.

Schreiner, P. (2001) 'Towards a European oriented religious education', in H. Heimbrock, C. Scheilke and P. Schreiner (eds) *Towards Religious Competence: Diversity as a Challenge for Education in Europe*, Münster: Comenius Institute.

Skeie, G. (1995) 'Plurality and pluralism: a challenge for religious education' *British Journal of Religious Education*, 17: 84–91.

Smith, J.Z. (1998) 'Religion, religions, religious', in M.C. Taylor (ed.) *Critical Terms for Religious Studies*, Chicago: Chicago University Press.

RECOMMENDED READING

Chidester, D., Stonier, J. and Tobler, J. (eds) (1999) *Diversity as Ethos: Challenges for Interreligious and Intercultural Education*, Cape Town: ICRSA, University of Cape Town. A useful collection of international perspectives on this topic.

Copley, T. (1997) *Teaching Religion: Fifty Years of Religious Education in England and Wales*, Exeter: University of Exeter Press. A comprehensive history of religious education in England and Wales.

Cush, D. (1999) 'Potential pioneers of pluralism: the contribution of religious education to intercultural education in multicultural societies', *Diskus*, 5(1), available online http://www.uni-marburg.de/religionswissenschaft/journal/diskus/.

Cush, D. and Francis, D. (2001) 'Positive pluralism to awareness, mystery and value: a case study in RE curriculum development', *British Journal of Religious Education*, 24: 52–67. How the theory of positive pluralism underpins a Locally Agreed Syllabus for religious education.

Grimmitt, M. (ed.) (2000) *Pedagogies of Religious Education*, London: McCrimmons. A very useful collection, with a critique of the major pedagogies of religious education in Britain today.

Jackson, R. (1995) 'Religious education's representation of "religions" and "cultures"', *British Journal of Educational Studies*, 43: 272–89. A very clear examination of the concepts of religion and culture within a context asking why religious education has been less successful than it might be in combating racism.

Jackson R. (1997) *Religious Education: An Interpretive Approach*, London: Hodder. One of the best theoretical discussions of religious education, from one of the leading UK professors, with much on religion and culture, taking an ethnographic approach.

SCAA (1994) *Religious Education: Model Syllabuses*, London: SCAA. The non-statutory 'models' for religious education from SCAA (now QCA).

Part II

Teaching, educational settings and policy

7 Government Policy on Education in England

Stephen Ward

Education is political because it is concerned with values and beliefs. This chapter explains the party politics of education. Much of the story is similar across the United Kingdom (UK), but there are complex differences between England, Scotland, Wales and Northern Ireland so, for brevity and accuracy, reference is restricted to England. You might want to compare policies in the Pacific Rim countries, the United States of America (USA) and Europe in Chapters 1 and 3.

The chapter introduces:

- trends in government policy in England since 1870
- some political theories and their effects on education policy
- the development of market forces in education.

THE BEGINNINGS OF EDUCATION POLICY

We take government education policy for granted, but national governments don't have to be involved in education. They are often keen on controlling the 'distribution of knowledge' but the *degree* of control varies in different countries and it has varied in England over time. In the 1830s and 1840s there was schooling for factory and workhouse children and some schooling provided by church foundations (see Chapter 5). But education was mainly for the rich who could send their children to independent schools and it was not until 1870 that the Forster Education Act introduced compulsory state schooling for all.

Once a government provides compulsory education through taxation, it is likely that it will want to control what goes on in schools, to make the service *accountable* and to ensure that the taxpayer is getting 'value for money'. The first attempt at education policy was simple: children were taught a basic curriculum of reading, writing and arithmetic and given moral and religious instruction, as set out in the Ministry of Education's *Handbook for Teachers*. To ensure that children were taught the curriculum,

Her Majesty's Inspectors (HMI) tested them in order to determine the level of teachers' pay: the so-called 'payment-by-results scheme'.

1902 saw the abolition of payment-by-results, effectively handing over control of the curriculum and methods to the teaching profession. It was an implicit statement of faith in teachers to do what was right and, for the greater part of the century, left England with no national curriculum and no structure for monitoring education. Midway through the century the 1944 Butler Education Act introduced compulsory secondary education, but again did not stipulate the curriculum, except for religious education. The 'hands-off' approach to education stemmed from the so-called 'liberalism' of nineteenth-century politics. In the interests of 'freedom' the government does not intervene in society and industry: people should be free to generate wealth, and those who don't manage to do so remain poor. So, from its beginnings, government intervention was limited, introducing the Board Schools for the poor in 1870, but leaving the voluntary, independent sector in place for the rich (Green, 2001).

The two main political rivals in the UK are the Conservative and Labour Parties. The right-wing Conservative Party has been committed to 'freedom' in the liberal tradition, whereas the left-wing Labour Party has been inclined to an interventionist programme in which state-funded services – schools, hospitals, social workers – protect the welfare of all members of society. The Labour Party would have the country pay more tax in order to fund welfare services, whereas the Conservative Party would charge lower taxes to leave people with more personal wealth to spend on services as they wish. Conservatives criticise Labour for wanting to intervene too much in people's lives, thereby creating a 'nanny state'.

THE 'POLITICAL CONSENSUS' ON EDUCATION

During the first three-quarters of the last century, political interest in education lay mainly in debates about types of schools, social class and access to schooling. Conservatives argued for selective grammar schools to preserve high standards for an elite, usually middle-class, group. Labour wanted to see equal access for all, regardless of social class, and from 1965 tried to introduce secondary comprehensive schools open to all pupils regardless of income or ability. However, schools were controlled by Local Education Authorities (LEAs) and some Conservative LEAs retained selective grammar schools. Independent fee-paying schools, of course, also continued.

During this long debate about access and social class, central government took little or no interest in the curriculum, in teaching or in the running of schools. The administration and monitoring of education was left to the LEAs and a small number of HMIs. It is as though the political parties were so concerned with social class and equality that they disregarded other aspects of education. In effect, the two parties were in tacit agreement not to interfere with schools and what went on inside them. This is known as the 'political consensus' on education (Lawton, 1992). Another reason for lack of control through a national curriculum was the fear of the politics of the totalitarian regimes which rent Europe during the twentieth century. Nazi and Communist governments had controlled their education policies, making them into propaganda machines to support the state. Politicians in the UK were anxious not to be seen to be anti-democratic and it led to some reluctance to have national control of the school curriculum. Another factor was the continuing success of the UK economy in the period after World War II. There was no need to bother teachers and schools when everything was going well.

EDUCATION AND THE GLOBAL ECONOMY

The oil crisis of the 1970s brought this indifference to an end. Until then, things had gone well economically for Britain. But conflict in the Middle East led to increasing oil prices which hit production in the European economies. At the same time, there were concerns about rising crime, lower moral standards, breakdown of traditional moral codes and racial conflict in the cities. Politicians looked around for solutions, and sent the first shots across the bows of the education professions. In 1973 Anthony Crosland, Labour Secretary of State for Education, famously complained that the school curriculum was 'a secret garden in which only teachers and children are allowed to walk'. Jim Callaghan, Labour Prime Minister, in a speech at Ruskin College, Oxford in 1976, stated that he was concerned about the quality of teaching in primary schools and whether schools were equipping young people for industry. These were signs that the government was unhappy with education and wished to take its control away from the LEAs and the teachers. 'Moral panic' set in, with schools portrayed as failing their children, and falling standards described as the cause of the nation's economic and social ills.

By the 1980s the effects of the global economy were being realised. The 'Asian tiger' economies of Japan, South Korea and Taiwan were producing better industrial goods more cheaply and were sucking away customers from Britain. Their education systems appeared to benefit from teaching basic skills through traditional methods (see Chapter 1). Controlling the curriculum to make it more suited to industrial production was seen as one of the means of enabling Britain to compete. Multinational companies, such as the Ford Motor Company, invested in Britain by establishing manufacturing plants and providing jobs. But they threatened to go elsewhere if the workforce was not suitably equipped. The government now began to treat education as the principal means of training industry for competition in the world, and it had to become more vocationally oriented.

A REVOLUTION IN EDUCATION

It took another ten years after Callaghan's warning speech for there to be significant action, but it came in a massive attack by the Conservative government with the Education 'Reform' Act of 1988. The act is well known for introducing a national curriculum and testing, but it also introduced the so-called 'local management of schools' (LMS). This took financial control away from the LEAs by delegating the spending budget directly to schools. In principle, schools were to use the money as they wished: to appoint teaching staff or non-teaching assistants, purchase more computers or repair the roof. Such decisions were now to be taken by the headteacher and the governing body of the school, not by local authority officials. While the National Curriculum had immediate impact on schools, LMS was a bigger change, making schools into business corporations which had to balance their books. The role of school governors was strengthened in order to ensure that schools were not run exclusively by the education professionals.

LMS at first seemed contradictory (Coulby, 1996). On the one hand, the government had taken central control of the curriculum and national testing, but had *de*-centralised spending and management. In fact, the so-called devolution of funding was designed to reduce the power of the LEAs. It was the Conservative government's political intention to limit the power of left-wing Labour-controlled local authorities, particularly the Inner London Education Authority (ILEA). Some had exercised strong equal opportunities policies with action against racism and sexism, which the Conservative government saw as dangerous 'social engineering' and against the liberal tradition. So while the 1988 Act appears to devolve power from government to schools, it actually increased the power of central government by disempowering the LEAs. The noose tightened around the education service with legislation in 1992 to introduce the Office for Standards in Education (Ofsted) with powers to inspect every school in the state system every four years. The Ofsted Framework for Inspection gives a detailed list of every possible dimension of a school's work and it can be seen as part of a general trend in society towards increased accountability and 'surveillance' (Bottery, 2000).

It is difficult to convey the magnitude and complexity of the systems which were put in place for education by the legislation of the late 1980s and early 1990s. They generated prodigious amounts of consultative documents, legislation and government agencies. (See the list of government education websites at the end of the chapter.) They also led to furious debate among professionals and politicians, particularly in setting up the content of the National Curriculum (Coulby, 1996; Chitty, 2002). It is important to understand what was going on in the government mind in devising all this, because it was never entirely evident to teachers at the time.

The politics of 'the New Right'

Many economists argue for a 'free market'. Providers compete with each other to give the best at the lowest price, and the more freedom of consumer choice the better. The logic underlying the 1988 Education Act was the attempt to make education accountable to the rest of society and to put it into the market place with freedom of choice for parents – the consumers. The primacy of market forces was the view held by Margaret Thatcher when she came to power as Prime Minister of the new Conservative government in 1979. Her plan for the country was to reduce taxation, 'roll back the state' and to allow people to have greater personal control over their own lives. This was the birth of the so-called 'New Right' politics, derived from nineteenth-century liberalism and so known as 'neo-liberalism'. Its ideas are based on the social philosopher Friedrich von Hayek (1899–1992) who argued that the welfare state disables people's creative energy and that individual freedom, while it appears to be self-serving and greedy, actually brings public good.

Thatcher did not try to scrap education as a social service altogether, but she tried to make it a service that people could select and use as they wished. 'Freedom of choice', then, was crucial to her policy and the 1988 Act introduced 'open enrolment' in schools. In the past the LEAs had set and limited the number of pupils schools could take; now schools would be able to accept any number of children and to grow as the market demanded. It also meant that parents could, in principle, choose any school for their children and that schools would have to compete with each other for pupils. Education was to be like shopping for clothes: if they're better at Next than at Marks and Spencer, you'll go there to buy.

But for parents to be able to choose, the goods need to be on display. The idea was to bring the performance of schools and teachers out into the open and away from the private control of the education professions. This was the real reason for setting up the machinery of a national curriculum, testing, league tables and Ofsted inspection – to make education into a market. It is more accurate to describe education as a 'quasi-market', a kind of market, but not fully so. State education is still free to all those who choose it; it is not properly 'privatised'. However, the ambitions of the Conservative Hillgate Group (1987) have now been realised in the sense of taking the control of education away from the 'self-interested professionals'. Of course, parental choice is not simple in that schools are not adjacent to each other like shops in the high street and a family may need to be equipped to transport children to the school of their choice. But the principle was that education must be accountable to its 'customers'. The move from education as a public service provided by professionals, to education as a commodity which can be purchased freely by all, is often attributed to Margaret Thatcher and referred to as 'Thatcherism'. In fact, it is part of a broader political movement taking place in many parts of the world (see Chapter 1).

Improving schools and controlling teachers

In Japanese education (see Chapter 1) teachers try to ensure that the whole class 'marches along together'. In contrast, one of the notions about education in England has been that schools cannot compensate for society: some children are bound to achieve less because of cultural background, poverty and 'low intelligence'. Another plank in the Conservative government's strategy in the 1990s was to seize on research such as Mortimore's (Mortimore *et al.*, 1988). He showed that children in some London schools learned more than in others. The differences were due to the quality of teaching and management, not just to the pupils' backgrounds. As part of the marketing of schools, the notions of the 'Effective School' and 'School Improvement' were introduced. The role of the headteacher is re-cast as a manager who can produce the goods and attract customers. The well-managed school concentrates on pupils' learning and achievement in the national tests. Another marketing message was for educationalists to use the terminology of business: 'auditing' and 'delivery' of the curriculum, 'target-setting' and schools as 'providers'.

In the National Curriculum there was an explicit statement that the legislation was to cover only content, not the way in which the curriculum was taught. However, the 'hands-on' approach to education had begun and by December 1991 the Secretary of State, Kenneth Clark, was unable to resist the temptation to interfere in teachers' methods. In a statement expressing his concerns about the quality of teaching in primary schools he announced an inquiry into primary teaching and requested a report to be made available by January 1992. Those appointed to the task, Alexander, Rose and Woodhead (1992), had to work over the Christmas period and their efforts became known as the Three Wise Men Report. They made a brief summary of the findings of 1980s research on primary teaching which indicated weaknesses in individualised teaching and group work in primary schools. They recommended an increase in the level of whole-class teaching, more subject-specialist teaching and grouping by ability.

Ofsted inspection enabled the government to control the practice of teachers. If a school was not operating in the prescribed way, then it could fail its inspection and be threatened with closure. The appointment in 1994 of Chief Inspector of Schools Chris Woodhead as the 'scourge of poor teachers' ensured that the tightest control was exercised and a bitter campaign against the profession was under way. The so-called 'naming and shaming' of schools began to create a climate of fear which had been unknown to teachers before.

NEW LABOUR AND THE 'MODERNISERS'

The Conservatives had enjoyed four terms of office until 1997 when Tony Blair swept Labour to power in a landslide election victory. Teachers looked forward to a return to the consensual days when they would again be able to control education and the criticism of schools would end. They were soon to be disappointed. For this was 'New Labour' and Blair soon showed that his three priorities – 'education, education, education' – meant more of the same politics of education as under the Conservatives. The first shock for teachers was that the Chief Inspector, Chris Woodhead, was not sacked, but given a salary increase. Blair claimed he had not been elected to return to 'Old Labour' methods. His 'modernisation' of Labour policies meant continuing the marketisation of education, keeping the pressure on schools to deliver education fit for a modern industrial society. This does not mean that the politics of New Labour were identical with the Conservative New Right. New Labour modernisers did not see market forces as a philosophical doctrine as the neo-liberal Conservatives did. Instead, Blair claimed that market forces were simply a pragmatic and effective way of operating to get the best from the system and termed it 'the Third Way'. The political philosophy is different, but the effect was much the same.

There were always contradictions in Conservative policy, in 'the Conservative mind' (Lawton, 1992). Neo-liberal Conservatives believed in the free market, so there should be as little government involvement as possible. On the other hand, there was the need to intervene to control things with a national curriculum, testing and inspection. With New Labour there was no such contradiction. Blair's 'modernising' approach to government meant *intervention*. The government should have the political will to take on big issues such as child poverty, inequality and underachievement and to attack them through a mixture of legislation, funding and persuasion. But central control did not mean the abolition of the quasi market. In fact, New Labour proved to be an even more enthusiastic proponent of market forces and privatisation than the Conservatives. Assessment and school league tables were strengthened with the setting of targets at all levels: national government targets for literacy and numeracy, as well as targets for LEAs, for schools and for individual pupils. Performance-related pay for teachers was introduced with the threshold scheme, failing LEAs were taken over by private companies and school building was financed by profit-making organisations in the Private Finance Initiative.

New Labour's shift went even further. Old Labour's commitment to equality of opportunity through comprehensive education faded with the refusal to abolish independent and grammar schools. The 2002 Education Act encouraged diversity, with specialist schools allowed to select through admissions tests. All this, Blair claimed, makes sense 'because it works' in increasing quality and standards to create an education system which provides an educated workforce for industry in globally competitive markets. Even if this allowed inequalities, it was thought to be worth it.

New Labour's strongest intervention was to take up the Conservative government's desire to prescribe teaching methods. *The Three Wise Men Report,* summarised in Gipps (1992), had pointed to the need for more whole-class teaching in primary schools. One of New Labour's first acts was to set up the National Literacy and Numeracy Strategies which required primary teachers to take a one-hour daily lesson in each subject, with a high proportion of interactive class teaching: the 'three-part' lesson from Japan and Taiwan, described in Chapter 1. Such prescription of methods was previously unknown, and it is interesting that the teaching profession should have been forced to allow it to occur. It is unlike the prescription made to any other professional body and a result of the lack of response of the educational profession to its own research findings which largely failed to a make significant impact on teachers' practice.

EDUCATION FOR THE ECONOMY

Old Labour policy had been to reduce inequalities both in society and in education by providing high levels of resources to schools. Labour governments in the past, though, had not succeeded in actually producing funds. Labour was characterised by Conservatives as the 'tax and spend' party, the idea being that with high income tax the general economy tends not to flourish. Blair's policy was to ensure that the economy was successful and Labour's first actions in education were economically careful, not increasing income tax and keeping to the former Conservative government's spending plans. The economy did quickly expand after 1997 and, without raising the level of income tax, there was sufficient funding for increases to both the education and health services, permitting a higher level of spending on school buildings, salaries and additional teachers.

New Labour's policies might be seen as simply an extension of the neo-liberal policies of the Conservative governments in that they were designed to enhance the economy through the use of market forces and they reduced the Old Labour agenda of social equality. However, Whitty (2002) notes that a number of actions were taken which were designed to improve the conditions of the socially disadvantaged. The reduction in class sizes in Key Stage 1 was funded through the removal of the Assisted Places Scheme where the government funded places at independent schools for high-achieving pupils. Other egalitarian actions were the Social Exclusion Unit in 1997, which was to concentrate on eradicating disadvantage, Education Action Zones and Excellence in Cities, which were designed to bring industrial investment into inner-city schools; there was also a target to expand access to university education to 50 per cent of the student cohort by 2010.

Another aim of New Labour was to promote *social cohesion* through 'joined-up' government with co-ordinated health, welfare and education policies. It has been argued for some time that it is no use simply providing good schooling for children who are unhealthy or undernourished. The SureStart Scheme was introduced to co-ordinate the physical, intellectual and social development of young children (see Chapter 9). It was also believed that social cohesion could be achieved if all members of society are literate and numerate, and a rationale for the primary Numeracy and Literacy Strategies was to ensure that these two subjects were taught 'properly'.

After achieving the control of primary school teaching, and later of secondary teaching with the Key Stage 3 Strategy, there was a softening of attitudes towards the profession. Estelle Morris, Secretary of State from 2001–2, was seen to be a more approachable figure, as an ex-teacher, and took a number of actions to demonstrate that the profession was again being listened to. The 2002 Education Act allowed for successful schools to be inspected less frequently and David Bell, a more 'teacher-friendly' Chief Inspector, was appointed. Morris's successor, Charles Clarke, while maintaining a bullish front, continued the softening process by reducing the testing regime in primary schools and calling for 'enjoyment' in the curriculum (Department for Education and Skills [DfES], 2003).

However, the DfES continued to be highly directive, dictating to schools what should be done and what is to be allowed. Teachers were surprised and amused to read a statement from David Milliband, the Standards Minister (2003), calling on schools to remember that 'creativity' is essential to a good education for industry: this after years of policy which reduced creativity and the arts in the curriculum (see Chapter 17). In short, the government perceived its duty to 'micro-manage' schools with almost daily guidance, direction and exhortation about their day-to-day business. The Teachernet website for school documents gives a view of the extent of this.

SHOULD GOVERNMENTS INTERVENE IN EDUCATION?

Government policies have been to employ market forces to introduce efficiency in education and to equip the labour market for a global economy. The assumption is that a vocationally-educated workforce will improve the economy and the economy will provide a good education system in a virtuous circle. However, Wolf (2002) demonstrates that there is no evidence of a link between education and a successful economy. She argues that the emphasis on vocational education and investment in extended higher education does not improve the economy in itself. The emphasis on numeracy and literacy has had the effect of narrowing the curriculum in primary schools, supposedly to suit vocational needs. But the government's perception of literacy and numeracy to meet the challenges of the global economy is questioned by Coulby (2000) who suggests that a twenty-first century economy needs a curriculum which emphasises *breadth* of skills and knowledge.

The tensions between the education professionals as the 'providers' and the government as paymaster and manager look set to continue as the economic forces in the global economy make increasing demands. Pupils' rights as consumers in the market place are protected by competition between schools, but Whitty (2002) points out that their rights *as citizens* are not protected, and the weak are exposed to inequalities:

... education policies in Britain can ... be seen as part of that broader project to create a free economy and a strong state ... In other words, as far as democratic citizenship is concerned, this may even be the worst of both worlds.

(Whitty, 2002: 89)

CONCLUSION

So how far should governments control schools? If education is not so closely related to the success of the economy, and governments have got it wrong anyway about the curriculum needed for the knowledge economy, we might ask whether their direction of education is either necessary or desirable. How you decide on this for yourself comes down to a view of education and democracy. Democratic governments will tend to control education along the lines of the popular view of education held by voters: traditional teaching and a basic skills curriculum. But you might want to argue that professionals know better: that there are wider possibilities for education, both in its curriculum and the way it is learned. Do we leave the direction of education to the professionals or to the popular vote?

QUESTIONS FOR DISCUSSION

- Should education be a public service, or be left to market forces?
- Should independent schools be allowed to continue?
- Should the government direct teaching methods?
- Does assessment and target-setting improve education?
- Can schools compensate for social disadvantage?
- Should the curriculum be designed to produce a skilled workforce for industry?
- Do teachers know best about education?
- Should teachers be good technicians who can effectively teach the national curriculum, or should they have a critical understanding of government policy?

REFERENCES

Alexander, R., Rose, J. and Woodhead, C. (1992) *Curriculum Organisation and Classroom Practice in Primary Schools: A Discussion Paper*, London: DES.

Bottery, M. (2000) *Education Policy and Ethics*, London: Continuum.

Chitty, C. (2002) *Understanding Schools and Schooling*, London: RoutledgeFalmer.

Coulby, D. (1996) 'The construction and implementation of the core National Curriculum', in D. Coulby and S. Ward (eds) *Primary Core National Curriculum: From Policy to Practice*, 2nd edition, London: Cassell.

Coulby, D. (2000) *Beyond the National Curriculum: Curricular Centralism and Diversity in Europe and the USA*, London: RoutledgeFalmer.

DfES (2003) *Excellence and Enjoyment: A Strategy for Primary Schools*, London: DfES.

Gipps, C. (1992) *What we Know about Effective Teaching*, London: Institute of Education.

Green, A. (1991) 'The peculiarities of English education', in Education Group II, Department of Cultural Studies, University of Birmingham, *Education Limited: Schooling, Training and the New Right since 1979*, London: Unwin Hyman.

Hillgate Group (1987) *The Reform of British Education*, London: Claridge Press.

Lawton, D. (1992) *Education and Politics in the 1990s: Conflict or Consensus*, Lewes: Falmer Press.

Milliband, D. (2003) Speech to the National Campaign for the Arts, 27 March 2003.

Mortimore, P., Sammons, P., Stoll, L., Lewis, D. and Ecob, R. (1988) *School Matters*, London: Open Books.

Whitty, G. (2002) *Making Sense of Education Policy*, London: Paul Chapman Publishing.

Wolf, A. (2002) *Does Education Matter?* London: Penguin.

RECOMMENDED READING

The following will take you further in the theoretical issues introduced in this chapter:

Bottery, M. (2000) *Education Policy and Ethics*, London: Continuum. Gives thought-provoking critiques of managerialism in schools (Chapter 3), the school improvement movement (Chapter 5) and the effects of Ofsted in the 'surveillance' culture (Chapter 7).

Chitty, C. (2002) *Understanding Schools and Schooling*, London: RoutledgeFalmer. Gives a detailed account of the history of education policy in England and Wales.

Green, A. (1991) 'The peculiarities of English education', in Education Group II, Department of Cultural Studies, University of Birmingham, *Education Limited: Schooling, Training and the New Right since 1979*, London: Unwin Hyman. Gives a detailed explanation of why independent schools have retained such a strong role in English education.

The Journal of Education Policy provides international perspectives on education policy.

Lawton, D. (1992) *Education and Politics in the 1990s: Conflict or Consensus*, Lewes: Falmer Press. Explains the background political theory in education policy.

Phillips, R. (2001) 'Education, the State and Reform', in Phillips, R. and Furlong, J. (eds) *Education, Reform and the State: Twenty-five Years of Politics, Policy and Practice*, London: RoutledgeFalmer. Gives a summary of political developments in the last 25 years.

Whitty, G. (2002) *Making Sense of Education Policy*, London: Paul Chapman Publishing. Outlines the tensions between pupils as consumers and as citizens (Chapter 5) and explains New Labour policy (Chapter 8).

Wolf, A. (2002) *Does Education Matter?* London: Penguin. Challenges the idea that vocational education helps the economy.

GOVERNMENT WEBSITES

Basic Skills Agency: www.basic-skills.co.uk.

DfES documents sent to schools: www.teachernet.gov.uk/Mailing.

DfES: www.dfes.gov.uk.

DfES Research: www.dfes.gov.uk/research/pubs.cfm.

Education Action Zones: www.standards.dfes.gov.uk/eaz.

National Education Statistics: www.dfes.gov.uk/statistics.

National Grid for Learning: www.ngfl.gov.uk.

Ofsted: www.ofsted.gov.uk.

Qualifications and Curriculum Authority: www.qca.org.uk.

Standards and Effectiveness Unit: www.standards.dfee.gov.uk/seu.

Standards Site: www.standards.dfee.gov.uk.

Sure Start: www.surestart.gov.uk.

Teacher Training Agency: www.canteach.gov.uk.

8 The Effective Teacher

Andy Bord

The aims for this chapter are to introduce you to:

- The importance of interpersonal skills in any notion of the effective teacher, including those of building self-esteem, active listening, communication, and working competently in groups
- Pedagogical skills that are needed by teachers in a range of professional contexts
- Ways of thinking about your own ideas about yourself as a future teacher.

The relationship between teaching and learning can appear deceptively simple: you teach – they learn. But being a learner is a more complex and active process than this simple *input* model implies. Learning is certainly the necessary outcome of teaching, indeed it is the core objective, and yet teaching is neither a necessary nor sufficient condition for learning. To be effective teachers we must recognise what it is to be a learner – the importance of self-esteem, the social nature of learning, the skills needed to work co-operatively in groups and the importance of imagination are all elements that play a key role in effective learning. Placing the learner at the heart of all teaching would mean starting from what we know about learning rather than from a body of knowledge to be learnt, the curriculum. David Fontana (1997) suggests that 'education for being' supports children in their self-actualisation. By this he means offering children:

> … the right to express their own feelings, to give their own views of events, to explain themselves, to reflect upon their own behaviour, to have their hopes and their fears taken seriously, to ask questions, to seek explanations in the natural world, to love and be loved, to have their inner world of dreams and fantasies and imagining taken seriously, and to make their own engagement with life.
>
> (Fontana 1997: 13)

This person-centred approach to education does not necessarily mean disregarding the curriculum, nor does it mean adopting any one particular teaching style, but rather bearing in mind at all times that at the centre of any classroom activity is learning for understanding which is owned by the learner. The prime responsibility of educators would be to provide for children the intellectual and emotional nourishment that will match their growing and developing powers.

SELF-ESTEEM: AT THE HEART OF ALL LEARNING

One of the fundamental questions that education asks is: Who are you and what are you about? Only when you can give a clear answer to 'Who am I?' can you help others to contemplate that question. Education is one of the contexts in which you learn about the values and norms of society. You learn what is expected of you and what is appropriate behaviour. Education plays a significant role in childhood socialisation and teachers are in a powerful position to influence children's understanding of themselves. How you conceptualise 'self' is crucial because it affects not only how you see your students, but also how you teach.

A view in which the individual is seen as 'separate' and 'self-contained', in which a sharp boundary exists between the self and others, would see an aim of education to create autonomous, independent individuals. A contrasting view in which the self is seen as being interdependent and part of a whole might consider an aim of education to be to strengthen ties between individuals, families and communities, to recognise the importance of relationships rather than separateness.

How we feel about ourselves, how we value what we do and how we think others judge us are each fundamental to our understanding of who we are. Self-concept is the image we build up of ourselves as we grow and mature. We tend to accept information that confirms our self-concept and ignore or reject that which challenges what we believe. Other people are a mirror by which we know ourselves and teachers have an important role in defining children's self-concept. Research has established that there is a relationship between self-concept and school achievement. Not only does self-concept affect achievement, but also achievement affects self-concept (Muijs and Reynolds, 2001). Those who generally feel good about themselves achieve more, those who lack confidence achieve less.

Self-esteem is the evaluation you make of yourself, whether positive or negative. When you are repeatedly good at something, self-esteem increases; if you are repeatedly unsuccessful, negative self-esteem is likely to follow. Self-esteem is about confidence, the confidence you have in your personality and your abilities. Students with low self-esteem will lack confidence and be reluctant to take risks, and are often particularly resistant to change of the self-concept. They may try to avoid particular situations that could lead to failure or humiliation and may compensate with over-confident behaviour to mask what they are feeling.

Skills needed for enhancing self-esteem

Supporting the positive development of self-esteem in others is an important skill for teachers to develop and Carl Rogers (1961) identifies three personal characteristics of *acceptance*, *genuineness* and *empathy* as being crucial to this process. Rogers explains that acceptance means being non-judgemental and accepting a personality as it is. The secret is to make a distinction between a person and their behaviour. Often when we dislike someone's behaviour we blame the person, which leads to further hostilities. The person then feels attacked and rejected. In the situation of a teacher responding to a child who is misbehaving it is important that the child is still accepted, even though her/his behaviour needs criticism. Genuineness requires an honest appraisal of one's self. It is the ability to be spontaneous and present in situations without being defensive or hiding behind role behaviour. It means really being yourself in any interaction rather than hiding behind one of your masks. Empathy involves putting yourself in someone else's shoes and getting a feel of what is actually going on for them. When people feel really accepted for who *they* are, that you are letting them see the real *you*, and you are trying to understand *their feelings*, much more meaningful interactions become possible.

If you can develop these three qualities – acceptance, genuineness and empathy – you will gain the trust of your students. It is not necessarily an easy thing to do, but it lies at the heart of effective teaching. In addition to developing these personal qualities as a teacher there are a number of classroom practices that you can implement to improve your students' self-concept. It is important to recognise that for all students, having high expectations of what they can achieve will improve self-concept as well as performance. Muijs and Reynolds (2001) suggest that the most important aspect of successful teaching is to ensure that all students experience success. Teachers should emphasise successes by telling students what they are doing right as well as correcting their mistakes and to show they value their contributions.

There will inevitably be occasions when a student's behaviour is not acceptable. It is important in such circumstances that the focus remains upon the behaviour and the reasons why it is not appropriate and that personal criticism is avoided. The message to convey is that 'I am disappointed in your behaviour and want you to change what you are doing', rather than 'I don't like you and wish you were different'. Undermining children and embarrassing them in front of others will contribute to the identification of certain children with certain behaviour. Labelling can follow from this, such as 'She's a spiteful girl' or 'He's a bully.' The classroom should be a place in which everyone has the opportunity to make a positive contribution. By giving students responsibilities for the day-to-day management of the classroom and other areas in the school it is possible to build up students' self-worth, particularly when these contributions are seen to be valued. Active participation in establishing the class rules, being reading partners for younger children, exercising real choices in how or when aspects of the curriculum are accomplished can each contribute to students' sense of personal worth which will enhance their self-esteem. The use of 'circle time' is now well established in many primary classrooms as a regular whole-class experience in which students are able to say something positive about themselves and others or something of which they are proud. Mosley (1996) gives a range of activities designed to encourage students to explore their feelings about their experiences and to understand how to express these to others.

LEARNING IN GROUPS

Groups are an important part of our everyday experience. We spend nearly all of our time in groups of one sort or another, be they groups of friends or families, groups in work or sports, religious groups and political groups, crèches, playschemes, schools and universities. Groups frequently need to achieve or complete a specific chosen or given task. As soon as we are in a group that collectively has to make a decision, other factors come into play. Did you choose that group? Maybe you don't like being in groups. Maybe you're with someone you don't like. How you behave in a group arises directly out of your sense of self, your degree of self-awareness, your sense of self-worth and your modes of self-presentation. Everything you've ever learnt, mostly unconsciously, about being with other people in groups comes into play. All sorts of roles, helpful and obstructive, are played out in groups from being a victim, using flattery, stirring it up and being dogmatic, to being supportive, getting a spread of opinion, getting things clearer and keeping the group on task. It is because you have so many negative and/or positive experiences in groups in the past that you will bring these behaviours to any group you are in today. So the first thing is to become more aware of what happens for you when you are in such a group.

For a group to work effectively, people must become aware of the needs and wants that they each bring. Maslow (1954) suggests a hierarchy of interrelated needs, of which the higher can only be met after the lower needs have been satisfied (see Figure 8.1).

Maslow proposes that the satisfaction of the needs on each level, starting with the lowest, frees a person for higher levels of satisfaction. In other words, when someone feels satisfied in the earlier levels, they can go on to learn for self-esteem, individual achievement and self-development purposes. If learners lack basic comfort needs – the room is too cold, or they have insufficient space to sit – then the teacher should focus on helping them to satisfy these needs before going any further. All people need to feel safe in their learning environment; if they feel vulnerable or afraid they may make mistakes or make fools of themselves, and be unable to learn.

> To feel good in a group, everyone needs three things: inclusion, control, and appreciation. Inclusion means feeling that you're part of the group, a member of the 'in' crowd. Control means feeling that you have some say in the group, that you will be heard and your views will be taken seriously. Appreciation means feeling accepted and liked.
>
> (McKay *et al.*, 1995: 263)

Behaviour which helps people to interact effectively, such as reconciling disagreements, praising, encouraging, co-operating and listening, all contribute to successful

Figure 8.1 Maslow's hierarchy of needs

Self-actualisation
Self-esteem
Love, affection and belonging
Safety needs
Physiological or survival needs

group work. However, fundamental to the success of any group is the acknowledgement of the needs of the individual group members. The teacher needs to ensure that the classroom provides a secure physical and emotional environment in which to learn.

Understanding conflicts

One inevitable consequence of being in a group is that conflicts will arise between individuals. Conflict is an inescapable part of the human condition because people have different perceptions, beliefs, needs and purposes in life. Conflict should not, therefore, be seen as 'bad' but rather as a normal part of everyday life. The principles involved in conflict formation, whether in the classroom or in the wider community, are often similar. Isenhart and Spangle (2000) suggest that because of its many overlapping and dynamic processes, conflict is a complex process and defining it in a specific situation can be a difficult task. However they list the following as common features:

- Conflict is an inevitable consequence of social life
- Patterns of conflict behaviour perpetuate themselves
- Conflict may appear chaotic, but many elements can be understood
- Conflict is maintained by a series of moves and countermoves
- Conflict affects the relationships of the parties involved
- Communication plays a central role in the management of conflict.

A number of key sources of conflict are likely to be present in the interactions in schools. Differences of opinion about information: who actually said what to whom in the playground? Clashes over different interests: who has the most right to use the computer to research their project? Who has access to that fabulous hat in the creative play area? Disagreement about the best way to do things, about the procedures used to resolve a problem: does the teacher always decide in favour of a favourite pupil? Does one child's view always dominate in a group? Refusing to co-operate because people do not trust others: children's distrust of other's motives in the playground. Disputes that arise from poor communication: how things are said or not said; language in the playground that sounds threatening or insulting.

To be able to pre-empt conflicts in your professional life, with students and with colleagues, is an essential skill. It is important to consider why children may wish to use or to perpetuate conflict. What do they gain through the process and are there other ways in which the child can feel important, involved and valued? It is important to recognise that many conflicts may be symptomatic of a lack of self-valuing experiences. The role of the teacher in resolving conflicts is to help achieve a sense of justice, an end to the anger, pain or sadness that is being experienced and a restoring of self-esteem.

Mediation is an approach to dealing with conflicts and peer mediation schemes in schools have been successful in responding to the kinds of conflicts which usually focus on swearing, insulting or hitting. More severe forms of bullying are less likely to be responded to in this way (Musgrove, 1999).

ACTIVE LISTENING

A crucial skill in resolving conflicts is to be able to listen attentively and actively to enable what people are saying to really be heard. Often when we are listening to someone else we do not really hear them because we are doing other things at the same time, which act as blocks to fully listening. Some of the blocks to listening are:

- *Comparing:* trying to decide who is smarter, more honest
- *Rehearsing:* planning what you are going to say next
- *Filtering:* listening to some things and not to others
- *Judging:* making value judgements about what is being said
- *Advising:* always having answers to other people's problems
- *Arguing:* jumping in to say why and how you disagree
- *Pleasing:* agreeing with everything because you want to be liked.

First we need to learn to watch our own behaviour, to become aware of what we actually do when we are listening to someone else that stops us from really hearing them. Second we need to learn the skills of active listening which convey our commitment to the other person. Hargie (1997) describes how the skill of active listening can be developed through six elements of interaction.

Paraphrasing   Stating in your own words what you think the other person said: 'What I hear you saying is … So what you actually felt was … Now let me just get this clear.' This stops miscommunication and the speaker really appreciates being heard.

Clarifying   Asking questions so that you get as complete a picture as possible of the situation. The speaker then knows that you are really trying to understand them. 'Tell me a bit more about that … So how did you feel?'

Giving feedback   The honest sharing of your own responses in a supportive and non-judgemental way: 'I wonder if that could have been handled in another way?' not 'That was a stupid thing to do!' 'What happens when you ignore me is that I feel unloved,' rather than 'I know you don't love me and I hate you!'

Having empathy   Trying to be in the other person's shoes, even if you don't actually agree with them. Ask yourself 'What is actually going on for *them*? What feelings lie *behind* that statement: anger, fear? What is the person *actually* asking for?'

Listening openly   Being able to face up to the fact that you might be wrong or that someone really disagrees with your point of view and being able to accept that without an emotional outburst.

Body language   An important element of active listening, requiring good eye contact, leaning forward slightly, nodding, showing that you are committed to understanding what is being said even if you feel angry or hurt.

WHY SHOULD WE CO-OPERATE?

The classroom climate will have a significant effect on the engagement of those students who are expected to learn within it, and classrooms can be organised in a number of different ways, each of which will encourage different ways of learning. Borich (1996) identified three distinctive types of classroom. In competitive classrooms pupils are encouraged to compete with one another to achieve goals which are usually set by the teacher. In individual classrooms the emphasis is on pupils working alone with individualised support from the teacher. In co-operative classrooms the emphasis is on pupils working together, with the teacher guiding groups towards shared goals. In such classrooms the term *collaborative learning* is used to describe the academic tasks and activities undertaken by groups of children, and which involve some degree of discussion, reflection and co-operation. Why might teachers wish to encourage children to learn collaboratively?

'Because it helps children to learn'   Many educators stress the importance of the social setting in classroom learning in that it provides opportunities for discussion, which is seen essential to long-lasting understanding. The Soviet psychologist Lev Vygotsky believed that children's interaction with others through language was a crucial influence on the development of conceptual understanding. He suggested that learners have a *zone of proximal development*: the gap that exists between what a person is able to do alone and what is possible to be achieved with the support of a more knowledgeable other. By intervening in this zone it is possible for teachers or peers to bring the child's learning to a higher level. For Vygotsky co-operation is the basis of successful learning (Muijs and Reynolds, 2001).

'Because it is part of what education is all about'   Co-operation can also be seen as a contribution to education's broader aims – the development of the individual to enable them to participate in society at large, to become active citizens. This requires opportunities to explore relationships with others. Collaborative learning can have far-reaching implications for relationships within a class. It can allow young children to experience their class, not as a collection of separate individuals, but as an interrelated system in which the actions of each member affect, and are affected by, the actions of others. Placing children in collaborative learning situations can encourage them to develop friendships from beyond their own gender and ethnic group (Whitaker,1995). Some teachers may be concerned that an emphasis on collaborative work will not adequately prepare children for the demands of an increasingly competitive world. However, today's students will need the skills to work co-operatively with others to achieve common goals in almost any field of work they choose to enter. Indeed schools could be criticised for emphasising an individualistic approach to work and failing to take into account the collaborative, sharing nature of most working groups. Even in highly competitive industries, there is an increasing trend towards co-operation and worker participation in goal-setting and decision making.

'Because teaching should support creative social change'   It can be argued that escalating competition has in many ways led the planet to the brink of destruction. Competition

for military superiority has led to the stockpiling of weapons capable of destroying human life many times over; at the same time budgets for housing, education and health fail to keep up with increasingly urgent demands. The race between multinational corporations for ever-increasing profits has led to the depletion of irreplaceable resources, while alternative energy sources remain largely under-researched. The effects of this type of competition on a global scale touch the lives of every person on the earth. If competition continues to be seen as the preferable way of relating to others, we risk maintaining the *status quo* which threatens our very existence as a species. Therefore teaching co-operative skills can be seen as part of teaching for creative social change (Hicks and Holden, 1995).

Activities to encourage co-operation

In small groups, children are more often prepared to be tentative, to take chances in exposing what they are unsure of, and to use language exploratively. Understanding is more likely to be achieved when children are allowed to express their ideas in their own words and to check this against the understanding of others. They need the freedom to explore at their own level without the fear of not doing the right thing, without having to work out what the teacher wants. Therefore, in addition to opportunities to work individually, paired, group and whole-class contexts are also important.

There are various activities to encourage co-operation in the classroom. Students can work together on individual tasks, thereby extending the challenge of their own learning. Working in a group on a task with a joint outcome, such as problem-solving or construction, will also develop co-operation, for example in designing a school sweatshirt. Groups can discuss open-ended problems or situations and decide between possible courses of action, such as surviving on a desert island following a shipwreck.

Students may work together on activities which contribute to a joint outcome: chapters of a story, or a dance or drama performance, or interpretative discussion. Groups can investigate and discuss a given focus, such as devising classroom rules for working together (Fisher, 1995).

The classroom organised around promoting opportunities for co-operative small group learning can also produce a beneficial teacher–student relationship. The role of the teacher changes from that of the person who imparts knowledge to that of the person who is responsible for carefully structuring the learning experiences and assisting children in their learning. The teacher can listen carefully to small group discussion, monitor individual children's talk to gauge the level of their understanding and provide more focused assistance when necessary (often immediately). When the class is working in small groups, the teacher is free to work with individuals in a way that is not possible when teaching the whole class and therefore the teacher has more time for personal interaction with children.

Peer tutoring, commonly seen in schools in reading partners and maths buddies, is a form of co-operation where the helping child (tutor) can benefit from taking on a nurturing role. Putting skills and knowledge to some purpose may help the 'tutor' to consolidate their thinking as well as help the child to understand more about the learning process. The child being helped (tutee) gains extra attention with regular and responsive feedback. Children may not be as good as teachers at 'scaffolding', that is offering the structured support appropriate to the learner's level of understanding. But they do offer direct help in learning and can provide a model of how to learn as well as emotional support.

CONCLUSION

I suggest the following principles to consider if you are thinking of yourself as a future teacher:

- Effective teachers understand that learning is not a consequence of what *teachers* do, but rather is the result of the active engagement of children with ideas and experiences that have significance for them.
- Learning can be greatly encouraged through the enhancement of self-esteem: the need for acceptance, genuineness and empathy in interactions.
- Much learning takes place in groups and how you behave in groups is directly related to your sense of self. Co-operation is crucial to any group task and is a process by which individual learning is enhanced through the communication of ideas.
- Conflict may appear chaotic and undesirable, but it can be understood, and the management of conflict through active listening and good communication will play an important role in learning in group.
- Collaborative approaches to learning help to create a climate in which children can work with a sense of security and self-confidence which, in turn, promotes a spirit of co-operation and mutual respect within the classroom.

QUESTIONS FOR DISCUSSION

- Is the development of positive self-esteem in pupils a more important role for the teacher than imparting knowledge?
- In what ways do schools encourage or impede learning?
- What kinds of learning are best achieved through working co-operatively?
- What are the main skills that are needed to be able to participate in a group activity?
- Each child has unique abilities and a way of learning which is all their own. If all learners are individuals, should all learning be individualised?

REFERENCES

Borich, J. (1996) *Effective Teaching Methods*, New York: Macmillan.

Fisher, R. (1995) *Teaching Children to Learn*, London: Stanley Thornes.

Fontana, D. (1997) 'Childhood and an education for being', *Caduceus*, 34, Winter 96/97, Caduceus Publications Ltd.

Hargie, O. (1997) *The Handbook of Communication Skills*, London: Routledge.

Hicks, D. and Holden, C. (1995) *Visions of the Future: Why We Need to Teach for Tomorrow*, Stoke on Trent: Trentham Books.

Isenhart, M. and Spangle, M. (2000) *Collaborative Approaches to Resolving Conflict*, London: Sage.

Maslow, A. (1954) *Motivation and Personality*, New York: Harper and Row.

McKay, M., Davis, M. and Fanning, P. (1995) *Messages: The Communication Skills Book*, Oakland, CA: New Harbinger.

Mosley, J. (1996) *Quality Circle Time*, Wisbech: LDA.

Muijs, D. and Reynolds, D. (2001) *Effective Teaching*, London: Sage.

Musgrove, R. (1999) 'Creative conflict resolution: a workshop approach in schools', in S. Decker, S. Kirby, A. Greenwood and D. Moore (eds) *Taking Children Seriously: Applications of Counselling and Therapy in Education*, London: Cassell.

Rogers, C. (1961) *On Personal Power*, London: Constable. Cited in D. Lawrence (1996) *Enhancing Self-esteem in the Classroom*, London: Paul Chapman.

Whitaker, P. (1995) *Managing to Learn: Aspects of Reflective and Experiential Learning in Schools*, London: Cassell.

RECOMMENDED READING

Burke, C. and Grosvenor, I. (2003) *The School I'd Like: Children and Young People's Reflections on an Education for the 21st Century*, London: RoutledgeFalmer. Gives children's perspectives on teaching and learning.

9 Early Years Education:

Children from Birth to Five

Karen McInnes and Jill Williams

This chapter is concerned with some of the historical and contemporary views of children and childhood and with how the social and educational systems in England provide for the care and education of young children. It is hoped that through questioning, reflection and analysis you will:

- Challenge popular and stereotypical views in order to understand more about the diverse experiences of children
- Understand that children's development is not fragmented but is holistic in nature
- Gain insight into the complexities of working with children from birth to five years.

In the first part of the chapter, on the nature of childhood, awareness is raised of historical, social, economic and cultural effects on young children and the differing perspectives of childhood that have followed. In order to recognise the importance of upbringing we have used examples from other countries to highlight the different roles that children play in society. It is important to recognise that the context in which young children find themselves will affect their potential. The perception of those who care for them will in turn have been affected by personal experience of being a child.

In the second and third parts we consider the holistic nature of children's development and the skills needed to understand how to provide children with a firm foundation for learning. We hope to illustrate that, although the nature of provision for young children is changing, it should be underpinned by a sound set of principles such as those set out in the Curriculum Guidance for the Foundation Stage (Qualifications and Curriculum Authority [QCA], 2000). Professionals are required to work sensitively with young children and their families and to value the social and cultural understanding that children bring to school with them. Observation, critical evaluation, the development of sensitivity and an understanding of the professional role of all those working for the benefit of young children are included.

PERSPECTIVES ON CHILDHOOD

Personal views

We all have memories of being children, some happy and some disturbing. Even within a 50-year time span, collective experiences of being a baby will have varied considerably. We may have had parents who were influenced by the behaviourist views of Truby King or the child-centred theories of Susan Isaacs (Boushel *et al.*, 2000). We will not remember whether we were 'breastfed', 'fed on demand', 'fed at regulated intervals', 'left to eat all our greens', 'allowed to choose our own diet', 'left to sleep on our own' or encouraged to share our parents' bed. But the ethos of bringing children up is an established part of family life and changes may cause tensions between the generations and between friends and other relatives. Food and sleep are two of the major concerns. In sophisticated societies, such as our own, we have choices and are subject to fashion and popular influences. In less sophisticated societies, where there is little choice, the time-honoured way of bringing up children is handed down from one generation to another. Whatever the influences have been on our early years they will have contributed to our personal history:

- How will our consequent views of childhood differ?
- What will have caused those differences?
- What was our status when we were children?
- Will our view of childhood vary according to our sex, our economic background, our ethnic origin or the decade in which we were born?
- How will our personal view of childhood affect our relationships with the children with whom we work?

Boushel *et al.* (2000) have written about the variety of perspectives of childhood and children. Mills and Mills (2000: 9) provide a similar overview and offer a note of caution about '... the problems of defining childhood, with its shifting visions, its lack of watertight compartments, its illusory and elusive nature ...'

Historical reflections on childhood

The western concept of childhood has been socially constructed or devised and modified according to economic and social changes in society. The evolution of childhood has not been straightforward and the changes are not clear-cut. John Locke, writing in 1693, introduced the idea of the *tabula rasa*, comparing the child's mind to a blank slate on which adults contribute information. Evidence of the blank slate, or transmission, model has remained in aspects of childrearing and early education. An example is the current rigorous interpretation of programmes for literacy and numeracy in some early-years settings which leave little scope for autonomy or for learning through experience. Jean-Jacques Rousseau in his novel *Emile* (1762) suggested that children developed purity and strength as long as they did not encounter diversity. The fictitious child, Emile, learned through play and was allowed freedom to have practical experience in the natural environment. Rousseau's views influenced parents from the middle classes at the time and provided a perspective on childhood that influences aspects of the care and education of young children today.

From the mid-Victorian period until the end of the nineteenth century, childrearing was strongly influenced by religion and moral beliefs. The printed word as well as popular illustrations served to publicize the state of childhood. Religious tracts and Sunday School publications had titles such as *Edgar's Pride*, *Little Miss Pry*, *Wilful Madge Marshall*. The home and family were seen as the focus of family life, and religion, duty, order and hierarchy were advocated. There was a marked difference, however, between the experiences of the rich and those of the poor. While Wordsworth and Coleridge celebrated the special nature of children, Charles Dickens and Charles Kingsley recognised the vulnerability of working-class children and the way in which society was exploiting them. This difference has not disappeared. 'The UK [United Kingdom] has the fourth largest economy in the world and yet we have … the highest level of child poverty in the EU [European Union]' (End Child Poverty, 2003: 8). Many children are seriously affected by poverty and are still vulnerable today.

The Industrial Revolution required people to leave their rural lives in favour of a search for work in manufacturing towns. Young children became employed in factories and it was not until 1870 that the Elementary Education Act aimed to make education compulsory until the age of 10. There was a need at this time for working-class children to be 'apprenticed' or to receive an education suited to their practical role in working alongside mentors (Mills and Mills, 2000). Although the idea of formal apprenticeship has now declined in the UK, many children serve a type of family apprenticeship with requirements made of them to care for younger siblings or to take responsibility for aspects of daily life such as going to the local shops. This is similar to the expectations of children in developing countries where each family member plays an important role in the survival of the group. Children of the Hmong tribe in Northern Thailand have competent use of bush knives as a result of early training in the art of hunting, under the guidance of adult males (Williams, 2003). Similarly in Malawi, Central Africa, young girls can be observed carrying siblings on their backs from about eight years old. Peru is an example of a country that has certain geographic locations where tourism is of economic importance. Beautiful, wistful, traditionally dressed children have a role to play in exploiting the attractiveness of the location. They stand, holding llamas, sitting at the feet of women who are spinning or men who are knitting and hold out their hands for tourist remuneration in return for photographs.

The role of children in their familial environment has strong cultural and social overtones. How much do we need to know about children's personal experiences in England? What cultural and economic factors are influencing childrearing? What criteria do adults use to judge one aspect of childrearing against another? Family values and cultural expectations are an integral part of children's development and, as such, are an important factor in their knowledge and understanding of the world and the way that they will be perceived in the wider environment.

The United Nation (UN) Convention on the Rights of the Child (1989) sets out 39 articles concerned with the entitlement for all children. As has been pointed out there is a disparity in these rights between children from different societies. Those working with young children in our own country need to question the assumption that children born in wealthy societies do not have their rights violated. 'To varying degrees, at least some children in all nations face unemployment, homelessness, violence, poverty and other issues that dramatically affect their lives' (United Nations Children's Fund [Unicef], 2002).

THE DEVELOPMENT OF CHILDREN

Article 6 of the UN Convention on the Rights of the Child (1989) states that children have a right to survival and development: they should be able to develop to their full potential in all areas. To ensure this, adults working with young children need to understand children's development: what is meant by development and what influences it. Blenkin and Kelly (1996) found that, for early years staff, knowledge of child development was highly valued by head teachers. First, however, it is important to explore how our own personal knowledge of children's development has arisen. We have already explained that childhood itself is socially constructed. We would argue that knowledge about child development is also socially constructed. This view arises from our own upbringing and cultural experiences, from images in the media and from books about childcare.

As discussed earlier, the culture into which you were born and the experiences you have as a child all impact on your beliefs and understanding. Whether or not you were breastfed, taken on outings, encouraged at school, all influence your view of child development. Articles that you read in the popular press can also influence your views as well as the multitude of books on childcare and development. Dr Spock influenced a generation in the 1960s about childrearing; and today's childcare guru, Gina Ford (2002), is having a dramatic effect on how we bring up babies and children and how we consequently view development. Our assumptions are significant and will influence how we work professionally with young children.

Children's development may be classified as:

- Physical development: gross motor skills, such as running and walking, and fine motor skills concerned with eye/hand co-ordination
- Intellectual development: skills concerned with reasoning, learning, remembering and concept formation
- Language development: receptive and expressive language
- Emotional development: emotional well-being and understanding and response to the emotions of others
- Social development: skills to become a socially acceptable member of society
- Spiritual development: 'awe and wonder' and the understanding of right and wrong in relation to others.

However, it is important not only to view the child under these headings, but also to view the child holistically and in context. 'Holism' is the notion that all areas of development are inter-related and that no one area is more important than others. It also means that the different areas can impact upon and influence each other. For example, a child with limited language skills may have difficulties with social development and interacting with others. This in turn may impact upon cognitive development. The 'contextualised' child refers to the importance of taking into account a child's cultural and social environment and how that may impact upon development. A child growing up as part of the Baka community in West Cameroon may exhibit a different developmental pattern from that of a child growing up in a small village community in England.

UNDERSTANDING AND WORKING WITH CHILDREN

Understanding and working with young children necessitates the development and use of core skills. These are:

- observation, evaluation and assessment of young children
- the ability critically to evaluate practice, resources and learning environments
- understanding the need for sensitivity and professionalism
- understanding the role of other professionals.

Observation, evaluation and assessment

Assessment refers to all the activities undertaken by adults which enhance understanding of the child and its learning and development. The key to effective assessment is observation (Drummond, 1994). QCA (2000: 11) states 'practitioners must be able to observe and respond appropriately to children informed by a knowledge of how children develop and learn and a clear understanding of possible next steps in their development and learning'. However, it is important to understand why we observe young children as this informs how to observe them. Observations of children enable us to:

- understand children
- assess their development
- highlight strengths and pinpoint weaknesses
- share our understanding with parents
- have dialogue with other professionals
- provide resources and an environment to support individual needs and learning.

In order to observe effectively it is necessary to try out and test different observational techniques. These can then be evaluated and critiqued to evaluate their effectiveness. A range of effective observational methods can then be used to observe individual children in depth. They include:

- spontaneous observations
- running records
- checklists
- timed observations (Harding and Meldon-Smith, 1996).

Practice, resources and learning environments

'The beliefs and values of teachers are the primary influences on the way classrooms are organised and managed' (Williams, 2003: 75). Through analysing our beliefs we can go some way towards understanding and evaluating the resources we choose and use and the learning environment we provide for children. In order to achieve this it is necessary to:

- observe children working
- discuss ideas with colleagues
- complete an audit of resources
- ask questions of children, colleagues and ourselves
- be honest about what we do and why we do it.

Carrying out these tasks and reflecting on the answers we find will enable us to improve our practice, choose appropriate resources and provide an effective learning environment.

Sensitivity and professionalism

The term 'sensitivity' when working with young children means taking each individual child's needs into account based on their home background and the experiences they have had. As already stated these have an enormous impact on development and we need to understand them. In order to be sensitive we need to have or to develop the following skills:

- listening to children and families
- giving children time to feel secure and to make relationships with others
- giving children space to explore and feel secure in the environment
- showing respect for children and their families
- having empathy with their experiences.

Developing 'professionalism' is about taking our own role seriously and improving and developing our own skills when working with young children. We need to be continually updating and increasing our knowledge of children, both how they develop and how they learn. We need to develop our communication skills so that we can communicate with others professionally. Understanding, respecting and practising the need for confidentiality demonstrates our professionalism. Using language that is respectful to others is a mark of our professionalism and indicates the respect that we give to others.

The role of other professionals

As early years professionals working with young children, we come into contact with professionals from a range of disciplines, such as paediatricians, health visitors, speech and language therapists, physiotherapists and educational psychologists. It is important that we have knowledge of their roles and how they work with children so that we can work with them effectively. For example, all children under five have a named health visitor who has known them and their family from birth. He or she will have carried out developmental checks on the child and advised the family if necessary. Knowing this, we are then in the position of being able to talk to the health visitor about any child who may concern us to gain a more complete picture of that child. This may then inform our own planning and work with the child and the family.

In addition, knowledge of other professionals and their roles enables us to have meaningful conversations with them about the children we work with. Good communication skills are crucial to ensuring meaningful dialogue. Working alongside and in partnership with other professionals is becoming increasingly important with the introduction of Children's Centres and is a part of the Government agenda through the work of the SureStart Unit. SureStart supports families from pregnancy until children are aged 14, and for those with disabilities up to age 16. The work of the unit is underpinned by seven guiding principles:

1   Working with parents and children to ensure better outcomes for all
2   Services for everyone based on individual family need
3   Flexible at point of delivery, all health and family support services should be designed to encourage access and be available through a single point of contact
4   Starting very early, services should start at the first antenatal visit
5   Respectful and transparent services should be customer driven
6   Community driven and professionally coordinated, all professionals should listen to the community
7   Outcome driven: all services for children and parents need to have as their main purpose better outcomes for children.

'All professionals with an interest in children and families should be sharing expertise and listening to local people on service priorities' (Department for Education and Skills [DfES] and Department for Work and Pensions [DWP], 2002: 23).

PROVIDING FOR CHILDREN

'Education for the under fives takes place as part of a continuum which links the home, non-statutory provision and compulsory schooling. In this continuum parents have a central role, particularly in helping bring about smooth transitions from stage to stage' (Department of Education and Science [DES], 1990: 8). Children under the age of five develop and learn in a variety of places depending upon their age, parental wishes and the local provision. These settings may include the home, a childminder's home, a playgroup, a day nursery, a nursery class in a primary school, a nursery school, a reception class or an early excellence centre. Each type of setting will offer a different type of provision and this in part will determine parental choice. Since September 2000, children between the ages of three and the end of the Reception Year are a part of the Foundation Stage, which is now a part of the National Curriculum. This distinct phase is subject to its own curriculum framework: *Curriculum Guidance for the Foundation Stage* (QCA, 2000).

The framework gives a clear definition of the term 'curriculum' for this age group. It is used to describe 'everything children do, see, hear or feel in their setting, both planned and unplanned' (QCA, 2000: 2). Adhering to this and providing an environment and practice that is true to this is challenging for many early years practitioners. The framework outlines six interrelated, curriculum areas:

1   Personal, social and emotional development: fostering positive dispositions and attitudes to learning, self-esteem and confidence, social relationships, behaviour and self-care
2   Communication, language and literacy: interacting with others, listening and speaking, language for thinking, reading and writing
3   Mathematical development: numbers, shapes, space and measures
4   Knowledge and understanding of the world: incorporating science, design and technology, history, geography and information and communications technology (ICT)
5   Physical development: including gross motor skills, fine motor skills and health
6   Creative development: including art, music, imagination and role-play.

Early years practitioners have generally welcomed the six broad areas of learning. The inclusion of emotional development alongside personal and social development has been particularly welcomed as it recognises the importance of this area and how it underpins all other areas. If children are not emotionally, personally and socially secure then learning, in general, will be hindered. An emphasis on communication alongside language and literacy has also been well received as it allows practitioners to concentrate on the important skills of speaking and listening, a recognition of a key way in which young children learn.

'Knowledge and understanding of the world' is probably the most controversial area. For some it tries to cover too many areas – science, design and technology, history, geography and ICT – and does not enable any to be covered in depth. For others the breadth and diversity of potential learning allows connections to be made between different subjects. It enables the curriculum to be learned in a holistic way, again recognising a key way in which young children learn. Indeed, the Scottish Early Years Curriculum actually includes mathematical development under knowledge and understanding of the world (Scottish Consultative Council on the Curriculum, 1999).

The curriculum guidance also refers to the different ways in which children learn and allows practitioners to draw upon a range of strategies for teaching and caring for children. Overarching this is the need for a play-based approach. This is stated within a separate section on play within the principles for early years education and is a constant theme running throughout the six areas of learning. Siraj-Blatchford and Siraj-Blatchford (2001) analysed the document to identify underlying pedagogic principles. Their analysis found that there was an emphasis on direct teaching involving practical skill development and on practitioner 'modelling' through the use of appropriate language, values and practices: '… throughout the guidance document the emphasis upon practitioner modelling is striking and suggests a general acceptance of "emergent" learning in all six areas of the Early Learning Goals' (Siraj-Blatchford and Siraj-Blatchford 2001: 8).

This can only be good news for all of us who wish to provide for young children in a play-based, developmentally appropriate way.

CONCLUSION

We have considered the effect that the social, economic and cultural environment has on young children. Although perspectives of childhood have changed over time there are constant reminders that children are still vulnerable and that those who work with them must consider all aspects of a child's life and recognise children as individuals. To ensure that this is achieved, adults working with young children need to understand how children learn and their role in ensuring that the climate is right for holistic development.

Developing the professional role of the early years practitioner is about taking our role seriously and improving and developing our skills when working with young children. We need continually to update and increase our knowledge of children, both how they develop and how they learn. By raising your awareness of the development of children from birth to five years we hope you will challenge stereotypes and modify personal assumptions. With a broad understanding of childhood and young children you will be able to use your voice and stand up for the rights of the children with whom you work.

QUESTIONS FOR DISCUSSION

- What are the key aspects of your personal view of childhood? What has influenced some of these views?
- How might your personal construction of childhood and children influence how you view and work with young children?
- Consider the three themes listed at the start of the chapter. Write a short paragraph identifying how the themes would help you to articulate a way of working with young children.

REFERENCES

Blenkin, G. and Kelly, V. (1996) *Principles into Practice in Early Childhood Education*, London: Paul Chapman Publishing.

Boushel, M., Fawcett, M. and Selwyn, J. (2000) *Focus on Early Childhood Principles and Reality*, Oxford: Blackwell Science.

DES (1990) *Starting with Quality: The Report of the Committee of Inquiry into the Quality of the Educational Experiences Offered to 3- and 4-year-olds*, London: Routledge.

DfES and DWP (2002) *SureStart*, Nottingham: DfES Publications.

Drummond, M.J. (1994) *Assessing Children's Learning*, London: David Fulton Publishers.

'Editorial', (2003) *End Child Poverty*, Spring (4): 1.

Ford, G. (2002) *The New Contented Little Baby Book*, London: Vermilion Press.

Harding, J. and Meldon-Smith, L. (1996) *How to Make Observations and Assessments*, London: Hodder and Stoughton.

Mills, J. and Mills, R. (eds) (2000) *Childhood Studies: A Reader in Perspectives of Childhood*, London: Routledge.

QCA (2000) *Curriculum Guidance for the Foundation Stage*, London: QCA Publications.

Scottish Consultative Council on the Curriculum (1999) *A Curriculum Framework for Children 3–5*, Edinburgh: The Scottish Office.

Siraj-Blatchford, I. and Siraj-Blatchford, J. (2001) 'A content analysis of pedagogy in the DfEE/QCA 2000 guidance', *Early Education*, 35, Autumn: 7–8.

UN (1989) *The Convention on the Rights of the Child*, New York: UN.

UNICEF (2002) www.unicef.org/convention.htm. Accessed 8 October 2003.

Williams, J. (2003) *Promoting Independent Learning in the Primary Classroom*, Buckingham: Open University Press.

RECOMMENDED READING

Bruce, T. and Meggitt, C. (2002) *Child Care and Education*, London: Hodder and Stoughton.

Fisher, J. (2002) *The Foundations of Learning*, Buckingham: Open University Press.

Smith, P., Cowie, H. and Blades, M. (2003) *Understanding Children's Development*, Oxford: Blackwell Publishers.

10 Inclusion and Special Educational Needs: Doing a Case Study in School

Mim Hutchings

This chapter is designed to help you to develop your research skills in one of the most sensitive and debated areas of education: the inclusion of pupils with special educational needs (SEN) in mainstream schools. It introduces case study research using examples drawn from examples written by third year undergraduate students in the module, 'Inclusivity and SEN'. The first part of the chapter includes some tasks to help with the early decisions that need to be made in writing a case study. The second part moves to using examples from other studies to illustrate the process of analysing data and structuring a report. Links are made to further reading for more detailed insights into methodology. The examples of case studies are anonymous as they are often in sensitive contexts.

INCLUSIVE EDUCATION

The idea is for you to be able to research inclusion as a part of life in a mainstream classroom or school, to research SEN as one aspect of social and cultural diversity and to consider how it is translated into everyday interactions in a school. There are differing perspectives on what is meant by the term 'inclusive education'. Corbett (2001: 2) argues that inclusion at an *ideological level* is about shared values and beliefs and at a *structural level* about strategic planning and coherent service delivery, but also that it 'requires a close analysis of pedagogy'. Current views also suggest that inclusive education is about creating a school which is supportive of *all* pupils, not just those with special needs.

Established policies about inclusive education (Department for Education and Skills [DfES], 2002) seek to remove barriers to learning and participation, to maximize the use of resources, to support learning and to remove discrimination. However, 'inclusion is a complex and contested concept and its manifestations in practice are many and various' (Lindsay, 2003: 3). You will need to understand conflicting perspectives, recognize consistency or gaps between beliefs and practice, and appreciate the general messy 'humanness' of change. For this you need a theoretical and historical basis for looking and listening which will help you understand the issues, tensions and successes from the point of view of the people involved, such as teachers, pupils, parents and pressure groups. The case studies in this chapter have tried to do this in different ways. What they have in common is that the writers viewed their studies as a learning experience which increased their awareness and understanding of inclusive education.

CASE STUDIES

A case study offers the opportunity to look, listen, learn and evolve your understanding of a particular context. It also allows for commitment to a particular perspective on inclusion. Although your study is unlikely to lead to generalisations that transfer to all contexts, it may allow you to make what Bassey (1999) calls 'fuzzy generalisations': ideas and understandings that will be relevant to you in the future.

Case study research creates a detailed picture of 'real people in real situations' (Cohen *et al.*, 2000: 181). It might include an individual or group within a class, a teacher, or relationships between parents and a school. Cohen *et al.* also suggest that 'case studies investigate and report the complex dynamic and unfolding interactions of events, human relationships and other factors in a unique instance' (2000: 181). The evidence collected draws on a variety of data-collection methods which seek to explore the 'how and why' of what happens in the everyday life of schools. Learning how to look, listen and see school life from a variety of points of view is an important part of learning how to understand and to meet the needs of all children in any classroom.

Bassey (1999) outlines three main types of case study.

Story-telling and picture drawing   In this instance, the researcher sets out to clarify what is happening within a classroom or school by compiling an accurate picture of events. One case study compiled a picture of the 'workings of a class' and how the teacher's values, attitudes and ways of organising the class helped to create an ethos of sharing, supporting and participation amongst the pupils. The student looked closely at how barriers to learning and participation were minimized and what resources were used to support learning and participation. The data collected were observations of teachers, classroom assistants and children at different times, follow-up discussions with teachers and classroom assistants and participant observation through helping with activities in the class. Her findings showed how the teacher had built an ethos within the class of valuing and treating each other with respect which permeated the social relationships within the class. She concluded that acceptance and sense of social belonging are an important part of inclusive education. It helped her write a report which 'saw' the class from different points of view. This is the category that many students seem to favour. It allows them to take their current views and knowledge into school and learn from the experience of others.

Evaluative   This second type of study is concerned with the effectiveness or value of particular interventions, ways of working in a classroom or systems within a school. A case study evaluated a primary school's claim that they took 'a fully inclusive approach to education' by looking in detail at the systems and procedures which existed in the school to support the inclusion of pupils. The findings suggested that staff were aware of, and in agreement about, the systems and procedures that contributed to effective inclusion, and viewed inclusive practices as those which met the needs of all children. Evaluative case studies can seem problematic for undergraduate students who are aware of their relative inexperience. However, with careful preparation, making evaluations can allow you to recognise the inevitable gaps between how we would like things to be and how they actually are at this moment in time.

Theory seeking and theory testing   Bassey's third type of study begins with a hypothesis or tentative statement. A case study examined whether support from local education authority (LEA) professionals helped a teacher with strategies to include a child with emotional and behavioural difficulties. Data collection methods were selected to test this theory, or hypothesis.

   However, a warning: research is seldom as tidy as these types of case study suggest. So do not give up on a good research question just because it does not fit neatly into one of these categories. At the heart of writing a good study lies the ability to describe clearly what you have heard, seen and read and to analyse why and what is important. A focus on the type of case study you wish to do will help in thinking about the purpose of study and what you might learn from it for the future.

DESIGNING THE CASE STUDY

The design of a case study should follow a logical sequence that links the research questions to information collected in schools (the data), your analysis and findings through 'an action plan for getting from here to there' (Yin, 2003: 20). What follows is a step-by-step procedure. However, there are two warnings. First, you will find that the steps sometimes merge, and even change order, as you prepare, collect data and analyse it. Second, you will need to supplement this simple outline with wider reading. The recommended reading will help you start the latter.

   There are five stages in writing a case study:

1   Identifying an issue, problem or hypothesis to explore as a starting point for your research questions.
2   Asking research questions and drawing up ethical guidelines for how you will work in school.
3   Preparing for and collecting data in school.
4   Analysing and explaining the data collected.
5   Writing the case report.

Identifying an issue problem or hypothesis to explore as a starting point for generating research questions

Clough and Nutbrown (2002) suggest that all research sets out from a particular position; so begin with a careful consideration of what you know and believe is important about inclusion. Think about the following statements and use them to help you write about what inclusion means to you and the sources of your current view, such as your reading and personal experience:

- Every child has the right to attend its local school.
- Teachers should try to sort out difficulties with behaviour without wanting children to leave the class.
- Inclusive schools welcome and accommodate all children, regardless of their physical, social, emotional, linguistic and other abilities and needs.
- I hope we can build a fairer more inclusive society.

The next step is to identify what issue or hypothesis you will explore. Here are some examples.

An issue
How does a class work together with a diverse range of special educational needs?
or
How does a nursery include and support a child with physical disabilities?

A hypothesis
The systems and procedures associated with statementing pupils with special educational needs creates a preoccupation with labelling which impedes this school's ability to meet a child's needs inclusively.
or
Pupil participation in writing Individual Education Plans is tokenistic because it is not part of a children's rights agenda.

At this stage, think about why you are doing the study and the kind of issue or hypothesis you are starting with. It will help you to recognise the type of case study you will write.

Research questions and ethical guidelines

Having decided on your area of interest you can begin to formulate some research questions. Bassey (1999: 67) calls the research question 'the engine which drives the train of enquiry'. Be aware that the questions you start with may need to be modified or even replaced as your understanding develops through the data collection. You will also need to 'test' your questions in order to decide how manageable they will be. Clough and Nutbrown (2002: 34) suggest you should subject draft research questions to the 'Goldilocks test'. Is this question 'too big' to be answered in the case study or is it 'too small' to generate enough relevant information? Alternatively, is this question 'too hot'? Maybe your questions are too sensitive or potentially damaging to the class or school you are a guest in. This will help you identify those questions that are 'just right' for investigation at *this* time, by *this* researcher in *this* setting.

Task

- Think of five or six research questions to focus the direction of your study.
- Ask yourself, are any of the questions 'too big', 'too small', 'too hot' or 'just right'?
- Decide how you might break up the bigger questions into suitable questions to take into school.

At this stage it helps to stand back and do what Clough and Nutbrown (2002) call radical listening, reading and questioning or 'making the familiar strange'. It involves understanding and questioning assumptions about your topic and systematically searching for different views. For example, looking at the role of classroom assistants might lead you to consider other research (Corbett, 2001), current policy and training (DfES, 2002) and the views of parents and pupils (Alliance for Inclusive Education, 2001). This part of the process will help in refining your questions, adding information and in selecting data-collection methods most suited to your topic. As your definitions of inclusion are refined and compared with others, you will begin to develop an awareness of some of the possible indicators of the relationship between the theories you have been thinking and reading about and what you will find in school. At the same time you will be exploring potential frameworks, such as the *Index for Inclusion* (Booth *et al.*, 2000) and National Curriculum Inclusion Statement (DfEE, 1999), to decide what you are looking for.

You will also need to think about how to look and listen: what kind of observations and interviews will help me explore my issue, problem or hypothesis? Do I need to look at the learner, at the teacher or the learning environment? Frederickson and Cline (2002) give ways of thinking about the needs of learners in relation to the curriculum, school environment and teaching methods.

During this time ethical guidelines for the study should be drawn up. Your university will have ethical guidelines about approaching schools, protecting the rights of informants and ensuring anonymity. Alongside your right to do research there are two responsibilities which make case study research ethical. The first is a respect for truth in collecting data and reporting your findings. This means checking that your report is honest and does not attempt to deceive either intentionally or unintentionally. The second is respect for the people you are observing and interviewing. The way in which you collect data should recognize their initial ownership of the data and respect them as fellow human beings who are entitled to dignity and privacy (Bassey, 1999).

Preparing for and collecting data

The most frequently used types of data collection in case studies are:

- documentary evidence, such as school policies and Individual Education Plans
- interviews with teachers, classroom assistants, parents and pupils
- direct observation of individual and groups of pupils and classes and meetings
- participant observation through working with individuals and groups of children.

There is a wealth of literature about data collection methods: Bell (1999) and Cohen *et al.* (2000) are some examples. This section concentrates on some of the principles, processes and decisions that are made as evidence is collected.

The following three principles will help you to collect data that yields sufficient evidence to answer your questions. First, data should come from a variety of sources, such as observation in a range of settings (different lessons, playground), interviews with different people (teacher, classroom assistant, parents) and documents. You should build up information that represents a range of perspectives about your research questions. Second, setting up a data-base (filing and storing) will help you to see how well interviews, observations and documents are answering your research questions. You need to be systematic in recording dates, times, places and who is involved. Finally, you need to keep track of how your chain of evidence is evolving by keeping a diary or log and writing notes on your evidence. Writing up after each session in school will help you reflect on how your ideas are forming and changing over time and help you pose questions and identify gaps and contradictions in the information you are gathering for analysis at a later date. Experienced researchers often begin their data analysis within the field. Novice researchers are often so caught up in just recording events as they happen that there is little time left to begin the analysis.

The following suggestions, adapted from Bogdan and Biklin (1998), help both the process of collecting data and making decisions about what is relevant:

1   Beginning with an exploratory broad focus will help you decide what you can do, what is of interest and who your key informants are likely to be. The key headings in the *Index for Inclusion* (Booth *et al.*, 2000) may help you to get a feel for the school or class you are in.

2   As you start to see what themes and information are most important to your questions, narrow the focus of your data collection. The more information you have on specific aspects of your questions the easier it will be to think more deeply when you come to the final analysis.

3   Early on, assess the usefulness of your questions in relation to the school or class you are in. Consider whether you need to reformulate your questions.

4   Review and write notes in your diary or log, and plan what you need to follow up on your next school visit.

5   Write comments and notes to yourself about what you are learning. Look for links and contradictions between the different sources of information. Use the notes to begin to think about emerging themes and ideas that can be explored more deeply.

6   Continue to explore literature relevant to your area. What are the main issues identified by other researchers? How does your perspective differ from theirs? How did they collect and analyse data?

7   Try representing some of your insights visually through charts, diagrams and rich pictures (Frederickson and Cline, 2002: 216). These will help you bring together key information and impressions of the school or classroom, views of people and themes.

In one case study initial exploratory observations led a student to look more closely at how children worked and played together. The sudent was observing an art group sharing out tasks to complete an activity:

I was aware that one of the children might need help with the use of scissors during this particular lesson. When I turned my attention to observe him, I found that the children on his table had altered their working method. Instead of working on their own they had shared out the tasks for the art class according to what they could offer. On another occasion I observed that the children had taken it upon themselves to share the cutting for him. It is worth noting that I never heard a 'thank you' pass between the children for the help they received from each other. There is certainly a culture in existence where helping each other is expected to be the norm.

At the same time, she had started to draw sociograms (diagrams of choices pupils made about who to work or play with) for activities during lessons and in the playground. These included:

- where children sat to do their daily work – decided by teacher
- quiet reading – self-selected, where children talked quietly
- activities in class – children self selected the groups in which they worked
- in the playground.

Using different kinds of observations helped her recognize more clearly the social interaction within the class and how these did not conform to the stereotypes she had anticipated. For example, boys and girls in the class chose to work together and children worked and played in mixed ability friendship groups. Her discussions and observations of the class teacher's influence on social interaction helped her draw conclusions about how this had been achieved.

Analysing and explaining the data

This is the stage when your data analysis becomes the systematic sifting and sorting of evidence. By now you have probably built up a great deal of data and are probably not quite sure what is relevant. You have to work through all your notes, observations and interviews and try to code them and condense them into statements which answer your questions. The aim is to ensure that you have considered all the evidence and thought about rival interpretations before deciding on what are the most significant aspects of your study. Finally, you need to relate what you have found out to your reading, other research and prior knowledge. Coding categories are used to test out and verify the truthfulness of your statements. The aim is to heighten your understanding of the evidence collected in order to present your findings. At this stage do not be afraid to speculate about key themes and ideas but always go back to the data to test out their accuracy. The initial statements you generate should be cross-referenced and checked with evidence in the raw data.

One student analysing the inclusion of an autistic child in a mainstream class drew together information from classroom observations, interviews with the teachers, classroom assistant and parents and school documents into a chart using coding categories to search for patterns and topics within the data (see Table 10.1). All of the categories were focused on creating a picture of how this child was supported within the class. The principle categories were:

- Setting and context codes: these set the scene and gave general information from school and LEA policy documents on inclusion and on the class.
- Perspectives held by subjects about:
    the child's language development, personal qualities, behaviour;
    the child's inclusion and support from the LEA.
- Activity codes: about regularly occurring activities in the classroom.
- Strategy codes: about the tactics and methods used with the child.
- Relationship codes: about how the child related to other children, adults, and relationships between the adults.

The codes and categories led on to statements about how the patterns of strategies and close relationship between the adults were promoting the child's independence in the classroom.

The categories and codes discussed here are only suggestions, but using some kind of coding system will mean that you interrogate your evidence thoroughly and base your findings and conclusion on data. The codes and categories selected will be influenced by the perspectives and theoretical frameworks you hold. What you have read, and the beliefs and values you bring to your topic, will influence the meaning you create from the data. You should recognise this as you shape your interpretations and explanations of your analytical statements.

Having coded, tested and refined some statements, and rejected others, you are now at the stage when 'how' and 'why' questions become important. You will begin to interpret information from groups and individuals and seek to explain the causes underlying your statements.

Another student chose to present part of her interpretation in the form of a narrative which drew on the coding of her interviews, observations and diary. This conveyed how her learning was shaped by what she saw and heard in school. One of the themes

Table 10.1 Extract from case study data

Data collected from	Strategies and techniques used with the child
Observation	Classroom Assistant (CA) sits with child to get him started on a task.
Observation	CA asks child to repeat what teacher has asked him to do – strategy known as recall (also from interview with CA).
Interview with teacher + document	Teacher differentiates curriculum to fit each member of the class. CA encourages child to put up hand to ask for clarification rather than always relying on CA being present. Part of current Individual Education Plan (IEP).
Observation + document	Teacher and CA both praise child on his work and what a good reader he is. Token economy – child given two tokens a day for good behaviour. Ten tokens in a week equals extra playtime or a treat. Part of current IEP.
Interview with teacher	Important that child becomes increasingly independent of CA. Applies learning from applied behaviour analysis with rest of class.
Interview with parent	When child gets home he has to repeat two things he has done in school today.

in the narrative was how different places and activities in the class made it more or less difficult for a child in a wheelchair to interact with his peers. There were some tentative generalisations about classroom management:

> After literacy hour carpet time we moved on to group work. Each table was grouped by ability and the child had no trouble finding his way and place at the table. I worked alongside him and was asked to keep the group on task. I was greatly relieved to see more interaction taking place during the group work and it was quite clear that it was because the children were all on the same level enabling eye contact.

The narrative was followed by statements and an analysis of other key themes such as group work and friendships.

Writing the case report

Although generally case study reports do not have prescribed format, two examples illustrate possible structures that are commonly used.

Example of an evaluative case study: how a primary school supported the inclusion of all pupils.

Introduction   Outlines the writer's rationale for the study and sets the scene on inclusion and her study school.

Aims and content   Includes the research questions and more general aims about what she hoped to learn from the study. The main research question is subdivided to focus on school policies, the implementation of the code of practice for SEN and how children were actively encouraged to participate within the school.

The literature review   Builds a theory of what needs to be described and evaluated through key propositions about what inclusion is. Discussion of inclusion as a process of change within a school provides a conceptual framework for evaluating whether it was an effective learning environment for all children.

Methodology   Establishes a framework for observations, semi-structured informal interviews and readings of policy documents. It includes the use of an existing questionnaire designed to help schools identify aspects of their policies and practice which needed further consideration.

Findings   Uses the research questions as headings to describe and evaluate how the culture, classroom practice, management and deployment of resources (including classroom assistants) met all children's needs.

Conclusion   Discusses the outcomes, refers back to the literature review and suggests that the school had a strong shared understanding of the systems and procedures which contributed to effective inclusion, a problem-solving ethos as a basis for further development.

Example of a descriptive case study: how a school included a Year 6 boy with emotional and behavioural difficulties

Introduction   Sets out the issues and areas to be described and analysed.

Brief literature review   Focuses on concepts of inclusion and exclusion.

The context   Introduces the school and relevant policy statements.

Rationale and methodology   Introduces the research questions and methods.

Pen portrait of the child   Draws together information from school documents and interviews with staff, illustrating the school's perspective on the child and inclusion.

Literature review   Looks at literature, emotional and behavioural difficulties and raises the issue for inclusive education and key characteristics of successful provision in mainstream settings. This provides key points for observation in the class.

Observations and analysis   Presented as a chronological account with each observation being analysed and related to themes in the literature review, such as behaviour management strategies used in the playground and classroom.

Conclusion   States the key factors that contributed to the successful inclusion of this child, such as clear views on acceptable behaviours and the supportive ethos of all staff and pupils.

CONCLUSION

However you decide to structure your final report it needs to be organized, display your thinking and reading and make explicit the links between the issues investigated, the evidence and outcomes. As you draft your final report try asking yourself these questions:

* Is my report a truthful account of what I have seen and heard?
* Have I made clear the links between reading, the context studied and the evidence?
* Will the readers of this study be convinced that I have selected relevant evidence?
* Is my report engaging and clear?

QUESTIONS FOR DISCUSSION

- How did you respond to the statements about inclusion? How do you think your current values and beliefs will influence your case study?
- How do you think schools can foster an inclusive climate?
- What are the advantages and limitations of case study research?
- What methods will you use to investigate your research questions and how do you justify them?

REFERENCES

Alliance for Inclusive Education (2001) *The Inclusion Assistant: Helping Children with High Level Support Needs in Mainstream Education: Report and Video*, London: Alliance for Inclusive Education.

Bassey, M. (1999) *Case Study Research in Educational Settings*, Buckingham: Open University Press.

Bell, J. (1999) *Doing Your Research Project*, Buckingham: Open University Press.

Bogdan, R. and Biklin, S. (1998) *Qualitative Research for Education*, Boston: Allyn and Bacon.

Booth, T., Ainscow, M., Black-Hawkins, K., Vaughan, M., and Shaw, L. (2000) *Index for Inclusion: Developing Learning and Participation in Schools*, Bristol: Centre for Studies on Inclusive Education.

Clough, P. and Nutbrown, C. (2002) *A Student's Guide to Methodology*, London: Sage.

Cohen, L., Manion, L. and Morrison, K. (2000) *Research Methods in Education*, 5th edition, London: RoutledgeFalmer.

Corbett, J. (2001) *Supporting Inclusive Education: A Connective Pedagogy*, London: RoutledgeFalmer.

DfEE (1999) *National Curriculum for England: Key Stages 1–4*, London: DfEE.

DfES (2002) *Valuing Teacher Time, Developing the Role of Support Staff*, London DfES.

Frederickson, N. and Cline, T. (2002) *Special Educational Needs: Inclusion and Diversity*, Buckingham: Open University Press.

Lindsay, G. (2003) 'Inclusive education a critical perspective', *British Journal of Special Education*, 30(1): 3.

Yin, R. (2003) *Case Study Research: Design and Methods*, 3rd edition, London: Sage Publications.

RECOMMENDED READING

Bell, J. (1999) *Doing Your Research Project*, Buckingham: Open University Press. This is a practical guide for first-time researchers which includes advice on methods and strategies for completing a study.

Rose, R. and Grosvenor, I. (2001) *Researching Special Education: Ideas into Practice*, London: Fulton. A number of researchers and practitioners discuss methods of research and recent studies in special education.

The British Journal of Special Education and *Support for Learning* published by National Association for Special Educational Needs (NASEN). These journals are a useful source for current thinking and research on inclusion and special educational needs.

11 Gender and Educational Achievement

Christine Eden

This chapter introduces you to:

- the debates about gender and educational achievement
- recent data on gender in relation to educational achievement
- explanations that help to account for the relationship between gender and educational achievement
- gender formation and attitudes towards educational achievement and entry into the labour market.

The media interest in education tends to focus on the information which it is believed parents are most interested in: how different schools have performed in relation to various tests and examinations, and their place in the published league tables. During the last 20 years, equality of opportunity debates have focused on performance and the extent to which schools are able to affect test results irrespective of the social background of children. These debates are often discussed in relation to issues of parental choice but are rooted in education's importance to the social and economic development of society.

To understand the complexities of the relationship between gender and achievement requires identifying patterns and facts, but also seeks the explanations that account for these patterns. These explanations will describe the processes that occur within the school and classroom, but there will also be discussion of the way in which the expectations young people have about their role as adult men and women may influence their understanding of educational achievement from a very early age. Research in this area does not give neat, definitive answers, so much of this discussion will be speculative.

THE CHANGING DEBATE

Gender has always received attention in discussions on pupil attainment and on debates about the socialisation processes within and outside schools. But the focus changes at different historical moments and is located in wider debates about the position of men and women in society as a whole. In the nineteenth century the Schools Enquiry Commission of 1868 compared girls' and boys' school performances and suggested that differences could be attributed to characteristic mental differences between the sexes. The Commission did not argue for a differentiated curriculum for boys and girls, but reports during the twentieth century did argue for such differentiation. In the mid-twentieth century two government reports, Crowther in 1959 (*15–18*) and Newsom in 1963 (*Half Our Future*), argued that the prime destination of girls was as wives and mothers and so their curriculum should reflect the nature of their ambitions and inevitably be affected by their future domestic role.

For many years in the mid-twentieth century the concerns centred on working-class male pupils. Various explanations were given for their disadvantage within the school system ranging from the characteristics of the home background through to the mechanisms within the school which stratified pupils on the basis of social class. The 1960s and 1970s saw significant changes in social values and education systems with the introduction of comprehensive schooling and the Sex Discrimination Act of 1975. Within this framework it was possible to challenge female underachievement.

The feminist movement of the time tried to tackle female underachievement by promoting subject choices for girls, and there were a number of projects which aimed to break down traditional assumptions and promote greater access across the curriculum. Projects such as Girls into Science and Technology and Women into Science and Engineering aimed to challenge stereotypical choices within the curriculum and drew attention to the importance of enhancing girls' achievement. Feminist writers made issues of gender equality very visible and tried to confront the reasons and the need for change. They argued that girls and women were disadvantaged in education and within the labour market. They were not prepared to accept that there were fundamental differences in the biological capacities of males and females. Instead they offered social explanations for gender inequality in educational achievement and recommended strategies for change.

The Education Reform Act of 1988 had considerable implications for gender equality in that it established a common curriculum to General Certificate of Secondary Education (GCSE) level for boys and girls. While stereotyped subject choices continue to be made at A-level, the climate of the national curriculum has led to at least the theoretical assumption that the sciences, technology and mathematics are as much part of the curriculum for girls as they are for boys.

These developments and associated changes in approaches to the importance of girls' education may help explain why girls' educational attainment is now higher than that of boys' and it is the underachievement of boys that is currently seen to be the problem. This has become increasingly visible since the early 1990s, initially revealed through GCSE results. The gap between female and male attainment has continued to widen in favour of females and even the traditional advantage of males over females in science areas is reducing. So after a relatively short focus on girls' achievements, any discussion of gender inequality now focuses on boys and strategies that will address their underachievement, usually without looking at the wider society and its economic and power structures where men and women have unequal opportunities.

Whether the focus has been on boys or girls, explanations for inequalities have explored the internal processes of the classroom, teacher expectations and interaction, the nature of the curriculum, resources and assessment strategies. What much of the debate fails to identify is the context within which young people understand themselves and their identities and the way this may impact upon their willingness to learn. Attention has been given to changes in the labour market and the extent to which that impinges upon boys' sense of masculinity. But there has been less interest in the extent to which young girls still see themselves as tied to a future which gives them the main responsibility for childcare. The significant expansion of women working has not been accompanied by any radical shift in the responsibilities that men and women, particularly working-class women, take for childcare responsibilities and domestic tasks.

GENDER DIFFERENCES IN EDUCATIONAL ACHIEVEMENT

In looking at patterns of educational achievement it is clear that both boys' and girls' educational performance has significantly improved during the last 20 years. But the rate of increase for females is greater than that for males and has occurred rapidly. This is particularly visible in relation to the proportions of boys and girls who achieve five or more grade A–C GCSE passes. Gender differences became obvious at the end of the 1980s and within four years the position had changed from near equality between the sexes to a clear gap. In 1988, 32 per cent of girls achieved five A–C GCSEs while 28 per cent of boys achieved these levels. By 1999 the gap had increased to 9.1 per cent with 60.2 per cent of girls scoring at least five top grades compared with only 51.1 per cent of boys. The differences in educational achievement vary across pupils' school careers. The achievement of girls in relation to boys actually widens as pupils get older, and in the last few years the gap in performance that had existed in favour of boys at A-level has also been eliminated. There are, though, continuing differences in subject entry to A-levels with stereotypical female-dominated and male-dominated subjects (Arnot et al., 1998: 16).

The provisional results for Standard Assessment Tests (SATs) and GCSEs in 2001/2002 confirm girls' achievement as greater than that of boys and this can be seen both in terms of overall achievement and level of achievement (Department for Education and Skills [DfES], 2003a; 2003b). Some key points from the DfES website illustrate this:

Key Stage 1

- The percentage of girls achieving Level 2 or above is greater than that of boys in reading, writing, spelling and mathematics.
- The widest gap – of 10 per cent – is in spelling.
- Girls continue to outperform boys at Level 2b and above in all subjects, with the largest gap – of 15 per cent – in writing.
- At Level 3 and above, boys outperform girls by four percentage points in mathematics. In the other three subjects girls have maintained or extended their lead.

Key Stage 2

- Performance in mathematics is equal.
- Girls continue to outperform boys in the other subjects at Level 4 or above.
- Girls have continued to extend their lead in English and reading.
- At Level 5 or above, boys have extended their lead over girls in mathematics and outperform girls in science by one percentage point.
- Girls outperform boys in all aspects of English.

These statistics illustrate the complexity of making blanket statements about gender performance in that both subject and level reveal different stories.

The patterns continue at Key Stage 3 and GCSE:

Key Stage 3

- Girls have a 17 per cent lead over boys in English at Level 5 or above.
- In both mathematics and science girls have a 1 per cent lead over boys.
- Girls have a 15 percentage points lead over boys in English at Level 6 or above. In mathematics boys and girls have the same level of achievement, and boys have a 2 per cent lead over girls in science.

GCSE

- 57 per cent of girls achieved five or more grades A–C compared to 46 per cent of boys.

There is also gender differentiation within the subject range taken by boys and girls who achieved grades A–C within GCSE. This is particularly pronounced within design and technology where 10 times as many boys take electronic products while the number of girls taking textiles is 60 times greater than that of boys. Approximately four times as many girls follow food technology, while over twice as many boys choose resistant materials and seven times as many boys follow systems and control. In overall achievement in design and technology girls appear to have been more successful in that 41 per cent of them have achieved grades A–C compared with 31 per cent of boys. Differences of subject choice which are strongly stereotyped can be concealed within a subject such as design and technology (DfES, 2003b).

GCE AS/A-level

The same pattern can be seen at higher level. Figures for 2001–2 show that over half of those attempting two or more AS/A-levels were female and they achieved higher point scores than males. At General Certificate in Education (GCE) A-level, 45.8 per cent of females achieved two or more passes compared with 36.2 per cent of males. The gender gap has widened significantly over the last 10 years.

As suggested above, it is at A-level where students make choices that follow traditional stereotypes. Over three times as many males took computing at A-level, twice as many males took economics, twice as many males took technology subjects, while over twice as many females took English. In mathematics and physics there is again a strong differentiation along gender lines with four times as many males taking physics and a third as many males taking mathematics. But in terms of grades, in the traditional male areas of computing, mathematics and physics, girls were achieving at a higher level than boys. Females dominated the entries in design, biology and communications studies, expressive arts and drama, modern foreign languages, psychology and sociology (DfES, 2003c; EducationGuardian, 2003).

This confirms a different set of choices for boys and girls in relationship to A-level, although girls are increasing their participation in such traditional stereotypical areas as mathematics and physics. These really are important choices as they help determine access to different degree courses which in turn can significantly affect the opportunities available within the job market (Arnot et al., 1998).

These differences in gender attainment are significant but do not give a complete picture of educational inequalities. Differences in attainment appear to be considerably smaller between genders compared to those associated with ethnic origin and social class background (Gillborn and Mirza 2000: 23). Gender, class and ethnic identity undoubtedly interact with one another and should be seen as part of any initiatives that aim to address educational achievement. When looking at the way in which race and gender interact, Gillborn and Mirza (2003) draw on research that shows consistent and significant inequalities of attainment between ethnic groups regardless of pupils' gender, although, as with gender patterns, these are complex. For example, African Caribbean girls do relatively well in comparison to both their white male and female peers. But gender continues to be significant in that overall patterns show girls more likely to achieve five higher-grade GCSEs than boys of the same ethnic origin. While the gender gap appears to be present within each ethnic group regardless of social class background, ethnic inequalities remain even when controlling for gender and class. This is worth remembering in all the fuss about boys' underachievement (Gillborn and Mirza, 2000: 26).

EXPLANATIONS OF DIFFERENCES IN ATTAINMENT

Children do not enter the classroom as a blank sheet but bring with them a wide range of expectations about how it is appropriate to behave and what is expected of them. Young children at the age of three are able to identify themselves by their gender and are learning the sort of behaviour which is approved or disapproved by parents and teachers. Research into three-year-old children playing with Lego showed significant gender differences in both the process and the actual constructions made, with girls building houses, and boys cars and guns (Browne and Ross, 1991). Schools have an important role in either countering such stereotypes or helping to reinforce them.

But it is also clear that children resist and challenge the expectations they encounter and select what they choose to adopt and act on in their own lives. So when we are looking at the influence of gender within the school we have both to be aware of the power of traditional models of male and female, but also of the capacity of children to resist and confront these images and adapt them. Some girls insist on joining the football team in spite of initial opposition from the boys and some boys refuse to join the competitive so-called 'laddish' culture. You may well be one of those who resisted stereotypical behaviour or know those who did. Add to this the variety of teachers and experiences that pupils encounter and we have a complex mix in the process of gender formation.

Notwithstanding the complexity of gender differences, the achievement patterns identified above have given rise to concern about boys' underachievement. Some writers such as Mac an Ghaill (1994) have set this within a wider debate about changing patterns of masculinity. He argues that the loss of working-class manual occupations has undermined traditional models of masculinity, which in turn has led to an erosion of confidence and a sense that education lacks relevance and value. This helps explain the culture which rejects educational success and gives status to achievements in sport (Francis, 1999).

Laddish culture leads to male students' negative approach to education: a group culture which gives power to the idea that education is undesirable. It accounts for greater rates of truancy, greater rates of exclusion and the fact that teachers regularly report that male students exhibit greater behaviour problems within the classroom. A five-year study by Davies and Brember (2001) argues that issues associated with discipline and authority should be given far more attention in relationship to boys in considering their academic achievement.

The other side of this debate points to the fact that women now expect to continue to participate in the labour market when they have children. With this trend comes enhanced independence. A greater emphasis upon a career as the focus of gender identity is seen to feed back into young women's educational aspirations, motivation and achievements. The labour market itself has grown in the areas of clerical and service work which have traditionally been women's work. These jobs are not well paid and women still remain underrepresented in positions of power and management within society as a whole. But there has been a shift in the general expectation that young women have of themselves of participating in the labour market even if not necessarily seeking high-flying careers. It is, though, still males who remain advantaged in employment opportunities and levels of pay and this is not always recognised in discussion about boys' underachievement.

Within the school itself, factors such as the curriculum, assessment techniques, teaching styles, teacher expectations, behaviour management and the organisation of teaching groups have all been seen to contribute to gender differences. There appear to be gender differences in learning styles which benefit girls where discussion and collaboration are involved. Boys and girls appear to have different orientations towards different types of task, with girls doing better at open-ended tasks and boys more responsive to memorising abstract facts (Howe, 1997). Powney's review of gender and attainment in Scotland reinforced the argument that girls seem to do well in coursework and essays whereas boys do better at multiple-choice questions. So different teaching styles and a range of teaching strategies may be needed to address the differences in preference between boys and girls (Powney, 1996).

In addition there are more complex explanations associated with the creation of sexual identities and a sense of appropriate gender behaviour which may also be significant in affecting gender performance. This links to the way that particular subjects appear to be associated with notions of masculinity or femininity, reflected in the A-level choices discussed above. Where there is evidence of a breakdown in gender stereotypes it appears to be largely girls who are prepared to address what were seen as masculine subjects, while boys continue to be suspicious of anything that could be seen as feminine.

It also seems that within gender cultures girls concentrate and focus on schoolwork and boys engage in the more destructive behaviour which gives status within the peer group. There also seem to be distinct differences in the way in which boys and girls interact with teachers and teacher expectations. Ofsted (1996) suggested that definitions of pupils' ability appeared to relate more to teacher expectations and behaviour than academic performance. Such expectations are transmitted in the classroom, in the corridors and through the many organisational aspects of the school which give messages about appropriate gender behaviour. These expectations are crucial given that, throughout their school career, pupils are actively engaged in constructing their gender identities and expectations of others.

GENDER IDENTITY AND EDUCATIONAL ACHIEVEMENT

Debates about the curriculum and teacher expectation all add to our understanding of how gender and educational attainment interact. But there is a further body of research that points to the importance of understanding what are seen as appropriate models of masculinity and femininity amongst pupils and their peer groups: how these develop and how they help to fashion responses to learning and gaining educational qualifications.

Pupils' expectations of their roles within the labour market and in relation to future domestic responsibilities are critical factors. Awareness of their futures is a continuing and permanent part of the way in which boys and girls see themselves growing into young men and women and this is informed by the patterns of gender that they see within both the labour market and the family. Expectations of future domestic responsibility are a major factor in working-class females' expectations of themselves. These factors help to shape the way education is perceived. For secondary pupils their sexual identity is a key factor that contributes to expectations of themselves (Mac an Ghaill, 1994, 1996; Lees, 1993).

Recognizing the constraints and culture within which young people develop does not have to lead to a deterministic position. Pupils do challenge traditional stereotypes. Research into primary school playgrounds (Eden, 1995; Thorne, 1993) shows how gender relations and ideologies are actively negotiated and resisted and that children are not passively socialised into a sex role. Pupils moved in and out of gender groupings according to their choices and on occasions actively intervened to enter into the other gender domain, particularly with regard to the football-playing which can dominate the playground. There is considerable crossing of gender-stereotypical behaviour. But even though gender ideologies were resisted, there were clear signs in the primary playground of boys dominating the physical space and frequently subjecting girls to sexual harassment. The subordination of femininity was acted out through the dominance of football and fighting within the playground environs with girls often sitting on walls acting as cheerleaders and vying for attention. Within the secondary context a number of research studies have shown that, while girls resist and construct their own lives and femininity, they are nevertheless constantly subjected to language and behaviour from the boys which places them in an oppressed position or one where they have to constantly challenge the boys' behaviour (Lees, 1993).

The complex definitions of masculinity that young males have to deal with make it easy for them to become reluctant learners. This is well illustrated by Frosh *et al.* (2002) who make clear the competitive hierarchy amongst boys and their concerns about being seen as feminine. Such concerns place consistent pressures on young men and the need to distance themselves from girls and the way in which girls respond to the educational system. There is a tension in this process in that young men also recognise the need to be well qualified and the significance of educational qualifications. The need to redefine what is seen as acceptable male behaviour within young male peer groups is one of the areas that schools need to address if they want boys' educational achievement to improve in the way that we have seen girls' performance improve over recent years.

This might also allow the inequalities that affect girls within the labour and domestic spheres to become part of the debate. As attention has shifted to boys' educational achievements, these inequalities have become privatised and about individual choice rather than recognised as part of structures of inequality within wider society. The issue of how women can balance family demands and career expectations is one that schools do not address. Without this perspective females will continue to find inequalities in the labour market and within the domestic sphere. The emphasis on male underachievement takes attention away from what are still profound inequalities associated with gender. It is undoubtedly the case that current patterns of educational achievement depict girls as the success story. But as soon as labour market participation and access to positions of prestige and power are considered, there is as yet little evidence to suggest that success at school translates into success in employment. Until that happens we should still be addressing the needs of girls and their future opportunities as much as those of boys.

Research by Daniels *et al.* (1999: 17) suggests that it is possible for boys' achievement to be enhanced by explicit teaching on how to collaborate through active interventions. They suggest that it is possible for boys to be moved away from 'conceiving of formal education in win/fail dualities'. In so doing they learn to benefit in terms of educational achievement. Ofsted (2003) review the success of various strategies to address boys' underachievement, including teaching strategies aimed at undermining laddish culture. Recent research by Tinklin (2003) also points to the power of attitudes towards education. Her research into high attainment emphasises the importance of peer group pressure and the fact that girls took school more seriously than boys.

However, an emphasis on boys' underachievement can also obscure differences between social classes and ethnic groups. Research has drawn attention to the fact that improvements in female achievement are not shared by girls from working-class backgrounds and may not be apparent across all subjects (Murphy and Elwood, 1998; Gillborn and Mirza, 2000). Any discussion of the school's role in promoting or challenging gender inequality should also look at the dimensions of class and ethnicity. Debates about inequality may therefore be more appropriately focused on which particular categories of boys and girls are underachieving and the extent to which teacher interaction and expectations vary across these different groups.

CONCLUSION

The research evidence in this chapter makes it clear that there is no simple explanation for the differences in boys' and girls' educational achievement. It is very important that the same emphasis is given to factors associated with ethnicity and social class and that all three dimensions of inequality should be monitored to ensure appropriate strategies are developed to challenge these.

QUESTIONS FOR DISCUSSION

- How can a 'laddish' culture be challenged in ways that do not impact negatively on other groups?
- What experiences have you had which help you understand the importance of teacher expectations?
- In what ways do notions of masculinity and feminity impact on approaches to learning?
- How do gender, social class and ethnicity interact in relation to educational achievement?
- Think of the women you know in positions of power. Does this suggest women are translating their educational achievements into the labour market?

REFERENCES

Arnot, M., Gray, J., James, M., Ruddock, J. with Duveen, G. (1998) *Recent Research on Gender and Educational Performance*, London: The Stationery Office.

Browne, N. and Ross, C. (1991) 'Girls' stuff, boys' stuff: young children talking and playing', in N. Browne (ed.) *Science and Technology in the Early Years*, Milton Keynes: Oxford University Press.

Central Advisory Council for Education (England) (1959) *15–18* (Crowther Report), London: HMSO.

Daniels, H., Creese, A., Fielding, S., Hey, V., Leonard, D. and Smith, M. (1999) *Gender and Learning, A Report for ESRC*, Birmingham: School of Education, University of Birmingham.

Davies, J. and Brember, I. (2001) *The Closing Gap in Attitudes between Boys and Girls: A Five Year Longitudinal Study*, Manchester: University of Manchester, School of Education.

Department of Education and Science (England) (1963) *Half Our Future* (Newsom Report), London: HMSO.

DfES (2003a) 'National Curriculum assessments for Key Stage 3 (revised), GCSE/GNVQ examination results (provisional)', available online at www.dfes.gov.uk/statistics/DB/SFR. Accessed 30 June 2003.

DfES (2003b) 'National Curriculum assessments of 7- and 11-year-olds in England, 2002 (provisional)', available online at www.dfes.gov.uk/statistics/DB/SFR. Accessed 30 June 2003.

DfES (2003c) 'Success rates of GCE A level', available online at www.dfes.gov.uk/statistics/DB/ SFR. Accessed 25 June 2003.

Eden, C. (1995) 'Gender in the playground'. Paper presented at the British Education Research Conference, University of Bath, September 1995.

EducationGuardian (2003) 'A-Level results 2002', available online at www:education. guardian.co.uk/ alevels2001/tables. Accessed 30 June 2003.

Francis, B. (1999) 'Lads, lasses and (New) Labour: 14–16 year old students' responses to the laddish behaviour and boys' underachievement debate', *British Journal of Sociology of Education*, 20(3): 355–71.

Frosh, S., Phoenix, A. and Pattman, R. (2002) *Young Masculinities*, London: Palgrave.

Gillborn, D. and Mirza, H.S. (2000) *Education Inequality – Mapping Race, Class and Gender: A Synthesis of Research Evidence*, report for Ofsted, London: HMSO.

Howe, C. (1997) *Gender and Classroom Interaction: A Research Review*, Edinburgh: The Scottish Council for Research in Education.

Lees, S. (1993) *Sugar and Spice: Sexuality and Adolescent Girls*, London: Penguin.

Mac an Ghaill, M. (1994) *The Making of Men: Masculinities, Sexualities and Schooling*, Buckingham: Open University Press.

Mac an Ghaill, M. (ed.) (1996) *Understanding Masculinities*, Buckingham: Open University Press.

Murphy, P. and Elwood, J. (1998) 'Gendered experiences: choices and achievement – exploring the links', *International Journal of Inclusive Education*, 1(2): 95–118.

Ofsted (1996) *Exclusions from Secondary Schools*, London: HMSO.

Ofsted (2003) 'Boys' Achievement in Secondary Schools', online. Available at www.ofsted.gov.uk. Accessed 15 July 2003.

Powney, J. (1996) *Gender and Attainment: A Review*, Edinburgh: The Scottish Council for Research in Education.

Thorne, B. (1993) *Gender Play: Girls and Boys in School*, Milton Keynes: Open University Press.

Tinklin, T. (2003) 'Gender differences and high attainment', *British Education Research Journal*, 29(3): 307–24.

RECOMMENDED READING

Arnot, M. (2000) 'Equal opportunities and educational performance: gender, race and class', in Beck, J. and Earl, M. (eds) *Key Issues in Secondary Education*, London: Cassell.

Delamont, S. (1999) 'Gender and the discourse of derision', *Research Papers in Education*, 14(1): 3–21.

DfES The Standards Site has a section on gender and achievement which gives references to books and journal articles, resources and links, available online at http:/www.standards.dfes.gov.uk/ genderandachievment/resources/publications.

Gillborn, D. and Youdell, D. (2000) *Rationing Education: Policy, Practice, Reform and Equity*, Buckingham: Open University Press.

Noble, C. and Bradford, W. (2000) *Getting it Right for Boys...and Girls*, London: Routledge.

Wallace, C. (1987) 'From girls and boys to women and men: the social reproduction of gender', in Arnot, M. and Weiner, G. (eds) *Gender and the Politics of Schooling*, London: Hutchinson.

12 Radical Education

David Hicks

What's wrong with schooling? Why have there always been people who want to set up educational initiatives *outside* the system? And why do some educators feel the system needs transforming from within? What, in short, is radical education all about? This chapter explores

- the importance of understanding ideology in education
- the radical critique of mainstream education
- radical alternatives both outside and within the system.

IDEOLOGY AND EDUCATION

The concept of ideology

Sociologists use the term 'ideology' to refer to a group philosophy. Meighan and Siraj-Blatchford (1997) write:

> Ideology is defined as a broad interlocked set of ideas and beliefs about the world held by a group of people that they demonstrate in both behaviour and conversation to various audiences. These systems of belief are usually seen as 'the way things really are' by the groups holding them, and they become the taken-for-granted way of making sense of the world.
>
> (Meighan and Siraj-Blatchford, 1997: 180)

The term 'ideology' can be used in many ways: political ideologies, economic ideologies, religious ideologies and, of course, educational ideologies. Where one ideology becomes prevalent it is known as the 'dominant ideology'. This happens when a dominant group makes its beliefs seem natural, normal or mainstream, and attempts to marginalise other ideologies. An ideology may become dominant through the use of overt repression (e.g. the army, police or courts) but more often this is done less overtly:

A softer form of legitimation is in the use of major institutions, such as education, mass media, religion, law and the economy, to put over a 'consensus', 'common-sense' or 'sensible person's' point of view as against the 'lunatic fringe' view, which turns out to be almost any view inconvenient to the group with the dominant ideology.

(Meighan and Siraj-Blatchford, 1997: 183)

Educators have drawn up various 'maps' of different educational ideologies. Askew and Carnell (1998) use a four-fold classification based on beliefs about knowledge and the role of education in society. Is knowledge extrinsic or intrinsic – external or internal to the individual? And is the task of education to fit people into existing society or to question the nature of that society? See Figure 12.1.

Dominant ideology

'Hegemony' means the way in which a dominant ideology embraces all aspects of life so that it achieves *rule by consent*. It is a form of ideological control in which dominant

Figure 12.1 Four educational ideologies
Source: Askew and Carnell, 1998

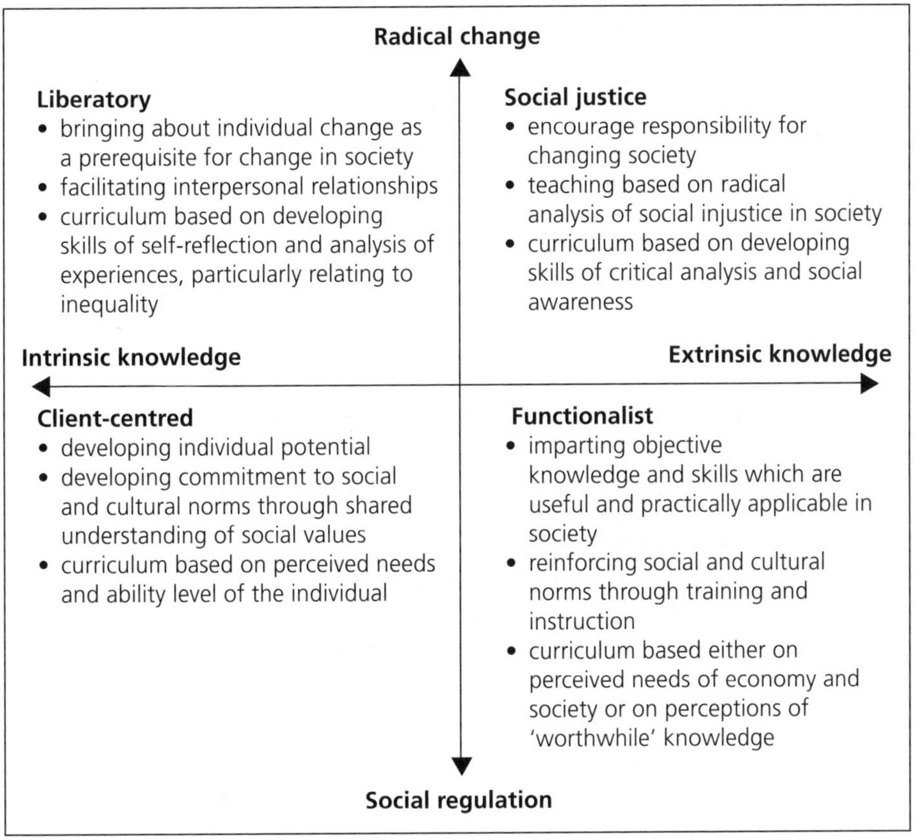

Radical change

Liberatory
- bringing about individual change as a prerequisite for change in society
- facilitating interpersonal relationships
- curriculum based on developing skills of self-reflection and analysis of experiences, particularly relating to inequality

Social justice
- encourage responsibility for changing society
- teaching based on radical analysis of social injustice in society
- curriculum based on developing skills of critical analysis and social awareness

Intrinsic knowledge   **Extrinsic knowledge**

Client-centred
- developing individual potential
- developing commitment to social and cultural norms through shared understanding of social values
- curriculum based on perceived needs and ability level of the individual

Functionalist
- imparting objective knowledge and skills which are useful and practically applicable in society
- reinforcing social and cultural norms through training and instruction
- curriculum based either on perceived needs of economy and society or on perceptions of 'worthwhile' knowledge

Social regulation

beliefs, values and everyday practices are created and disseminated throughout society via a range of institutions such as schools, family and mass media. Hegemony defines common sense by making particular ideas seem normal. It is not about indoctrination. It *saturates* society in such a way that it comes to be seen as common sense, reality itself. Ideology is therefore not something abstract since it powerfully shapes our perceptions of both self and society. Examples of western hegemonic beliefs would be: science is the measure of all things; war is inevitable; the individual is more important than the group; gender dictates opportunity; all children should go to school.

A key function of hegemony is to make inequality and hierarchy seem normal and acceptable – that's just the way things are. In particular, hegemony helps perpetuate inequalities of race, class and gender. Many people do challenge poverty, racism and sexism, and significant changes have occurred in the twentieth century. However, hegemony easily absorbs reformist tactics and blunts radical struggles for change.

The new right

From 1945 to the early 1970s capitalism experienced the longest period of sustained economic growth in history. In the United States of America (USA) during the 1960s and 1970s, however, the civil rights movement, the anti-Vietnam War movement and the Watergate political scandal shook society to its roots. For many it felt as if the nature of society was being threatened. This led to the rise of 'new right' politics which aimed to achieve a new consensus. The new right in the USA and the United Kingdom (UK) wanted to abandon the welfare state, return to 'traditional' morality, and oppose critical social movements. In particular they saw education as a tool for achieving this.

What Apple (2001) calls a 'new hegemonic alliance' emerged combining the interests of four major groups:

- dominant political/economic elites intent on 'modernising' the economy
- largely white working/middle class groups concerned with security, family and traditional values
- economic and cultural conservatives who want a return to 'high standards', discipline and social competition
- part of the new middle class whose professional advancement depends on greater accountability and efficiency.

In education over the last 25 years this has meant:

- attacks on the autonomy of professional educators
- tighter accountability and control of education
- increased marketisation and privatisation.

In the UK it has led to a national education system of standards, testing and curricula (see Chapter 7).

Radical ideology

The term 'radical' has a variety of meanings: fundamental (a radical error); far-reaching (radical change); a person holding radical views (a radical); a fundamental principle (getting to the roots of). Traditionally radicalism has been associated with the political left as this has been the main opposition movement during the twentieth century, challenging the conservative/liberal *status quo*. Button (1995) points out that in the popular mind radicalism is often identified with extremism, but this is not the meaning given to it here.

A radical ideology attempts to go to the root of things, to question the fundamental premises of dominant beliefs. Radical ideology comes into existence when a group begins to challenge the status quo in society in relation to politics, economics, religion, race, gender or education. A radical ideology is defined by what it is *against* as well as what it stands *for*. Radicals are driven by a vision of what a better society could look like and the need to act in order to bring it about. They oppose injustice and inequality and abuse of power and privilege. They challenge all forms of disempowerment (lack of control over one's life chances) and seek to promote empowerment (being fully responsible for one's life chances). Adherents to the dominant ideology will always see radicalism as dangerous, but over a period of time radical ideas and demands often become incorporated into the dominant ideology, such as the abolition of slavery and the establishment of votes for women.

In the nineteenth century radicals fought for the abolition of slavery and for better working conditions. Socialism and anarchism were the two radical ideologies challenging conservative and liberal ideas. Socialism emerged in the nineteenth century as a challenge to the liberal stress on individualism and the growth of capitalism. Anarchism emerged in the eighteenth century and in the popular mind is often equated with disorder and chaos. This is because anarchists reject the need for external authority, including that of government. Some of their key beliefs are:

- authority is generally used to take away people's freedom
- the potential goodness of human nature
- a stress on individual freedom, equality, co-operation and solidarity
- the organisation of society should work from the bottom up rather than top down.

During the twentieth century most radical groups drew on socialist or anarchist ideas and practice in their activism: the suffragettes; colonial struggles for liberation; social movements such as civil rights, the campaign for nuclear disarmament (CND), anti-Vietnam War, feminism, environmental activism and gay rights.

What is it about education that has attracted radicals in the twentieth century? To answer this question we need to know something about the rise of state schooling in the nineteenth century, i.e. education as part of the dominant ideology. In the UK this occurred during a period of major capitalist industrialisation, urbanisation and social class formation. Radicals argue that the development of compulsory state schooling was essentially *coercive*. It was the way in which the growing middle class sought to control the rapidly expanding urban workforce. Their purpose was essentially to train citizens and workers for life in the modern industrial state.

The main radical critique of education is that it reproduces the social, political and economic norms of the dominant ideology. In the west this is capitalist, technocratic, individualistic, materialist and patriarchal. A key question is: Whose knowledge is of most worth? Since radicals are suspicious of state education, many radical initiatives have taken place outside the mainstream system. Schools and education, the argument runs, can never be neutral. Apple (1993: 3) writes: 'Education is both a "cause" and an "effect"... The school is not a passive mirror, but an active force, one that also serves to give legitimacy to economic and social forms and ideologies so intimately connected with it.' All education is a political act in that it gives strong messages about the distribution of power and resources in society. Schools offer a particular selection from the sum total of knowledge, e.g. it is 'obvious' that science, maths, English, and information and communication technology are the most important subjects; that European history is more important than Asian history; that boys are better at many things than girls.

RADICAL IDEAS (OUTSIDE THE SYSTEM)

One of the debates at the heart of radicalism is whether it is individuals that need to change or society. The answer is 'both'. However, social activists look first at the individual and are concerned about how socialisation under a dominant ideology restricts a person's sense of self. They are concerned with the freedom of the individual. On the other hand, political activists are concerned with changing society first. They argue that if the unjust structures of society can be changed then people's life opportunities will be improved. These two different emphases are sometimes known as the 'libertarian tradition' and the 'social justice tradition'. They form the top two quadrants in Figure 12.1.

The libertarian tradition

This tradition raises questions about the nature of freedom. Political freedom means little, it is argued, if the individual's actions are limited by some internalised authority. Godwin, in *An Enquiry Concerning Political Justice* (1973), made one of the first attacks on the concept of the state. He argued that the state has no right to tell people what to do and was suspicious of a national system of education, feeling that government would only use such education for its own purposes.

Anarchists (or libertarians) are concerned with the way in which external authority, in all its forms, is used to oppress the individual. Libertarian educators wish to be free from the influence of the state and teachers. What children learn in school, they argue, is primarily to obey, to believe and to think in ways imposed by others. Libertarians oppose all forms of coercion believing true learning can only occur as part of a spontaneous process arising within the individual. Libertarians believe children should be given the same respect as adults and that they should not be looked down on or treated as inferior. Libertarians believe in the essential goodness of human nature. A.S.Neill was one educator who put these principles into practice.

A.S. Neill and Summerhill School

Neill began teaching in the early 1900s at a time when education was based on strict discipline, rote learning and frequent punishment and he became interested in experiments in progressive education. In 1927 he set up his own school, Summerhill, at Leiston in Suffolk. Neill believed that children sitting at desks studying useless subjects resulted in docile, uncreative children and citizens. Instead of making the child fit school he believed school should fit the child. He had a deep belief in the child and, in order to allow children to fully be themselves, he renounced discipline, direction and moral training. A timetable was posted but attendance at lessons was voluntary. Neill believed that learning should come after play and that children would come to learning when they were ready.

The school was run through the General School Meeting where all rules were voted on by the entire school. Both children and staff had a single vote on any issue. This was true equality and democracy in action. Such meetings decided on rules about safety and social behaviour. Pupils were loyal to their own democracy because they were being given real freedom. There was little fear or resentment because they were learning that self-government can actually work. Neill's principles (1962) have been summarised as:

- children are inherently good
- the aim of education is to work joyfully and find happiness
- education must be intellectual *and* emotional
- education must be geared to children's needs
- dogmatic discipline creates fear and hostility
- freedom does not mean licence
- true sincerity is needed from the teacher
- security comes from true independence
- guilt feelings create fear and bind child to authority.

Past pupils and employers have reported a greater self-confidence, greater maturity, greater self-reliance and tolerance than their contemporaries at other schools. Some pupils have reported feeling older than their contemporaries. After Neill died in 1973 the school was run by his wife and is now run by his daughter Zoë. This model of libertarian education has long had an international reputation and two-thirds of the pupils now come from overseas. It was recently in the news because of a damning report by Ofsted inspectors, but dominant ideology is never likely to be sympathetic towards radical principles and practice.

Challenging schooling

Writers in the 1970s (e.g. Postman and Weingartner, 1971) looked at formal education and found it seriously wanting. In particular, schools were seen as places which existed to reproduce the dominant ideology and which ignored the real needs of young people. Much of the critique hinges around the commonly accepted notion that learning can only really happen in school. Radical educators make a crucial distinction between 'schooling' and 'education'.

John Holt is famous for several books including *The Underachieving School* (1969). Having worked in schools himself he decided in the end that they were bad places for children. He gives as an example the small child's ability to learn language and what happens when he arrives at school:

> In he comes, this curious, patient, determined, energetic, skilful learner. We sit him down at a desk, and what do we teach him? ... First, that learning is separate from living. 'You come to school to learn', we say, as if the child hadn't been learning before, as if living were out there and learning were in here and there was no connection between the two. Secondly, that he cannot be trusted to learn and is no good at it ... He comes to feel that learning is a passive process, something that someone else does to you, instead of something you do for yourself.
>
> (Holt, 1969: 23)

Johnathan Kozol (1980) taught black American children in inner city schools. As a result of his experiences and the ways in which he saw schools perpetuating rather than challenging inequality he wrote this:

> There is no such thing as a 'neutral skill', nor is there a 'neutral education'. Children can learn to read and write in order to understand instructions, dictates and commands. Or else they can read in order to grasp the subtle devices of their own manipulation – the methods and means by which a people may be subjugated and controlled. Oppenheimer, working on the final stages of development of the atom bomb, and his co-worker Fermi [said] that they were 'without special competence on the moral question ...' It is this, not basic skills, but basic competence for basic ethical enquiry and indignation that is most dangerously absent in our schools and society today.
>
> (Kozol, 1980: 89)

What *is* education worth if it does not include discussion of moral and ethical dilemmas as one of its central concerns? A rich variety of alternative approaches to education emerged again in the 1990s. Interesting case studies can be found in Hern (1996), Gribble (1998) and more recently Carnie (2003). See also Shotton (1992) and Education Otherwise, the home-based education movement (www.education-otherwise.org/).

The social justice tradition

Radicals were also struck by the huge injustices and inequalities that they saw in society. Dominant ideology explains these as inevitable, but radical educators do not accept this. Issues of inequality are seen as a proper focus for education. Issues of injustice – prejudice, discrimination, abuse of human rights – are not ones that education should turn its back on. One of the leading figures in this tradition is Paulo Freire (Elias, 1994).

Paulo Freire

Freire was born and worked in north-east Brazil, one of the poorest regions in the world. In the early 1960s, when his work became internationally known, 75 per cent of people in this region were illiterate, with a life expectancy of 30. Half of the land was owned by 3 per cent of the population. Freire worked as a teacher in the slums and became interested in adult literacy. Since only literate people had the right to vote, literacy was the key to social reform. In 1963 Freire's literacy programme was extended to the whole country. However, opposition to his literacy methods grew amongst the political right who accused him of spreading subversive ideas. In 1964 a military coup overthrew the government and Freire went into exile rather than facing the risk of imprisonment. He was not allowed to return home to Brazil until 1980. His book, *Pedagogy of the Oppressed* (1972), is a classic of revolutionary education.

So what did Freire *do* that made him appear such an enemy to the political right? Firstly, he was appalled by the degree of poverty and injustice that he saw at first hand. People who lack the ability to read, he realised, lack the basic tool for understanding life in modern society for they can't understand any form of written communication. Learning to read was a first step in understanding more about their own social and political situation.

Freire and his team began by talking to people in the area where they were working. They chose a basic list of words that had the most meaning in those people's lives. They also chose words that would help people to understand the social, cultural and political reality that they faced every day, e.g. slum, plot of land, work, salary, government, swamp, wealth. Because Freire wanted to avoid traditional notions of schooling and imposed authority, the facilitator was known as a 'co-ordinator' and dialogue replaced old-fashioned rote learning. This process was known as 'conscientisation' or consciousness raising. Freire believed that people cannot be truly human until they have real freedom in society. This process enabled people to become subjects rather than objects in their own lives.

His approach to adult literacy was revolutionary, giving the oppressed the tools of their own liberation. It was a threat to oppressors (the landlords and those in power) because it unmasked the tools of oppression, the ways in which powerful groups kept others in subjugation. The aim was not to attack the oppressors, but to expose the social and political structures which perpetuated inequality and injustice.

RADICAL IDEAS (INSIDE THE SYSTEM)

Is it possible for radical ideas to work within mainstream education? Are there spaces within the dominant educational ideology where its practices can be challenged? Both libertarian and social justice traditions *do* have proponents within mainstream education. If schools are a major site of cultural reproduction, it is argued, then they need to be subverted from within as well as outside the system.

Libertarian ideas

In Askew and Carnell's typology (Figure 12.1) you will recall that one quadrant dealt with the client-centred model of education, also known as person-centred or child-centred education. UK primary schools were world famous for their child-centred approach to education in the 1960s and 1970s and this is still evident in early years teaching today. The key principles of early years teaching are seen as 'the holistic nature of children's learning and development ... the importance of developing autonomy, intrinsic motivation and self-discipline through the encouragement of child-initiated, self-directed activity, the value of first-hand experiences and the crucial role in children's development of other children and adults' (Whitebread, 1996: 1). Some of these principles resonate with elements of the libertarian tradition. The main difference is that they are implemented *within* the formal structure of schooling (see Chapter 9).

A leading figure in person-centred learning is Carl Rogers, best known in education through his classic work *Freedom to Learn* (1994). He sets out the three key teacher qualities that facilitate true learning.

Realness in the facilitator   The teacher needs to show her/himself as a real person, open to and sharing his or her own feelings with the group; students meet the person not just the role.

Prizing, acceptance, trust   This means prizing the learner, her feelings, her opinions, her person; it is a basic belief that this other person is fundamentally trustworthy (Lawrence, 1996).

Empathetic understanding   This means the ability to understand the student's reactions from the inside; it relates to the appreciation of being understood rather than being evaluated or judged (see Chapter 8).

These three attitudes require, like those of Rogers, Neill and others, a deep trust in human nature and its potential. This is based on a belief in the basic human tendency towards fulfilment, growth and self-actualisation. Such beliefs are the foundation upon which the school of humanistic psychology was developed in the 1960s and 1970s by psychotherapists such as Abraham Maslow and Carl Rogers. They also underpin important forms of counselling and therapy today.

Ideas about social justice

Robin Richardson

Robin Richardson was influenced by both Freire and Rogers and has played a major role amongst radical educators in the UK. In the 1970s he was concerned that the curriculum seldom helped pupils learn about current global issues and he played a major part in placing this on the mainstream agenda (Hicks, 2003) (see Chapter 2). From the 1980s his influence amongst UK educators with a radical bent has been considerable, particularly in the fields of anti-racist education and global education (Richardson and Miles, 2003). Both Carl Rogers (internationally) and Robin Richardson (in the UK) have shown how radical principles can be implemented within mainstream education in order to creatively change self, education and society.

Issue-based educations

During the 1970s and 1980s radical educators began to question whether mainstream education was really helping pupils to make sense of the world. The UK curriculum was largely focused on the dominant culture in a national and European context. As a result, a series of issue-focused educations emerged, all seeking to radicalise mainstream education. These included development education, global education, environmental education, anti-racist education (Goldstein and Selby, 2000), peace education, anti-sexist education, human rights education and futures education. In the 1990s these were joined by citizenship education and education for sustainable development.

Development education had its roots in the early 1970s when non-governmental organisations (NGOs) concerned with global inequality realised education had an important role to play in helping reduce public ignorance. Educators thus had to move deeper into the debate about causes of underdevelopment. As far as the UK public was concerned this was due to backwardness and low levels of economic development. However, NGO fieldworkers heard a different story – that European imperialism and colonialism had caused underdevelopment, continuing in the present through unfair trade and aid. Underdevelopment was seen as an ongoing process rather than a state or condition. Development education was influenced by Freire's work. There are major Development Education Centres in places such as Birmingham, Manchester, London and Leeds with significant educational programmes.

Whilst development education has as its main focus issues of inequality and injustice, global education focuses in particular on the notion of interdependence. Global education has traditionally been based in institutions of higher education. Richardson ran the influential World Studies Project in the 1970s, succeeded in the 1980s by the World Studies 8–13 project. Such projects worked with a large number of local education authorities and were internationally important because of their focus on global issues and person-centred learning. Also influential in the 1990s was the International Institute for Global Education (Pike and Selby, 1999/2000). More recently the Department for International Development has made funding available in the UK to help promote a global dimension in the curriculum (see Chapter 2).

Shared features

Lister (1987) referred to these initiatives as 'new movements' in education, acting as a vanguard, leading social and political education into new territory and new styles of teaching.

> The twin stresses on human-centred education and global perspectives constitute a radical shift away from the dominant tradition of schooling (which

is knowledge-centred and ethnocentric). Thus the vanguard educators seek to give education a new process and a new perspective on the world.

(Lister, 1987: 54)

He identified a series of common features shared by these new movements:

- Knowledge should have a social purpose aimed at improving the human condition; it should involve both understanding and action for change.
- The curriculum should deal with major issues, e.g. war and peace, poverty and development, human rights, a multicultural society, an interdependent world.
- Learning is about developing skills, not just about content.
- In order to develop skills, learning needs an active dimension, e.g. games and role-play.
- Attitudes and values are as important as knowledge and facts.
- There should be recognition of pluralism and diversity in our own society and globally.
- The curriculum should have an international and global perspective.
- Education should have a futures perspective.

Much of this has become accepted pedagogy today. Such 'vanguard educators', Lister noted, shared a common interest in an issue-perspective (content) and active learning (process) – two hall-marks of the radical tradition in education.

The advent of the Conservative government's national curriculum in the late 1980s had a major impact on these new movements. The right-wing emphasis on traditional subjects and the importance of English, maths and science meant that cross-curricular concerns all but disappeared for a number of years. From 1997, under New Labour, the climate has changed somewhat. There is recognition again of the importance of issues such as race, environment and citizenship. But the dominant ideology in education is still one of *teachers as technicians* in a market-led economy with Standard Assessment Tests and league tables used to measure performance of pupils, teachers and schools, the very antithesis of radical ideas. Currently global citizenship and education for sustainable development provide an important springboard for radical educators in terms of content and pedagogy. It is also possible to find radical educators working within most subject areas of the curriculum.

We need radical educators working within mainstream education because:

> Education in the modern world was designed to further the conquest of nature and the industrialisation of the planet. This tended to produce unbalanced, underdimensioned people tailored to fit the modern economy. Postmodern education must have a different agenda, one designed to heal, connect, liberate, empower, create and celebrate.

(Orr, 1992: x)

CONCLUSION

This chapter has explored two important radical critiques of mainstream education – the libertarian and social justice traditions – and explained these in relation to the notion of dominant ideology. Examples have been given of radical initiatives *outside* the mainstream, specifically the pioneering work of A.S.Neill at Summerhill and Paulo Freire's work in adult literacy. It has also been argued that radical ideas have an important part to play *within* mainstream education with examples given from the work of Carl Rogers and also the vital issue-based educations that emerged in the 1980s.

QUESTIONS FOR DISCUSSION

- In what ways has your outlook on life and education been shaped by dominant ideology?
- Which aspects of the radical critique attract your attention and why?
- In what ways can you see radical perspectives influencing your main subject and education more generally?

REFERENCES

Apple, M. (1993) *Official Knowledge: Education in a Conservative Age*, London: Routledge.

Askew, S. and Carnell, E. (1998) *Transforming Learning: Individual and Global Change*, London: Cassell.

Button, J. (1995) *The Radicalism Handbook*, London: Cassell.

Carnie, F. (2003) *Alternative Approaches to Education: A Guide for Parents and Teachers*, London: Routledge Falmer.

Elias, J. (1994) *Paulo Freire: Pedagogue of Liberation*, Malabar, FL: Krieger.

Freire, P. (1972) *Pedagogy of the Oppressed*, London: Penguin.

Godwin, J. (1973) *An Enquiry Concerning Political Justice*, Harmondsworth: Penguin.

Goldstein, T. and Selby, D. (2000) *Weaving Connections: Education for Peace, Social and Environmental Justice*, Toronto: Sumach Press.

Gribble, D. (1998) *Real Education: Varieties of Freedom*, Bristol: Libertarian Education.

Hern, M. (1996) *Deschooling Our Lives*, Gabriola Island: New Society Publishers

Hicks, D. (2003) 'Thirty years of global education: what have we learnt?', *Educational Review*, 55(3): 265–75.

Holt, J. (1969) *The Underachieving School*, London: Penguin Education.

Kozol, J. (1980) *The Night is Dark and I am Far from Home*, New York: Continuum.

Lawrence, D. (1996) *Enhancing Self-esteem in the Classroom*, London: Paul Chapman.

Lister, I. (1987) 'Global and international approaches to political education', in C. Harber (ed.) *Political Education in Britain*, Lewes: Falmer Press.

Meighan, R. and Siraj-Blatchford, I. (1997) *A Sociology of Educating*, London: Cassell.

Neill, A.S. (1962) *Summerhill: A Radical Approach to Education*, London: Gollancz.

Orr, D. (1992) *Ecological Literacy: Education and the Transition to a Postmodern World*, Albany, NY: State University of New York Press.

Pike, G. and Selby, D. (1999/2000) *In the Global Classroom*, Toronto: Pippin Press.

Postman, N. and Weingartner, C. (1971) *Teaching as a Subversive Activity*, London: Penguin.

Richardson, R. and Miles, B. (2003) *Equality Stories: Recognition, Respect and Raising Achievement*, Stoke-on-Trent: Trentham Books.

Rogers, C. (1994) *Freedom to Learn in the 80s*, 3rd edition, Columbus: Charles Merrill.

Shotton, J. (1992) 'Libertarian education and state schooling in England 1918–90', *Educational Review*, 44(1): 81–91.

Whitebread, D. (1996) *Teaching and Learning in the Early Years*, London: Routledge.

RECOMMENDED READING

Apple, M. (2001) *Educating the 'Right' Way: Markets, Standards, God and Inequality*, New York: Routledge Falmer.

Button, J. (1995) *The Radicalism Handbook*, London: Cassell.

Gribble, D. (1998) *Real Education: Varieties of Freedom*, Bristol: Libertarian Education.

Hern, M. (1996) *Deschooling Our Lives*, Gabriola Island: New Society Publishers.

Richardson, R. (1990) *Daring to be a Teacher: Essays, Stories and Memoranda*, Stoke-on-Trent: Trentham Books.

Richardson, R. and Miles, B. (2003) *Equality Stories: Recognition, Respect and Raising Achievement*, Stoke-on-Trent: Trentham Books.

USEFUL ORGANISATIONS

Educational Heretics Press: www.edheretics.gn.apc.org.

Education Otherwise: www.education-otherwise.org/.

Human Scale Education: www.hse.org.uk.

Libertarian Education: www.spinninglobe.net/libedessay.html.

Summerhill School: www.s-hill.demon.co.uk.

Part III

Knowledge, learning and the curriculum

13 Knowledge and Science Education

Alan Howe and Dan Davies

This chapter will help you to understand:

- beliefs about the nature of scientific knowledge and scientific method
- perspectives that have made science an educational priority for many economically developed countries
- concerns about the ways in which science has been represented and taught in schools
- the future for science education.

UNDERSTANDING THE NATURE OF SCIENCE

A tabloid newspaper recently published a problem page question and answer that went as follows:

> **Question**: *When I was in hospital having my new baby the doctor and midwife were talking behind my back about the lines on my baby's hands and feet. I read somewhere that lines on the palm of your hands might show up a mental problem. My baby's lovely and the health visitor says she's fine. She was OK at her six-week examination. I am still worried sick. What did those doctors see?*
>
> **Answer**: I am sure they didn't see anything because your baby is fine. What you've heard about is some new research showing that people with learning difficulties sometimes have distinctive lines on their hands. The lines – which include crease marks on the palm, as well as ridges and unusual fingerprint patterns – may also give clues to intelligence generally.
>
> (Daily Mirror, 2003)

This is a striking example of one of many science-based issues that can confront us in our lives. It raises a number of questions:

- Who did the research, when and where?
- What exactly does the research conclude about the link between hand lines and learning difficulties?
- Are the conclusions justified by the data and findings?
- Where was the research published?
- Have any other studies replicated the findings?

We can ask about the human factors lying behind the research:

- Who paid for it?
- What are the beliefs and values of the researchers?
- What are their assumptions about intelligence?

But we need to know something about science to ask the questions in the first place. We need an awareness of the *nature of science* as a body of changing, contested knowledge and as a human endeavour.

In order to cope with many of the decisions and dilemmas we face in our lives we frequently need to apply scientific knowledge, skills and understanding of how science *works*. Whether we are choosing food for a balanced diet, dealing with allergies, caring for a relative, seeking medical attention, deciding whether to eat genetically modified foods or what to do about global warming, the authors believe that science education *should* have a part to play in preparing us to cope. This implies a purpose for science education often called *scientific literacy* (Millar and Osborne, 1998). Scientific literacy is about being able to 'read' and make sense of the wide range of 'scientific' information with which we are bombarded, so we can take decisions from an informed, critical perspective.

This is a different rationale for teaching science than has been offered by the 'traditional' models of science education for those preparing to enter a university course and a subsequent career in science or engineering. The problem with the traditional approach is its *exclusivity*: many young people have left school not understanding or wanting to understand science. We can all get by without using scientific understanding in everyday life. We do not need to know about electrons to switch on a light; we do not need to understand chemical bonds in order to take paracetamol for a headache. Traditional science education focused on 'fact' and the recall of abstract ideas. Peter Fensham (1985) proposes *Science for All*, a science education that has social meaning and usefulness to the majority of learners and that assists them in sharing the wonder and excitement of scientific endeavour. *Scientific literacy* and *science for citizenship* are core purposes for a science curriculum in the twenty-first century.

WHAT COUNTS AS SCIENTIFIC KNOWLEDGE?

Imagine for a moment that all scientific knowledge could be contained in one huge book, or a CD-ROM. In the front is a recipe for doing science – follow this and you can't fail to make the same discoveries as some of the authors of the book. At each phase of education learners are permitted to read and remember some more pages of the book until they retain enough to pass a test and move on to the next chapter. This is the way science knowledge has been presented in school for most of the last hundred years. It is not surprising that few ever get beyond the first few pages and that many didn't bother trying.

This approach to knowledge derives from two sources: ancient Greek philosophers such as Aristotle, and the empirical scientists of the Enlightenment, such as Newton. Ancient Greek science was essentially *rationalist* and *deductive* in nature. It was based on applying the intellect to certain ideas about the nature of the universe which were themselves considered to be transcendent and not open to question. Aristotle's reasoning about the rate of fall of objects was deduced from his initial assumptions rather than induced from experiment. His conclusion that the rate of fall of a body was proportional to its mass (heavy things fall faster) was wrong. Yet it remained unchallenged until the time of Galileo because of the high status of such knowledge as 'natural philosophy'.

As more *empirical* approaches to scientific enquiry began to develop in Europe from the sixteenth century onwards, the natural philosophy of the Ancient Greeks began to be questioned. Despite opposition at various points in history by Church and State, the status of science has continued to grow. The values underlying the 'modernist' view of society grew directly from the dominant physical and mathematical theories of the seventeenth century. Modernist culture places great emphasis on scientific theories (such as Darwin's theory of evolution) to explain every aspect of life, bring social progress and lead us towards a 'perfect society'. This view, and the cultural arrogance that accompanies it, still dominates much of western thought, leading to the kinds of off-putting curricula experienced by schoolchildren.

If we see science as a body of high-status knowledge to be 'learned', there will always be debates about what goes in our science encyclopaedia. Some scientists seem to have reached an irreproachable status and their ideas always appear in new editions of the book of science, even though the discoveries were made several hundred years ago, whilst others struggle to have their ideas included. Who decides what goes in and what is left out? Why do Lamarcks' discredited ideas about evolution still get a mention when Jane Goodall's observations about primate behaviour are omitted? Should we put in Beatrix Potter's discoveries about the symbiosis of algae and fungi in lichens, even though eminent men of science (wrongly) dismissed them at the time?

The problem of what to include and what to leave out arises because traditional science education ignores the revolution in the ways scientists view their knowledge in the twentieth century. With less deterministic, more uncertain views of the universe, characterised in the world of physics by the theories of relativity, statistical thermo-dynamics and quantum mechanics, and more recently by the mathematical concepts of catastrophe and chaos, new patterns of thought have emerged. The old order was seen to be flawed, both in the macro-scale (Einstein's curvature of space–time due to gravity breaking the laws of Cartesian geometry) and the micro-scale (Heisenberg's uncertainty principle in quantum mechanics breaking Newton's laws). Many scientists have become less deterministic about the nature of the universe, and less certain about their abilities to decipher it: 'Our experience, both as individual scientists and historic-ally, is that we only arrive at partial and incomplete truths; we never achieve the precision and finality that seem required ...' (Ziman, 1968: 6).

This is a *postmodern* view of science: knowledge is provisional and subject to change. Though scientific knowledge is an extremely powerful way of making sense of many phenomena surrounding us, it cannot claim the status of 'truth'. Any review of science in the media reveals that the scientific community is constantly debating 'the facts'. For example: Is global warming a real phenomenon? If so, is human action to blame? If so, is there anything we can do about it? If so, what should we do to reverse it? Science is littered with such debates. It simply cannot be divorced from its human and cultural context. For example, we might ask who decides which topics are the most important for research scientists to address. Most scientific research is now done in military or pharmaceutical fields. Science is closely related to power and profit. Should the reader of our book of science be told about this?

Then there is the question of whether certain knowledge counts as science, pseudo-science, or not science at all. At one extreme is the universalist view that scientific knowledge is only provided by western modern science (WMS). WMS operates through an agreed set of rules and methods based on logic which give us knowledge that is claimed to be explanatory, predictive, based on empirical evidence, and communicated in written forms. This knowledge is only testable against the material world and is independent of human interest, culture, religion or the gender of the researchers. WMS has become so dominant that it acts as an effective 'gatekeeper', allowing in only the knowledge that passes every test of universalism. In the versions of science education found replicated in schools across the economically developed world, WMS is usually the only science taught.

Some knowledge is branded by universalists as 'pseudo-science' (including much complementary medicine and therapeutic practice) if empirical evidence is lacking or seen as 'flawed'. An educational example of the tensions between WMS and pseudo-science claiming equal legitimacy is provided by the *creation versus evolution* debate in several states of the United States of America. Creationism is taught alongside Darwin's theory of evolution by natural selection (teaching evolution is not 'banned' in any state). WMS scientists claim creationism simply has no scientific credibility, whilst creationists have attempted to use scientific (or at least pseudo-scientific) arguments to refute Darwin's theory. For example, carbon dating as a way of establishing the age of the earth beyond 4004 BC has been deemed 'flawed' by the creationists. So here is an attempt to challenge the dominance of WMS in the school curriculum through the use of the very science that is being called into question.

Emerging in this epistemological discussion is the question of whether the inclusion of knowledge from other sources outside WMS, such as indigenous, 'multicultural' knowledge, is valid. This movement is particularly prevalent in North America and Australia, continents with relatively large indigenous populations that have rich veins of oral-traditional knowledge (see Chapter 1). Snively and Corsiglia (2000: 6) argue that there is now a 'burgeoning science-based traditional ecological knowledge (TEK) literature' to enrich our understanding of the environment and sustainability. Irzik (2000) argues, however, that the problem is that such a conception of science is too broad; it 'lets in' not only TEK, but mythology and religion. It can lead to a science curriculum based on the principle of relativism – the view that there are no absolute truths and all beliefs and values are of equal worth (Poole, 1995). Irzik (2000) notes that the philosophical position of the teacher will be important here: will students be invited to judge for themselves which is the most 'true' account of nature, or will the teacher tell the student that different conceptions and world views are all equally valid?

Supporters of WMS such as Wolpert (1992) and Dawkins (1999) argue that if science does not defend its boundaries, superstition and harmful customs will retain credibility. They argue this is dangerous in developing countries where so much of basic education is about giving young people reliable advice on how to stay healthy and resist unsafe practices. Human health and diet, the spread of acquired immune deficiency syndrome (AIDS) and other communicable diseases, animal health and husbandry, and maintenance of the environment are all examples requiring the replacement of some superstitious beliefs with scientific knowledge. This raises the question: how can teachers value indigenous knowledge without reinforcing unsafe superstitions?

If we accept that all scientific knowledge is tentative and subject to change, it is surely more important to teach children how to *appraise* science-based information than teach the detail of such information. The next 'big idea' rendering half the knowledge in our book redundant may be just around the corner. To do this they need to know how science is carried out. Perhaps we need to throw our encyclopaedia away and concentrate on the *processes of science* rather than the content, resurrecting a debate that has raged in the scientific education community for decades (Murphy and Scanlon, 1994).

How is scientific knowledge generated?

Do scientists dream up theories (deduction), derive them from experiment (induction), 'discover' them (serendipity), a mixture of the three, or none of the above? Such questions are essential to grapple with if we are to make sense of or give credence to the stories they tell us, and if as educators we are to portray an authentic model of scientific enquiry in the classroom. Aristotle did not see a purpose for experimentation in the process of deriving scientific thought: it was to proceed by the pure operation of reason. In some senses Einstein returned to such a model with his use of thought experiments to imagine what would happen as one approached the speed of light. Modern science, however, is characterised by its empirical nature: the primacy of the 'experimental method' which enables the scientist to '...arrive at truth by logical inferences from empirical observations' (Ziman, 1968: 6). The empirical model of scientific discovery, first formulated by Francis Bacon in the sixteenth century, goes something like this:

- Science is founded on observations of the natural world.
- Observers perceive events and derive facts from them.
- Facts can be assembled into related ideas or concepts and so new explanations or theories about the world emerge.

This is the 'positivist' view of science, but it is open to criticism. Observers do not always perceive events in the same way: it is easy to interpret what we see, hear, smell, touch or taste in a number of different ways. Scientific methods try to eliminate as much subjectivity as possible, but always some remains. Contemporary scientists talk about probability and statistical significance, rather than certainty. No finite number of observations will 'prove' that something will always happen in the same way. Popper (1968) argues that science is founded on the recognition that we can disprove or *falsify* a theory by a single contradictory observation; by implication, any theory that cannot be falsified is not scientific. For example, Einstein's postulate that 'light rays will bend in strong gravitational fields' *is* falsifiable by an observation that shows light rays unbending in such conditions. The astrological observation that 'those born under Gemini often have a split personality' *is not* falsifiable because there is no qualification of the word 'often' (more than 50 per cent?) and the definition of the term 'split personality' is unclear.

One problem with the falsification principle is that it may not be the theory that is false; perhaps the observation is faulty (light did bend in the gravitational field, but you didn't notice) or the method is faulty (you didn't measure the direction of the light rays properly). Chalmers (1999: xxi) takes this a step further to claim that '... the idea that the distinctive feature of scientific knowledge is that it is derived from the facts of experience can only be sanctioned in a carefully and highly qualified form, if it is to be sanctioned at all.'

One of the problems with scientific curricula is that scientists are often presented as 'disembodied minds' (Sheldrake, 1990) and the methods they use as unemotional, unimaginative and value-free. Thomas Kuhn (1970) has placed more emphasis on the social and cultural nature of the scientific community in its acceptance of new paradigms (ways of seeing the world). He argues that scientists are innately conservative and reluctant to rock the boat. Far from seeking to falsify evidence, they maintain an emotional attachment to their theories and reject new ideas until overwhelming evidence forces them into a paradigm shift.

The very concept of a scientific method has been questioned and redefined as a range of approaches, varying in sophistication and dependent on the branch of science being studied. Feyerabend (1994) exposes the myth that scientific knowledge is only ever based on perfectly logical and methodical experimentation. He points out that progress is often only made precisely because scientists decide *not* to be bound by certain obvious methodological rules, because they unwittingly break them or choose to break them. He portrays Galileo, for example, as making full use of rhetoric, propaganda and various tricks to prove his point that the earth orbited the sun. Feyerabend has been labelled a relativist and therefore an enemy of science. He has, however, potentially liberated science educators to portray it as a rather more messy, creative and human endeavour than hitherto.

We would not go as far as Feyerabend in rejecting systematic enquiry. Scientists should investigate phenomena in ways that will open their findings to the scrutiny of others. It is possible to distinguish between published scientific studies by critiquing the methodology and the evidence base. However, there is plenty of room for creativity and intuition in the process. Sheldrake (2001) suggests that, for children, 'writing up' investigations has limited worth. The traditional ways of writing about science in a passive voice (the chocolate was melted), and in a sequence (apparatus, method, results, conclusion), does not acknowledge the real complexities of scientific enquiry and should be replaced by more active reporting on what really happened and what children think about it. Such an approach could make science more real to children and lead us towards a more positive response to our key question:

Can science education help us deal with real questions?

Given the debate and uncertainty, maybe science isn't so useful after all! However, in our view, if scientific knowledge is seen as tentative, ever changing, often challenged, debatable, based on incessant curiosity and human creativity, then it becomes more interesting and relevant, not less so. The question educators should be asking is not 'What should school students learn about science?' but 'What makes students want to learn science?' (Osborne, 2003).

One approach to the curriculum is to present scientific content as a series of explanatory stories (Millar and Osborne, 1998; Harlen, 2000). These narratives attempt to show the development of some of the big ideas in science (e.g. the particle theory of matter) through the story of the key people involved, the debates that have arisen, and the evidence that has been used to generate and refine scientific knowledge. The National Curriculum for England (Department for Employment and Education [DfEE]/Qualifications and Curriculum Authority [QCA], 1999) allows for this approach by including a section on 'ideas and evidence in science' under the general heading of scientific enquiry. However, there is little evidence that it forms a major component of classroom practice (Office for Standards in Education [Ofsted], 2003). One of the dangers of explanatory stories is that they perpetuate the impression of progress through the debates of 'dead white western males'. Another is that the content fails to engage with the issues facing people in the twenty-first century. How could an understanding of the behaviour of smoke particles in a gas help us to decide whether smoking cannabis is harmful or not?

This raises one of the fundamental problems with the scientific literacy movement. The science we most need to understand as scientifically literate citizens is at the 'cutting edge' – the hardest stuff! Most scientific content appropriate for learning at school is so far removed from that which is reported in the papers as to be entirely irrelevant. However, it is possible for even young children to have sufficient experience of *doing* science – behaving in a scientific way, exhibiting the 'virtuous' attitudes of curiosity, respect for evidence, willingness to change ideas. They can learn to tell the difference between good and bad science, even if they don't understand the concepts concerned. A child who has compared their results in a particular scientific investigation with a number of other children in the class will know about experimental error and issues of reliability. They could ask some pretty searching questions of a scientist who claims that sugar is good for us on the basis of one sample, despite having no knowledge of the chemistry of carbohydrates, and however much they may wish to believe the results! The type of scientific literacy that is most useful to children is that concerned with process rather than content – what we will call 'procedural scientific literacy'.

BUILDING A NEW SCIENCE EDUCATION

We offer some principles for the construction of scientific curricula which are derived from the discussion above:

1   They should emphasise scientific enquiry, rather than knowledge.

2   They should emphasise those elements of scientific enquiry leading to a procedural scientific literacy (ability to appraise critically the processes of science, rather than its concepts).

3   Conceptual content should, as far as possible, build towards understanding of those issues most relevant to children's roles as citizens (in other words, it needs to be flexible and shifting).

4   Conceptual content should be presented as tentative and subject to change. This may be achieved by means of 'explanatory stories', as long as it is done with acknowledgement of alternative cultural, traditional and indigenous knowledge.

These principles can be used for the evaluation of the National Curriculum for England (DfEE/QCA, 1999):

1   Scientific enquiry is one of four areas of the Programme of Study, with a 50 per cent assessment weighting at Key Stage 1 (ages 5–7) and 40 per cent at Key Stage 2 (ages 7–11). The National Curriculum does not do badly in this respect, so let us award it 7 out of 10.

2   In addition to the section on 'ideas and evidence' in science (see above), there is emphasis upon planning 'fair' tests (in which variables are controlled), collection and interpretation of evidence, all of which could contribute towards procedural scientific literacy. However, there is little emphasis upon reliability and validity in scientific enquiry, and neither is there any opportunity for pupils to critique existing examples of 'published research'. We award 5 out of 10 on this criterion.

3   It is in relation to conceptual content that the National Curriculum falls down badly. The remaining three areas of the Programme of Study are framed as fairly traditional biology, chemistry and physics respectively, with little to do with citizens in the twenty-first century. Some of the areas of Sc2 (Life and Living Processes) such as those concerned with healthy eating, drugs and medicines, heredity and ecosystems could be said to contribute to scientific literacy, but much of the rest is content for content's sake. It is what biologists, chemists, physicists and politicians felt that children 'ought to be taught'. Two out of 10.

4   The conceptual content is not framed in such a way that it is open to question, nor is acknowledgement made that ideas have changed over time. It could easily be presented as a set of explanatory stories, and the National Scheme of Work (QCA/DfEE 1998), with its emphasis on elicitation of children's existing ideas, allows for a process of conceptual change. But the fact that there is no invitation to problematise the content means that very few teachers will do so. Sadly, the National Curriculum scores zero on this count.

What would a curriculum look like that genuinely had the interests of the scientifically-literate citizen at heart? Some steps have been taken by Peter Fensham and a group of Chinese science educators working with citizens in China (Fensham, 2003). By questioning people about the issues most often confronting them in daily life, the team derived four areas for a relevant scientific curriculum, each of which would be differently emphasised for children at different ages, in different locations and situations:

Scientific knowledge   This is directed in the ways suggested by Point 3 above. One of the most common 'problems' identified by Chinese citizens was 'falling over'. Fensham argues that traditional science education focuses on the impact of forces upon rigid bodies, whereas what is important to understand in the context of humans falling is the impact upon *flexible* bodies.

Scientific awareness   This is closely related to an understanding of how science 'works' (the 'ideas and evidence' part of scientific enquiry in the National Curriculum). This is important to enable pupils to evaluate scientific information and make decisions about pragmatic issues, such as diet.

Scientific policy and legislation   Fensham argues that citizens need science to help them exercise democratic rights. We need to know how science is funded and what decisions are taken by governments in the framing of policies that directly impact upon our lives, society and the planet.

Scientific values and commitment   The presentation of science as an activity divorced from human feelings and culture risks alienating learners. If we can understand what drives scientists (and children) to want to explore further this will lead to a much richer scientific curriculum.

The four 'literacies' are obviously only embryonic in the construction of a science curriculum. Criticisms could be made of the examples Fensham uses: how could a knowledge of the impact of forces on flexible bodies possibly help you as you were falling downstairs? Yet he has pointed the science education community in the direction of a *multifaceted* science curriculum, in contrast to the *tetrahedron* (four-faced) model currently employed in England and other countries. As Fensham stresses, science looks very different from the outside (the lay perspective) than it does from within (the position of most scientists and science educators). Perhaps future curricula in science need to be constructed from the 'outside in', rather than, as currently, from the 'inside out'.

CONCLUSION

During the twentieth century, school science represented science as a body of undisputed facts that had been discovered by men rigorously applying the scientific method. It was thought that this served the nation well as it resulted in a relatively small number of carefully selected and highly trained scientists and technologists able to join the workforce in order to sustain the competitiveness and productivity of the nation.

Society now wants something different from its citizens, and its citizens need something different from education. Science educators are sure that science education must change. The development of new curricula and teaching methods, which emphasise knowledgeable and critical thinking about science, is the challenge.

QUESTIONS FOR DISCUSSION

- How could an appropriate science education have helped the mother in the extract at the beginning of this chapter?
- Do women need to be 'scientifically literate' in a different way from men?
- Is it more important for children to receive a science education relevant to their lives now, or to their future roles as citizens?
- Should there be a basic entitlement to scientific knowledge for all children by the age of 11?
- What is your understanding of 'procedural scientific literacy'? Is it important?
- Should Fensham's four areas (above) form the basis of a science curriculum? Would you add others?

REFERENCES

Chalmers, A.F. (1999) *What is This Thing Called Science?*, 3rd edition, Guildford: Open University Press.

Chapman, B. (1994) 'The overselling of science education in the 1980s', in R. Levinson (ed.) *Teaching Science*, London: Routledge.

Daily Mirror www.mirror.co.uk. Accessed 17 February 2003.

Dawkins, R. (1999) *Unweaving the Rainbow: Science, Delusion and the Appetite for Wonder*, Harmondsworth: Penguin.

DfEE/QCA (1999) *The National Curriculum: Handbook for Primary Teachers in England*, London: HMSO.

Fensham, P. (1985) 'Science for all: a reflective essay', *Journal of Curriculum Studies*, 17: 415–35.

Fensham, P. (2003) Keynote address at ICASE World Conference on Science and Technology Education, Penang 7–10 April 2003.

Feyerabend, P. (1994) *Against Method: Outline of an Anarchist Theory of Knowledge*, London: Verso.

Harlen, W. (2000) *The Teaching of Science in Primary Schools*, 3rd edition, London: David Fulton.

Irzik, G. (2000) 'Universalism, multiculturalism and science education', *Science Education*, 85(1): 71–3.

Kuhn, T.S. (1970) *The Structure of Scientific Revolutions*, Chicago: University of Chicago Press.

Millar, R. and Osborne, J. (eds) (1998) *Beyond 2000: Science Education for the Future: A Report with Ten Recommendations*, London: Kings College, London.

Murphy, P. and Scanlon, E. (1994) 'Perceptions of process and content in the science curriculum', in J. Bourne (ed.) *Thinking Through Primary Practice*, London: Routledge.

Ofsted (2003) *Science in Primary Schools: Ofsted Subject Reports Series 2001/2*, London: Ofsted.

Osborne, J. (2003) 'Making science matter', in R. Cross (ed.) *A Vision for Science Education: Responding to the Work of Peter Fensham*, London: RoutledgeFalmer.

Poole, M. (1995) *Beliefs and Values in Science Education*, Buckingham: Open University Press.

Popper, K. (1968) *The Logic of Scientific Discovery*, London: Hutchinson.

QCA/DfEE (1998) *Science – A Scheme of Work for Key Stages 1 and 2*, London: QCA.

Sheldrake, R. (1990) *The Rebirth of Nature: New Science and the Revival of Animism*, London: Rider.

Sheldrake, R. (2001) 'Personally speaking', *New Scientist*, 2300: 48–9.

Snively, G. and Corsiglia, J. (2000) 'Discovering indigenous science: implications for science education', *Science Education*, 85(1): 6–34.

Wolpert, L. (1992) *The Unnatural Nature of Science*, London: Faber.

Ziman, J. (1968) *Public Knowledge*, Cambridge: Cambridge University Press.

RECOMMENDED READING

Chalmers, A.F. (1999) *What is This Thing Called Science?*, 3rd edition, Guildford: Open University Press.

Cross, R. (ed.) (2003) *A Vision for Science Education: Responding to the Work of Peter Fensham*, London: RoutledgeFalmer.

Millar, R. and Osborne, J. (1998) *Beyond 2000: Science Education for the Future*, London: Kings College. Also available online at http://www.kcl.ac.uk/depsta/education/be2000/index.html.

Poole, M. (1995) *Beliefs and Values in Science Education*, Buckingham: Open University Press.

14 Learning and Mathematics

Malcolm Hanson

This chapter should give you an understanding of:

- anxieties about mathematics experienced by both students and the general public
- beliefs about the nature of mathematics
- research into effective teaching of mathematics
- the outcomes of international comparative studies into the performance of adults and children in mathematics and into the teaching of mathematics
- how the above interrelate
- the influencing factors behind the introduction of the National Numeracy Strategy.

ANXIETIES ABOUT MATHEMATICS

> As I was in the top set I found it hard as I was one of the poorer students in the class and felt that others were much better than me.
>
> (Undergraduate student 1)

> During the third year of secondary education I was given a test to assess ability. I was then put in a really low ability group (I was in high ability groups for other subjects). I did not understand maths and was scared to ask the teacher, as he was not at all approachable. I can still picture him all these years later.
>
> (Undergraduate student 2)

> I was terrified of my teacher who was incredibly strict and I generally worried constantly throughout lessons that I would be made to look and feel stupid in front of the whole class.
>
> (Undergraduate student 3)

All the above quotations are from students engaged in an undergraduate education module who were asked to relate their experiences of studying mathematics at school. The stories they tell are typical and although the negative experiences might have parallels in other subjects they seem to be particularly common and powerful in mathematics.

To many, mathematics is a subject which allows little negotiation (see Lim Chap Sam's research later in the chapter). Questions are perceived as having clear right or wrong answers, which means any inadequacies on the part of those attempting to answer the questions are quickly exposed. In the late 1970s a government inquiry into the teaching of mathematics in schools under W.H. Cockcroft (1982) commissioned a survey of adult attitudes to mathematics. The researchers experienced great difficulty in persuading members of the public to co-operate.

> Both direct and indirect approaches were tried, the word 'mathematics' was replaced by 'arithmetic' or 'everyday use of numbers' but it was clear the reason for people's refusal to be interviewed was simply that the subject was mathematics ... Several contacts pursued by the enquiry officer were adamant in their refusals. Evidently there were painful associations which they feared might be uncovered. This apparently widespread perception amongst adults of mathematics as a daunting subject pervaded a great deal of the sample selection; half of the people approached as being appropriate for inclusion in the sample refused to take part.
>
> (Cockcroft, 1982: 6)

The widespread anxiety about mathematics seems particularly prevalent in the UK. The Basic Skills Agency (1997) undertook an international basic numeracy survey in seven developed countries: United Kingdom (UK), France, Netherlands, Sweden, Japan, Australia and Denmark. Of the UK sample, 13 per cent refused to undertake the test involved without even looking at it, compared with 6 per cent in Japan (the next highest proportion) and 0 per cent in the Netherlands. Of those who went on to take the test the UK had the highest 'refusal to answer rate' for each of the 12 questions.

The reluctance to become involved appears to have been independent of factors such as age, gender and social grouping. So what can account for such a pervasive apprehensiveness on the part of the British public concerning mathematics?

THE NATURE OF MATHEMATICS

Lim Chap Sam (2002) identifies three 'myths' regarding mathematics. First, the belief that mathematics is difficult. This was the most common perception of the subject that emerged from a large-scale survey of adult images of mathematics. He found this belief prevalent both amongst those who enjoyed and appreciated the subject and those who disliked it and distanced themselves from it. 'I didn't have the brain power to actually use it and do it properly, so I just got bored with it ...' complained one of his respondents (Lim 2002: 268). Related to this is his second myth, that mathematics is only for clever ones. There was a common belief that only those with sufficient intellect could tackle the subject adequately and that the capacity to handle the subject is substantially innate. His third myth is that mathematics is a male domain. Although he found that 78.5 per cent of his respondents thought both genders could be equally good at mathematics, he discovered that there were subtle differences between respondents that gave support to this myth. For instance, a far greater proportion of females than males in his survey expressed concerns about the subject, saying that they found it confusing or that it made them feel nervous.

Where do you stand with regard to these 'myths'? What other beliefs do you have regarding mathematics? Take time to ponder these questions now.

Lim's myths may begin to explain why such a large proportion of the UK population has anxieties concerning mathematics, but we need to ask what experiences lead people to hold these beliefs.

Many respondents to the survey undertaken for the Cockcroft Report (1982) could relate their disquiet with the subject to experiences in schools. Some ascribed their difficulties to a change of teacher or of school, others to the set they were placed in and others to the attitudes and expectations of their teachers. These ascriptions are certainly consistent with the experiences of those students quoted at the start of this chapter. As well as affecting attitudes to the subject, school experiences appear to have led to sets of beliefs about mathematics that have hindered some adults' abilities to 'do' mathematics successfully. Some respondents to the Cockcroft survey believed there was always a single 'proper' method for solving mathematical problems, others thought that mathematics questions always had one exact answer. Others again experienced a conflict between the standard written methods they were forced to learn and recall (frequently with the injunction 'show all your working') and the mental methods, often of their own development, that they actually used to arrive at answers to problems.

Some 20 years later Lim Chap Sam (2002) identified five views regarding the nature of mathematics which he believed his research revealed. He characterised them as follows:

- *Utilitarian view:* mathematics as an essential tool for everyday life.
- *Symbolic view:* mathematics perceived as a collection of numbers and symbols, or rules and procedures to be followed and memorised.
- *Problem-solving view:* mathematics related to a set of problems to be solved.
- *Enigmatic view:* mathematics is seen as mysterious, yet something to be explored and whose beauty is to be appreciated.
- *Absolutist or dualistic view:* mathematics perceived as a set of absolute truths, or as a subject which always has right or wrong answers.

Take a moment to consider which of these views you would subscribe to. Is it possible to subscribe to more than one of these views? If so how?

The utilitarian view is perhaps the easiest to subscribe to. Whenever we check our change, estimate how much longer our journey will take or calculate the number of rolls of wallpaper the lounge is going to need we are using mathematics in this way. At a more advanced level, engineers, physicists and economists will be using mathematics to model a situation or predict an outcome. Lim found there was an almost universal perception that, through this role of mathematics, people came to view it as important and as an essential part of our education. It was true of respondents whether they liked mathematics or not, with some viewing it as a necessary evil and not enjoying the practice of it one bit.

People who subscribed to the symbolic view tended to be those who disliked mathematics at school and found it boring. Mathematics for them came across as ordered and rule-governed, but the logic of the rules and the purposes of the symbolic manipulation they had been required to undertake left them cold: 'rules (and) formulae learnt before understanding' (Lim, 2002: 254) as one respondent put it.

The 'problem-solvers' in Lim's study tended to have a far more positive attitude to the subject. Mathematics as problem solving was often seen as pleasurable with a sense of satisfaction to be enjoyed at reaching a successful solution. Again, problem solvers were inclined to view mathematics as an aid to logical thinking more generally and to see it as encouraging such powerful skills as 'tak(ing) small steps to understand difficult problems' (Lim, 2002: 256).

The enigmatic view of mathematics, as its very name implies, is far more difficult to characterize. '... I like the elegance of mathematics. The proofs and theories are very elegant. ... like recognising the patterns of mathematics, I found it very interesting' (Lim, 2002: 257) was how one respondent put it. Mathematics to this person clearly had aesthetic dimensions. There was a beauty to be appreciated, perhaps in the economy with which truths can be expressed or perhaps in the universality of those truths. Not surprisingly, this view of mathematics was often that of people whose jobs gave them a direct involvement in the subject.

The absolutist standpoint has elements of the symbolic and enigmatic about it in that mathematics is seen as having clear procedures and rules but of a coherent rather than arbitrary nature and which lead to incontrovertible conclusions. Some people enjoyed this certainty: 'I just like the fact that you could get a solution and that nobody could say that you have done wrong' (Lim, 2002: 258), said one respondent, whilst others were discouraged by this view, seeing mathematics as arid and lacking in creativity.

As Lim recognizes, these views of the nature of mathematics are somewhat idealised and people may well show evidence of holding elements of more than one view at any one time. However, they do help us to map the landscape of how mathematics is viewed and will help us to relate this to the teaching of mathematics.

EFFECTIVE TEACHING OF MATHEMATICS

In the mid-1990s a group from King's College, London, undertook research into the characteristics of effective teachers of numeracy in primary schools (Askew *et al.*, 1997). They used traditional tools to measure effectiveness through pre- and post-testing the children taught by the teachers who were selected for their research and took a 'value-added' measure. Through questionnaires, interviews and classroom observation they also set about trying to identify key features of the styles of teaching which the selected teachers exemplified. As a consequence they constructed three distinct and idealised 'orientations' of the teachers involved.

1   Transmissionists believed that:
    1.1   Being numerate involves an ability to perform standard, distinct, mostly written procedures and 'decode' problems to select the appropriate procedure;
    1.2   Children become numerate through being introduced to standard routines one at a time and that pupils vary in their capacity to become numerate;
    1.3   Children are best taught to become numerate by being given verbal explanations of teacher-determined methods.
2   Discovery-oriented teachers believed that:
    2.1   Being numerate involves finding an answer by any method, a reliance on practical methods and confidence in separate aspects of mathematics;
    2.2   Children become numerate through engaging in individual activities when they are ready to undertake them; this readiness is seen as varying from pupil to pupil and so children vary in their capacity to become numerate;
    2.3   Children are best taught to become numerate by engaging in practical activities so that they discover methods for themselves.
3   Connectionists believed that:
    3.1   Being numerate involves selecting, from a range of known possibilities, methods that are efficient and effective and which link different areas of mathematics, demonstrating confidence with mental methods and using reasoning and justification in reaching conclusions;
    3.2   Children become numerate through being challenged and then struggling to overcome difficulties, and nearly all pupils can become numerate;
    3.3   Children are best taught to become numerate by engaging in dialogue with the teacher to explore understanding.

Think of your most memorable (for whatever reason!) mathematics teacher at school. Which of the above characterisations best fits him or her?

Whilst all involved were deemed to be at least moderately effective teachers of mathematics, it was those who were best characterised as connectionists who secured the greatest gains, and by a significant margin over transmissionist- and discovery-oriented teachers. It was also found that the beliefs of the teachers, as characterized above, were far more influential than organisational factors such as whether there was 'setting' of classes or what texts were used.

It is interesting then to relate the beliefs regarding mathematics of the various teacher orientations outlined above with the more general images of mathematics revealed by Lim Chap Sam's work and the anxieties regarding mathematics touched on earlier.

The transmissionist approach could clearly lead to a symbolic view of mathematics. If skills are taught in discrete chunks and the connections between them not emphasised, mathematics might come to be viewed along the narrowly manipulative lines of the symbolic view of the subject. Those who viewed mathematics in this way tended to be alienated from the subject and see it as little more than mindless rule-following. Again the nature of the questioning used by transmissionist teachers, who sought answers in line with their preferred methods of solution, has the potential to create anxiety on the part of the pupils. Will what the pupil says fit with the teacher's expectations? If they produce a distinct, but nonetheless valid, explanation, will this be dismissed?

Some of the difficulties that adults experienced at the time of the Cockcroft Report (1982) could be laid at the door of transmissionism, which appears to have a long history in this country. When reviewing the responses they received to test questions, the authors of the report noted that

> … many individuals appeared to have only one method of tackling a problem. If this failed, or if the calculations involved became too cumbersome, they lacked the ability and confidence to attempt a different approach. Nor, in some cases, were they even aware that there might be alternative and possibly more straightforward methods which could be used.
>
> (Cockcroft, 1982: 8).

The discovery orientation does not link so obviously to any of Lim's identified views. As children are encouraged to seek and use their own methods it could be viewed as associated with a problem-solving stance. However, as discovery-oriented teachers tended to adopt a pragmatic approach, accepting any method their pupils used that worked, the opportunity to develop a coherent set of thinking skills required by Lim's broader understanding of problem-solving is unlikely to be achieved.

In contrast, the emphasis on reasoning and justification observed in the classrooms of connectionists is far more consistent with this extended conception of problem-solving. Connectionists encouraged a multifaceted approach to mathematics where, as with discovery-oriented teachers, different solutions to problems are actively sought. Unlike discovery-oriented teachers, the alternative solutions are not then viewed as equally valid, but instead are further analysed for their efficiency and associations with other areas of mathematical experience. This could involve considering which method is best in the context of the particular problem set and in what circumstances alternative approaches might better be used.

Connectionism can also be associated with at least one of the other views identified by Lim. Respondents he classed as holding the enigmatic view described mathematics as 'an exploration into another world' or 'a voyage of discoveries' that is 'fun and challenging' (Lim, 2002: 257). Connectionists were seen as challenging their pupils and drawing from them a view of mathematics as a coherent set of truths that can be accessed through reason.

I do not wish to argue that if all teachers adopted a connectionist approach to the teaching of mathematics then the anxieties identified by my students, by the Cockcroft Report researchers or by Lim Chap Sam would miraculously be eliminated. Learning mathematics inevitably involves challenge, but connectionists attempt to exploit the fruits of this challenge to aid learning. As one of my own students put it, 'Perhaps the mental space in which one practises mathematics is inherently anxious, perhaps that is something that mathematicians enjoy'. The challenge to the teacher is to create situations of mathematical challenge that all can enjoy.

So far, the evidence I have put forward to support this view is very much 'home grown'. What can we learn from international studies?

INTERNATIONAL COMPARATIVE STUDIES

Earlier I used an international survey of numeracy undertaken by the Basic Skills Agency (1997) to provide evidence that there is a high degree of anxiety about mathematics on the part of the UK public. What I did not mention was how British adults performed on the numeracy test administered through the survey. 'Relatively poorly' would be a generous assessment. In fact on any measure you might wish to use, UK adults did worse than any of the other six nations involved. For instance, in the UK 47 per cent of adults got 10 or more of the 12 questions correct. In Japan the proportion was 81 per cent and in Australia, the next worse performing nation, it was 58 per cent.

Such results create headlines. The same has been true of international comparisons at school level. The Third International Mathematics and Science Study (TIMSS) (International Association for the Evaluation of Educational Achievement [IEA], 1995) undertook a massive study of the mathematical performance of children at three different ages across 40 nations. What caught the attention of the media at the time, and when a follow-up study was conducted in 1999, were the rankings of UK children, which in most cases were close to, but nontheless below, the international average. UK children were seen as being significantly outperformed by children from France, Hungary and Switzerland, and massively outperformed by those from Pacific Rim countries such as Singapore, Japan and Korea. As we shall, see it was partly in response to such results that the National Numeracy Strategy was created (see Chapter 1).

What did not receive the same publicity were the results of sub-studies undertaken under the TIMSS umbrella but which looked in more detail at the relationship between performance and classroom practice. The UK was not involved in such studies, but the United States of America (USA), whose children performed at a very similar level to UK children in the tests, was included.

In one sub-study, The Survey of Mathematics and Science Opportunities (SMSO) (Kaiser *et al.*, 1999: 68–85), a team of researchers examined classroom practice in six different countries, including Japan and the USA. Through a combination of pupil and teacher questionnaires and classroom observations the research group arrived at descriptions of what they saw as typical patterns for teaching and learning activities in mathematics for each country. In fact they were struck by the consistency with which such patterns were observed within any one country and the qualitative differences between patterns observed in different countries.

In Japan, lessons typically centred on the solution of a carefully chosen single problem. Pupils were invited to provide multiple solutions to these problems, often working in small groups. Various solutions were subsequently presented by the pupils to the rest of the group. The teacher carefully orchestrated class discussion to draw out major points and develop the concepts involved. The problem focused upon in each lesson was judiciously selected to centre on a single major concept, which in turn related to other concepts addressed through a sequence of lessons. 'Topics were generally developed through subtly directed class discussion interspersed with periods for individual or small group reflection or practise' (Kaiser *et al.*, 1999: 80).

In contrast, lessons in the USA were typified by teachers presenting information and directing student activities and exercises. Lessons often encompassed a diversity of topics and activities, with a focus on basic definitions and procedures. 'Consistent with the cognitive emphasis found in textbooks, the preponderance of lesson discussion involved information about procedures, exercises and basic facts' (Kaiser *et al.*, 1999: 81). Pupil activity was individual in nature, consisting principally of skills practice without any substantive discussion. The emphasis was very much on the development of skills rather than concepts.

Another TIMSS sub-study involved the detailed analysis of videotapes of lessons in Japan, Germany and the USA (Kaiser *et al.*, 1999: 86–103). At least 50 mathematics lessons in each country, involving children in the equivalent of Year 9, were recorded and analysed in a variety of ways. The findings were remarkably similar to those of the earlier SMSO study.

Practice in Japanese classrooms was extremely consistent and followed the outline described above from the SMSO study. The single problem set was always 'non-routine' and yet accessible given the prior work the group had undertaken. This gave plenty of scope for alternative approaches, which in turn generated a variety of discussion points when solutions were presented to the rest of the group. Here is a typical example:

> It has been one month since Ichiro's mother has entered the hospital. He has decided to pray with his younger brother at a local church every morning so that she will be well soon. There are 18 ten-cent coins in Ichiro's wallet and just 22 five-cent coins in his brother's wallet. They have decided to take one coin from each wallet and put them in the offertory box, and continue the prayer until either wallet becomes empty. One day after they were done with their prayer, when they looked into each other's wallet, the brother's amount of money was greater than Ichiro's. How many days has it been since they started the praying?
>
> (Kaiser *et al.*, 1999: 95)

Have a go at this problem yourself. Try and approach it in a variety of ways. Characterise your approaches in different ways. Which is the easiest to understand? Which, do you think, is the most sophisticated? Which could you generalise for use in other cases?

Japanese lessons were reviewed at their end and major learning points emphasised. Homework was seldom set.

Practice in US classrooms was found to be less consistent but most typically followed the outline described above from the SMSO study. There was an acquisition phase, where the teacher provide a step-by-step solution to a routine problem, and an application phase where the pupils practised the procedures the teacher demonstrated by solving similar problems. Teacher 'discussion' tended to be limited to helping individuals who had difficulties during the application phase. Problems left unsolved at the end of the lesson were often set as homework.

As well as these descriptive analyses, the videotape study also attempted further analysis of the conceptual content of lessons. By relating the work undertaken in lessons to the analysis of national curricula undertaken by the main TIMSS study they reached the conclusion that the content of lessons in Japan was, on average, some 1.6 grades, i.e. over 18 months, in advance of that observed in the USA. Over 83 per cent of the concepts addressed in Japanese lessons were classified as having been 'developed' in those lessons as opposed to just 'stated'. In the USA the equivalent figure was 22 per cent. Again, an analysis of the time for which pupils were engaged in individual or small group work in a lesson concluded that 94.9 per cent of this time was taken with practising procedures in the USA as opposed to 42.5 per cent in Japan. In contrast, 43.8 per cent of the Japanese pupils' time was taken up with inventing their own solutions to problems, with a corresponding figure of only 0.2 per cent in the USA.

How do these sets of lesson descriptions for Japan and the USA relate to the King's College descriptions of teacher orientation? What beliefs about the nature of mathematics are they each likely to foster?

Japanese children have performed at or near the top of the pile in all the international comparative studies in which they have been engaged. In addition to the high level of their performance in studies mentioned above, Japanese children had the highest mean performance in a more recent survey of 'mathematical literacy' undertaken by the Organisation for Economic Co-operation and Development (OECD) (Programme for International Student Assessment [PISA], 2000). Here mathematical literacy was defined as 'the ability to put mathematical knowledge and skills to functional use rather than just mastering them within a school curriculum' (PISA, 2000: 22). Again, within a further sub-study for TIMSS, the abilities of Japanese and US children to solve more overtly mathematical problems were compared. Here Japanese children demonstrated a significantly higher success rate and were seen to achieve it through the use of more sophisticated problem-solving techniques (Kaiser *et al.*, 1999: 121–39).

   In looking for reasons why Japanese children (and adults) appear to perform so well across a wide range of measures of mathematical attainment, several factors are bound to be relevant. They will include cultural features, such as attitudes towards the importance of education in general, and mathematics education in particular. Again, organisational features in schools, such as the use of setting (classes in Japan, at least up the age of 14, are mixed ability with a strong cultural bias against grouping by attainment) will play a role. Such features are examined in some depth in yet another TIMSS sub-study outlined in Kaiser *et al.* (1999:104–20). However, classroom practices, as outlined above, must have their part to play in this success.

THE NATIONAL NUMERACY STRATEGY IN ENGLAND

David Reynolds and Shaun Farrell produced an influential booklet (Reynolds and Farrell, 1996) which reviewed a large number of international surveys of educational achievement. Whilst warning against the dangers of importing practices from abroad in the hope of improving educational performance 'at home' they nonetheless made recommendations concerning school practices which they felt could be beneficial to educational achievement in England. Amongst these was an emphasis on a more interactive style of teaching as witnessed in Pacific Rim and eastern European countries, which engaged children in debate about their learning (see Chapter 1).

   Reynolds went on to chair the Numeracy Task Force charged with developing the

National Numeracy Strategy (NNS). That strategy has now been in place in primary schools in England since 1999, and the influences of research via international comparisons and also into effective teaching of mathematics can clearly been seen in its structure.

Read the introduction to the NNS Framework for Teaching Mathematics (Department for Employment and Education [DfEE], 1999). In particular read the section on the influence of teaching on standards of numeracy (p.5) and the section 'Teaching Mathematics' (pp.11–15). How do the recommendations you find here relate to what you read above about effective teachers of numeracy? Compare the classroom practices recommended here with those observed in Japanese classrooms. (Copies of the Framework are available from the Department for Education and Skills, Tel: 0845 6022260, Ref: NNFT.)

The effectiveness of the strategy is inevitably a matter of some debate. The Office for Standards in Education, in their review of the first three years of the strategy, claim that 'The National Numeracy Strategy has had a significant impact on the standards attained in mathematics and on the quality of teaching over the last three years' (Ofsted, 2002: 2). However, in a further review of the strategy undertaken by researchers at King's College, London, only 'very minor' improvements in pupil performance were noted (*Times Educational Supplement*, 9 May 2003: 1).

There appears to be far less debate over the influence the strategy has had on attitudes towards mathematics and mathematics teaching, both on the part of pupils and teachers. Ofsted (2002) states that:

> Pupils' confidence, enjoyment of and involvement in mathematics have improved since the strategy began. They respond positively to the routines and clear structure of the daily mathematics lesson and they are motivated by the direct teaching which it requires. Many pupils understand their strengths and weaknesses in mathematics better, as well as the progress they are making.
>
> (Ofsted, 2002: 2)

Even the King's College researchers admit that teachers have been 'overwhelmingly positive' about the strategy.

For me, a further criterion for success will be the elimination, over time, of the sort of stories about mathematics teaching that I shared with you at the start of this chapter. As an outstanding teacher of mathematics put it nearly 60 years ago:

> The teacher of mathematics has a great opportunity. If he fills his allotted time with drilling his students in routine operations he kills their interest, hampers their intellectual development, and misuses his opportunity. But if he challenges the curiosity of his students by setting them problems proportionate to their knowledge, and helps them to solve their problems with stimulating questions, he may give them a taste for, and some means of, independent thinking.
>
> (Polya, 1945: v)

CONCLUSION

In this chapter we have seen that adults in the UK frequently experience anxieties regarding mathematics. We have further seen that these anxieties can often be traced back to experiences in school where not only are we taught the skills and understanding associated with mathematics but gain sets of beliefs about the nature of the subject. These beliefs, in turn, have a significant influence on our attitudes towards mathematics. We then saw that research into effective teaching of mathematics revealed that those teachers who were most successful in improving the attainment of their pupils in the subject were also those who held beliefs about the subject most closely associated to positive attitudes towards it. Finally, we saw that the National Numeracy Strategy embedded several of the tenets adhered to by successful teachers both in the UK and abroad and that initial examination of the influence of the Strategy on children's attitudes to mathematics show promising signs that it is having a positive effect on their feelings about the subject.

REFERENCES

Askew, M., Brown, M., Rhodes, V., Johnson, D. and Wiliam, D. (1997) *Effective Teachers of Mathematics*, London: King's College, London.

Basic Skills Agency (1997) *International Numeracy Survey: A Comparison of the Basic Skills of Adults 16–60 in Seven Countries*, London: Basic Skill Agency.

Cockcroft, W.H. (1982) *Mathematics Counts: Report of the Committee of Inquiry into the Teaching of Mathematics in Schools under the Chairmanship of W.H. Cockcroft*, London: HMSO.

DfEE (1999) *The National Numeracy Strategy: Framework for Teaching Mathematics from Reception to Year 6*, London: DfEE.

IEA (1995 and 1999) *Third International Mathematics and Science Study*, available online at http://isc.bc.edu/.

Kaiser, G., Luna, E. and Huntley, I. (eds) (1999) *International Comparisons in Mathematics and Education*, London: Falmer Press.

Lim Chap Sam (2002) 'Public images of mathematics', PhD thesis, available online at http://www.ex.ac.uk/~PErnest/pome15/lim_chap_sam.pdf.

Ofsted (2002) *The National Numeracy Strategy: the First Three Years 1999–2002*, London: Ofsted, available online at http://www.ofsted.gov.uk/publications/docs/3048.pdf.

PISA (2000) *Knowledge and Skills for Life*, Paris: OECD, available online at http://www.pisa.oecd.org/Docs/Download/PISA2001(english).pdf.

Polya, G. (1945) *How to Solve It*, Princeton: Princeton University Press.

Reynolds, D. and Farrell, S. (1996) *Worlds Apart? A Review of International Surveys of Educational Achievement Involving England*, London: Ofsted.

RECOMMENDED READING

In addition to the books listed in the reference section, the following could prove useful:

Burton, L. (1984) *Thinking Things Through*, Oxford: Basil Blackwell. This book provides a very accessible introduction to a problem-solving approach to mathematics.

Harries, T. and Spooner, M. (2000) *Mental Mathematics for the Numeracy Hour*, London: David Fulton. As well as providing lots of engaging mental mathematics activities, the second chapter of this book gives a brief outline of relevant theories of learning which link nicely to the styles of teaching identified in the above research into effective teaching of mathematics.

Jaworski, B. and Phillips, D. (1999) *Comparing Standards Internationally*, London: Symposium Books. This will provide you with a more detailed analysis of the results of the TIMSS research project.

15 ICT and Learning for the Future

Susan Haywood and Mim Hutchings

This chapter consider the ways in which information and communications technology (ICT) can play a part in developing learners' responses to the demands of the world today, as well as prepare them for the unforeseeable future.

THE RISE OF COMPUTERS IN EDUCATION

Estelle Morris, when Secretary of State for Education and Skills, stated that:

> ICT has huge potential to engage pupils in ways that will help to realise their individual potential whilst also offering teachers new opportunities to develop their professional skills in the classroom.
>
> (British Educational Communications and Technology Agency [BECTa], 2002: 5)

The period from the 1980s has seen the introduction of computers into classrooms. They may be organised as dedicated computer suites, clusters of computers to be shared between classrooms, as computers located in each classroom or as a combination of approaches. Some or all of these machines will be 'networked', that is linked together with cables or radio signal, and then connected via a dedicated computer, or server, to the Internet. By 2002 all British primary and secondary schools were connected to the Internet.

These developments are a reflection of an increasingly technological society, and the fact that capability in ICT is recognised as a key skill (Department of Education and Employment [DfEE], 1999). Our prosperity as a nation and as individuals will depend, at least in part, on our ability to use the tools of new technology effectively. The first computers in classrooms were financed, not by the education system, but by the Department for Trade and Industry, a recognition that children were growing up in a world in which technology would be an increasingly important source of employment and wealth. The emergence of so-called 'knowledge economies' has made this development, with its associated requirement for ICT capability, ever more urgent. Knowledge itself, rather than ownership of land, raw materials or manufacturing capacity, is becoming a primary source of wealth. The development of high-level skills, including the ability to use ICT as a tool, is becoming a priority (Coulby, 2000). The Stevenson Report (Stevenson *et al.*, 1997), commissioned by the Labour Party in opposition, commended the progress that had been made in introducing new technology in British schools, but cautioned that it was analogous to being in the lead after only 500 metres of a marathon race. Much still needs to be done if Britain is to maintain its place as one of the leading world economies.

It is not just that children growing up in an increasingly technological world need to be confident with, and knowledgeable about, technology. (Research shows that even amongst educators this remains the most common rationale for its inclusion in the curriculum [Twining, 2003].) More important is the fact that technology itself is a vital tool for learning. Technology changes the way we learn.

Think about what you are doing now. You are reading a book, itself a product of technology. You may be making notes, underlining key ideas in pencil, using a highlighter pen, making notes on a voice recorder or computer. All of these are technologies that influence the way you learn. If you did not have access to these technologies, in what ways would the process of learning change? The relationship between technology and learning is complex when powerful technologies are brought into the process.

The majority view is that the introduction of computers into schools is beneficial. However, not all agree and the use of ICT to support learning is still a subject of debate, decades after computers were first introduced to British schools. There is a view that computers are bad for children (see Chapter 6). Starting from Rudolf Steiner's developmental ideas and practice in the Waldorf schools (termed Steiner schools in Britain), Setzer and Monke (2003) argue that:

> … early computer use and an emphasis on computerlike thinking, is leading children's development to be dominated by the rigid, logical, algorithmic thinking, bereft of moral, ethical or spiritual content, that is characteristic of computer interaction. This accelerated, but isolated intellectual development brings a child's mental abilities to an adult level long before the emotional, psychological, spiritual and moral sensibilities have grown strong enough to restrain it and give it humane direction.
>
> (Setzer and Monke, 2003: 19)

RELATIONSHIPS BETWEEN ICT AND LEARNING

Two broad views of learning have inspired different approaches to the use of ICT. Each stems from different philosophical beliefs about how learning happens and what it is possible for us to know. 'Objectivists' see knowledge as being 'out there in the world'. It is real and exists independently of the human mind; there is a body of knowledge and core skills that society needs to pass on to the next generation. It is grounded in behaviourist psychology and information-processing strands of cognitive science research.

'Constructivists', on the other hand, believe that we build up knowledge by having experiences. When we integrate new experiences into our existing knowledge, new understandings are created and learning occurs. Constructivist theories have evolved from a variety of branches of cognitive science.

Whilst the debate between objectivists and constructivists inspires different approaches to teaching and learning, Roblyer (2002) suggests that taking an 'either/or' stance is unlikely to explain how all learning takes place, or to address all the problems inherent in learning. Both theories:

- try to clarify what makes learning happen
- are based on the research of learning theorists who have systematically studied the behaviours of learners
- have influenced curriculum design, teaching approaches and research into learning.

What teachers want children to learn in school is so complex that no single existing theory will account for how it is actually learned. A more relevant question is, 'How can research into learning help educators to support all children in learning with new technologies?'

A number of writers have proposed models of the relationship between the computer and the learner, or the process of learning. Kemmis *et al.* (1977) analysed computer use in terms of the experience of the learner. They identified four modes:

Instructional   The computer instructs the learner, who is given opportunities to practise tasks and is then provided with feedback from the program. This mode reflects the 'drill and practice' or programmed learning approaches, which were prevalent at the time.

Revelatory   The learner explores a model, simulation or adventure game, discovering the rules of the model through trial and error as he or she progresses through it.

Conjectural   The learner explores a model, devising and testing hypotheses by asking questions such as 'What would happen if...?'

Emancipatory   The computer is used to complete routine processing, leaving the learner to focus on analysis, interpretation and presentation of information.

A decade after Kemmis proposed this model, computers were commonplace in British schools. Anita Straker (1989), Director of the government-funded Micro-electronics Education Programme Project, proposed another model which focused on the impact on the curriculum. She suggests that computers have the capacity to support, enhance or extend the curriculum.

In supporting the curriculum, the computer could be used within existing frameworks to provide an alternative medium for the learner but without any significant change to the learning process. This would include activities such as using an encyclopaedia on CD-ROM for research, or a simple counting program to produce a graph.

Computers can enhance the curriculum by providing different approaches to existing activities that were already an accepted part of the curriculum. This could provide a better experience for the learner. Examples might be to use a word processor to draft and edit writing, a desktop publisher to produce posters or brochures, or a music program that would allow even a non-specialist to compose. In history, ICT can provide easy access to census records or, in geography, to aerial photographs, offering enhanced opportunities for learning.

Straker's final suggestion is for ICT to be used to extend the curriculum: to provide new opportunities for learning that would otherwise have been difficult or impossible. 'On the Line' was a project in which children along the Greenwich meridian across two continents exchanged information about their everyday lives. The use of remote sensing, web cameras, video conferencing with experts and Internet access to remote locations all provide opportunities that are only possible using ICT. Extending the curriculum does not always imply the use of very sophisticated technology. Using a computer-based historical model, a group of children can role play as a group of Roman soldiers. They can decide where to locate their camp, how to secure water supplies and defences, what crops to plant, and where, when and whether they can afford the materials and labour to put up buildings.

Somekh (Somekh and Davies, 1997) looks at ICT in terms of how the computer is used as a tool for learning. She suggests three possible approaches:

Computer as tutor   The computer 'teaches' the child, a process that, at its worst, is repetitive and not appropriate for all styles of learning. She suggests that Integrated Learning Systems (ILS) can be seen as an example, although some advocates of ILS would suggest that their use extends beyond that limited role.

Computer as neutral tool   Similar to Straker's 'enhancing the curriculum', the computer provides ways of completing tasks in different ways. It implies the ability to understand when ICT is the appropriate medium and when it is not, a key element of ICT capability.

Computer as cognitive tool   Here Somekh refers to the ways in which the use of ICT helps the learner to develop new skills and understanding. These skills may be in data analysis and presentation using spreadsheets, music composition, communication skills using presentation software, and so on. Within the category of 'cognitive tool' is included the way in which ICT can provide opportunities for the development of higher-order skills such as design, analysis, organising and classifying information, hypothesising or interpreting.

Each of these three models of the relationship between computers and learning can be linked to the objectivist and constructivist perspectives on learning introduced earlier. The objectivist view relates most directly to Kemmis's mode of 'computer as instructor' and Somekh's 'computer as tutor'. Two learning theories provide the basis for what is sometimes called 'directed instruction'. These are 'behaviourist' and 'information processing' theories of learning. They provide the foundations for directed instruction such as drill-and-practice and tutorial programs. The idea behind drill and practice software is to increase the number of correct responses to stimuli. They are frequently used to help memorise basic information within specific areas of learning difficulties, such as spelling. Tutorial software is designed to guide pupils through an instructional program in order to learn specific concepts. In each case the computer acts as a teaching aid, leading the learner step by step through a series of tasks. Tutorial software is also widely used in industry and commerce for training purposes.

Behaviourism suggests that we have control over our responses but that responses can be shaped by reinforcement. Behaviourist theories were developed through observing how desired behaviour can be achieved through reinforcement. In the example of drill and practice software this happens through the positive reinforcement of praise for correct answers, leading to the learner trying harder to be correct in future answers (desired behaviour).

Behaviourist principles were widely applied in classrooms and teaching was viewed as the process of organising reinforcement to achieve the desired behaviour, or learning. It was thought that one of the most effective means of teaching was to use stimulus–response reinforcement to fix patterns of behaviour. This system determines the design and structure of drill-and-practice programs.

Information-processing theories developed from a branch of cognitive psychology that focuses on memory. How people develop as thinkers and learners is seen to relate to how computers work. Information-processing theories concentrate on:

- how information is received and stored in the memory
- how memory connects new learning to previous learning
- how a learner retrieves information from short- and long-term memory and applies it to new learning.

Much software is based on information-processing views of learning and is designed to support pupils in storing newly learned information into the memory by:

- using questions or visuals that capture attention
- stressing important points in learning
- suggesting ways of remembering information
- making links to previous exercises
- setting practice exercises.

Directed instruction depends on well-designed materials which teach important skills through a structured learning environment, together with a clear plan for how ICT will be used. However, because skills tend to be broken down into small steps and taught in isolation, activities are often boring, repetitive and unrelated to real use. You may learn to spell a number of words in a drill-and-practice exercise, but not go on to spell them correctly when writing a story, and you may not develop the reasoning needed to use a spell-checker effectively. These skills are more suited to individual learning than co-operative group work.

The foundations of constructivism lie in a broad range of learning theories based on cognitive science. The theories draw on the developmental pyschology of Jean Piaget and the socio-cultural pyschology of Lev Vygotsky. Piaget saw meaning as actively constructed by the individual: the child constructs knowledge and relates new learning to previous learning. Piaget emphasises the individual. Vygotsky saw cultural and social contexts as the predominant influence on learning through interactions with people – parents, teachers and other children. However, it is the more recent research and development based on principles of constructivism and social constructivism that have been directly linked to ICT.

No discussion of ICT and learning could fail to include reference to the work of Seymour Papert, who studied with Piaget at Geneva, and whose application of constructivist approaches was to have enormous impact on the practical and theoretical approach to the use of ICT for learning. Papert coined the term 'microworlds' which he described as 'incubators for knowledge' to describe his vision of computer-rich environments in which children could learn using ICT. He suggested that such microworlds provide a real environment in which children can think and problem-solve, and his ideas were influential in challenging behaviourist approaches to the use of computers in education (Papert, 1993, 1994).

Jonassen (1996) suggests that microworlds are the ultimate example of active learning environments and explains their potential for the learner:

> The ideal associated with this approach is the feeling of 'direct engagement', the feeling that the computer is invisible, not even there; but rather, what is present instead is the world we are exploring, be that world music, art, words, business, mathematics, literature or whatever your imagination and task provide.
>
> (Jonassen, 1996: 239)

The notion of microworlds brings us to another model of the relationship between ICT and learning. Papert's model is the simplest, but arguably the most powerful. When you see a child using a computer, he asks, is the child controlling the computer, or is the computer controlling the child?

Generic, open-ended programs provide tools for thinking and can put the learner in control of the learning process. As well as communications tools, such as the Internet, these include word processors, desk-top publishers, spreadsheets, databases, music and graphics programs, multimedia and web-authoring programs, presentation software, digital recording and editing equipment, programmable devices and control equipment.

Papert contrasts this with the notion of the computer controlling the learner. Much content-specific software falls into this category. It seems as if the computer is controlling the child. Within this category are the tutorial programs and computer-based training packages found in industry as well as education. It also includes a great deal of the educational material aimed at the home market, 'edutainment' software, and computer-based assessment programs, which are relatively easy to set up, but limited in learning potential. Of course, there is a place for both types of computer use. The use of content-specific software to reinforce learning and provide opportunities for practising skills is a legitimate and valuable use of ICT. The structured, progressive and non-threatening environment provided by good software of this type is well-suited to some learning tasks.

Constructivist approaches have been adopted at the Vanderbilt Learning and Technology Centre (Roblyer, 2002). It produced software which encouraged children to develop complex problem-solving skills within familiar and authentic situations. The design of the materials means that the technology becomes a tool to scaffold thinking and activity so that learners solve problems and think together in more advanced ways. For example, *The Adventures of Jasper Woodbury* focuses on mathematical problem-finding and problem-solving through a series of videos that end with complex tasks (Bansford, 2003).

Scardamalia (2000) at the Institute for Knowledge Innovation and Technology suggests that children are capable of *socially constructing* knowledge and developing communities of learners. These are based on virtual learning communities within and between schools. In the *Knowledge Forum* children pose problems, suggest theories, build on and reference each other's ideas, and publish materials. In one *Knowledge Forum* database some elementary students developed an Inuit perspective on global concepts. Beginning with their own language, Inukititut, and their culture and community, they developed a deeper understanding of their own heritage as well as the world beyond.

In Britain, Mercer and Fisher (1993) have researched how computers can be used to develop ways of collective thinking (*interthinking*) in the classroom. Influenced by a neo-Vygotskian approach to understanding teaching and learning, they set out a conceptual framework for 'learning with help':

> … the essence of this approach is to treat learning and cognitive development as culturally based, not just culturally influenced, and as social rather than individualized processes. It highlights communicative aspects of learning, whereby knowledge is shared and understandings are constructed in culturally formed settings.
>
> (Mercer and Fisher, 1993: 340)

The work has resulted in two classroom approaches which combine software design with off-computer coaching of exploratory talk to enhance the quality of interactions at the computer. The aim is to use computers to stimulate high-quality discussion and collaborative learning.

Constructivism has moved beyond using software to learn isolated skills and memorise facts to an emphasis on solving problems, finding information and thinking critically. This illustrates how ICT can be a powerful pedagogical tool in supporting learning. Yet, in a similar way to any other tool, it functions within a social context and is mediated by the learning conversations that go on around it.

ICT CAPABILITY

ICT capability was identified as one of a number of specific attributes in the National Curriculum Orders published in 1995. ICT was recognised as a tool for learning across the curriculum. Skills were seen as important, but ICT capability could not be defined solely in terms of isolated skills, of knowing what buttons to press. The 1995 Orders emphasised the importance of understanding the impact of ICT in the world, and on learning. It stressed the application of ICT, when ICT is an appropriate tool to use and when it is not.

Implicit is the recognition of the attitudes and characteristics that help develop confidence and the ability in children to take risks as learners, individually and collaboratively. It includes the flexibility needed to learn and use new applications, but also the more fundamental capacity to recognise the potential of completely new paradigms or the creativity to use existing technology in new ways. For example, in

1993 the giant Microsoft website was 'hosted on three computers, located on a folding table in a hallway' (Abbott, 2001: 22). Even this world leader in technology development had not, at that stage, recognised the fundamental changes to access to information and the models of learning that would soon be commonplace.

Readiness for change, and what it means to be a learner with new technologies, is important if we are to understand what ICT capability is. For the learner, it is not a question of knowing all there is to know about any application. It is rather the flexibility and confidence to apply existing knowledge and skill to new applications, to explore, experiment, and learn from mistakes. Training in the use of new technologies is important, but even this is not straightforward. In an international survey of teachers' confidence with ICT, Italian teachers were shown to be relatively confident users, having received little formal training (Research Machines, 2000). A substantial ICT training program was provided for them. Rather than increasing confidence, it led to a decline in confidence as the training made teachers more aware of their shortcomings.

A learning activity does not have value simply because it is approached through a sophisticated technology. An activity which is educationally unsound and inappropriate for the learner does not become a good learning experience simply because it is computer-based. ICT can be used for impoverished as well as rich learning opportunities. However, ICT *is* a medium for developing a range of higher-order skills including collaborative learning, collective thinking and building communities of learners, whether local or global. It has the capacity to offer challenging and motivating opportunities when learners have access to powerful learning tools. Commercial games manufacturers have taken full advantage of this potential. 'Anyone who can draw as many people into situations related to learning as … Lego or Nintendo knows something that educators … ought to want to learn' (Papert, 1994: 87).

CHARACTERISTICS OF ICT

ICT has four distinct attributes that make it a powerful tool for learning:

- provisionality
- capacity and range
- interactivity
- speed and automatic functions.

Provisionality   ICT-based work need not be considered completely finished at any stage. Changes can be made and mistakes put right as the learner works. However, it is not just concerned with improving and refining work. The provisional nature of the medium encourages the learner to record ideas, even if tentative and imperfect. ICT can provide an environment which is safe for experimenting, thinking and sharing ideas. It is a particularly good medium for collaborative work, shared writing, presentation and planning. Mistakes can be seen as opportunities for learning and better understanding in an environment that is psychologically safe for the learner to experiment.

Capacity and range   This refers to the way in which the learner can have access to information of a variety and extent never before contemplated. He or she can research using the Internet, view the world revolving in space from a satellite web camera, look inside a wild game enclosure or a badger sett, visit an art gallery or a virtual museum, look at models and reconstructions of historical places, search public records, listen to music or listen to broadcasts from radio archives. The quantities of information available mean that research and information retrieval skills and the capacity to evaluate information are more important than ever, and must be taught. Critical judgement, as well as skills, is needed for the learner to access and make use of information effectively.

Interactivity   This is a key feature of the use of ICT resources for learning. Because of its interactive nature, learners can access information in whatever way suits their purpose or learning style. For example, when using an electronic source for research the learner has choices: read the text, have it narrated, use a glossary with text or narrated definitions, look at pictures, diagrams, animations or video. The material can be accessed in any order. The learner can make notes orally, on a notepad, or copy and paste text or images into their notes. When using generic software such as a word processor, desk-top publishing program or art package the learner can make changes to fonts, colours and backgrounds, and see the effect immediately. Learners can interact with their own, with other people's materials or commercial material such as branching stories and computer-based models.

Speed and automatic functions   These enable the learner to be free from routine, low-level processing and to focus on higher-order skills. For example, calculations can be copied across a spreadsheet and charts drawn using a chart wizard so the learner can concentrate on interpreting the data rather than presenting it. The same data can be presented in several different chart formats, selecting the most appropriate for the purpose. Instead of spending time looking though census records, counting and recording, the learner can search data automatically, looking for patterns, asking and answering questions. The tools in an art package can be used to distort, blur, re-colour, emboss, repeat and manipulate images in many different ways to create the desired effect. The learner can experiment easily with the dynamics, tempo, key or instruments used in a composition created with a music package.

CONCLUSION

Papert (1994: 1) invites us to imagine a group of surgeons and teachers, time travellers from a century ago, finding themselves in a modern operating theatre or classroom. Both would recognise their environment, but the changes in the operating theatre would far outstrip those in the classroom. The rate of change represented by the technology in the operating theatre is only just beginning to be paralleled in the classroom. The tools we learn with are changing. The children of the future will increasingly rely on their capacity to work with powerful learning tools. 'In times of great change learners will inherit the earth whilst the learned will remain perfectly equipped to deal with a reality that no longer exists' (MacGilchrist *et al.*, 1997: xiii, quoting Eric Hoffer, 1902–83).

QUESTIONS FOR DISCUSSION

- What ways of learning do you think are needed for the future?
- How has your own learning changed as you have used new technologies?
- In what ways have you seen technology used to support learning in classrooms and how does this link to theories about learning?

REFERENCES

Abbott, C. (2001) *ICT: Changing Education*, London: RoutledgeFalmer.

Bansford, J. (2003) *Anchored Instruction*, available online at http://tip.psychology.org/anchor.html.

Becta (2002) *Connecting Schools, Networking People: ICT Practice, Planning and Procurement for the National Grid for Learning*, Coventry: Becta. Available online at www.becta.org.uk.

Coulby, D. (2000) *Beyond the National Curriculum*, London: RoutledgeFalmer.

DfEE (1999) *The National Curriculum*, London: DfEE/QCA.

Jonassen, D. (1996) *Computers in the Classroom: Mindtools for Critical Thinking*, Upper Saddle River, NJ: Prentice Hall.

Kail, R.V. and Cavanaugh, J.C. (2000) *Human Development: A Lifespan View*, Belmont, CA: Wadsworth.

Kemmis, S., Atkins, R. and Wright, E. (1977) *How do Students Learn?* Working Papers on Computer Assisted Learning, Occasional Paper 5, Norwich: Centre for Applied Research in Education, University of East Anglia.

MacGilchrist, B., Myers, K. and Reed, J. (1997) *The Intelligent School*, London: Paul Chapman Publishing.

Mercer, N. and Fisher, E. (1993) 'How do teachers help children to learn? An analysis of teachers' interventions in computer based activities', *Learning and Instruction*, 2: 339–55.

Papert, S. (1993) *Mindstorms: Children, Computers and Powerful Ideas*, 2nd edition, Hemel Hempstead: Harvester Wheatsheaf.

Papert, S. (1994) *The Children's Machine*, Hemel Hempstead: Harvester Wheatsheaf.

Research Machines (2000) *The RM G7 (8) Report 2000: Comparing ICT Provision in Schools*, Abingdon: Research Machines.

Roblyer, M.D. (2002) *Integrating Educational Technology into Teaching*, 3rd edition, Upper Saddle River, NJ: Prentice Hall.

Scardamalia, M. (2000) Can schools enter a knowledge society?', in M. Selinger and J. Wynn (eds) *Educational Technology and the Impact on Teaching and Learning*, Abingdon: Research Machines PLC, available online at http://ikit.org/index.html and http://csile.oise.utoronto.ca/intro.html.

Setzer, V.W. and Monke, L. (2003) 'An alternative view on why, when and how computers should be used in education', available online at http://www.ime.usp.br/~vwsetzer/comp-in-educ.html, accessed 24 July 2003.

Somekh, B. and Davies, N. (eds) (1997) *Using Information Technology Effectively in Teaching and Learning*, London: Routledge.

Stevenson, D. *et al.* (1997) *Information and Communications Technology in UK Schools: An Independent Enquiry*, London: ICT in Schools Commission, available online http://rubble.ultralab.anglia.ac.uk/stevenson/.

Straker, A. (1989) *Children Using Computers*, Oxford: Basil Blackwell.

Twining, P. (2003) 'dICTatEd: discussing ICT, aspirations and targets for education', available online at http://www.med8.info/dictated/results.htm.

RECOMMENDED READING

Abbott, C. (2001) *ICT: Changing Education*, London: RoutledgeFalmer. This book gives a broad overview of trends and uses of ICT in education.

Kail, R.V. and Cavanaugh, J.C. (2000) *Human Development: A Lifespan View*, Belmont, CA: Wadsworth. This provides an overview of learning and development including the theories discussed here.

Roblyer, M.D. (2002) *Integrating Educational Technology into Teaching*, 3rd edition, Upper Saddle River, NJ: Prentice Hall. This provides an introduction to learning theories in relation to new technologies. It has an accompanying website with material linked to the book. Available online at http://www.prenhall.com/roblyer/.

16 Language, Power and Education

Howard Gibson

In this chapter we look at the following key points:

- We communicate our thoughts, feelings and ideas in language. But language offers us alternatives for doing this.
- In settling upon one alternative rather than another, meaning and structure become fused. Language can no longer be seen as a value-free conduit for communication. It holds the traces of our thoughts, feelings and ideas. It cannot be viewed as innocent, even if the choices made were done so unknowingly.
- One aim of this chapter is to see through language and to understand how educational discourses in particular are constructed and not arbitrary.
- Another aim is to explain that it is important to *de-naturalise* discourses and unearth their assumptions, because *de-naturalised discourses* can reveal power relations in the way teachers talk to their pupils.

LANGUAGE CHOICES

Recently I found a pen and handed it in to the receptionist. This was no smudgy Bic but the gold-plated proper sort you might get for a twenty-first birthday. As I left I wondered what would become of it and whether it would be claimed, whether I might even be able to claim it later. But as I passed the students' union a scenario gripped me. I imagined coming to the end of a lecture, whipping out *my* pen and jotting down the time of a tutorial, to look up and find horror on the face of the student at my scandalous possession of her lost love token, wedding gift, grandfather's keepsake or what have you – and pretending it to be mine! What would you say? 'I found it and got it back from the reception desk?' That'd take far too many words and would make one sound far too active, like trying to over-explain a theft you genuinely had nothing to do with. 'It was given me?' Better – makes you the passive object of someone else's action and, because it was given to us both in a weird sense, you could be seen to be an equivalent of the real owner. Umm, yes, that'd sound better.

Like me, you make language choices every time you open your mouth or write a word and every time you vet what you hear or read. Technically speaking, with regard to the pen, I suppose I envisaged trying to employ a passive construction that would help obfuscate my involvement in it. A child of four will do just this. They know how language choices make differences, like how to employ just the right auxiliary verb – 'must' or 'might', 'could' or 'may' – when petitioning for a flake in their ice cream or explaining why they couldn't possibly walk to the shops. What these youngsters don't know, however, are the reasons for their language choices. They know how to use language *implicitly* but they don't know why they're doing it *explicitly*. We can make explicit people's use of language so that we can look more critically at the reasons for the choices they make. The idea is to get you started on the process of *de-naturalising* these links and opening them up for scrutiny.

For example, had you noticed how I chose in the opening paragraphs to communicate in an informal, talkative manner, using a personal anecdote and contractions like 'that'd'? I even started a sentence with 'but', despite being told at school this was unforgivable. So why did I make these particular choices and pretend to engage you in conversation? Was I adopting the chatty, informal style that pervades many discourses these days, like those friendly mobile phone salespeople when they call just as you've sat down to watch Eastenders (Cameron, 2000)? And does the adoption of that conversational style have a history and that history an explanation? Does it, for example, signify the disintegration of boundaries between personal and public language and the rise of what has been called 'synthetic personalisation'? Perhaps you also noticed how I moved from using the pronoun 'I' to the pronoun 'one' and then 'you'. If you speak a little French then you'll know that the use of 'tu' or 'vous' is not arbitrary and that I can include or exclude you with the use of 'we'. 'We can look at that later' is designed to include you, in contrast to 'We don't do that here', which excludes you. Doctors, politicians and teachers use this simple pronoun for just this purpose. I also managed to get in technical terms like 'pronoun', 'contraction', 'passive' and 'auxiliary verb'. These may seem daunting, but the naming of terms is probably necessary if we are to be explicit about language constructions and talk about them. The point is that my language choices so far have been conscious and intentional. And what I have just done is *de-naturalise* them, make them look like choices and not just like natural language.

My next point is that language cannot be a simple conduit for transmitting meaning that lies somewhere else. It's not value-free and we need to be clear about this from the outset. (Actually, I first of all wrote '... we *have* to be clear about this from the outset ...' but I've just changed it to make it sound less authoritarian – 'we *probably* need' to build what is called 'modality' or the relationship I wish to establish with you as a reader. I was saying ...). From the outset we need to agree that the relationship between words and truth is tenuous and problematic, and that all representations of events, from explaining the finding of pens to the explanations offered by politicians for their educational policies, are 'polysemic', that is, ambiguous and unstable in meaning. So although we can describe language in terms of choices between a vast array of verbs, clauses, tenses and the rest, the purpose of choosing a particular form is interesting and significant because language carries meaning and constructs it at the same time. Sometimes the language is chosen consciously and reflectively. Think of yourself carefully writing an essay, or the wording of a zillion-pound advertisement for a glossy magazine, or a speech for Tony Blair (Fairclough, 2000b). But sometimes the language chosen is spontaneous, as in situations where the author or speaker is less self-reflective, like when speaking to a friend in the pub. But in both instances meaning and language are constructed simultaneously and the language structure carries meaning.

This happens in many areas outside education, in the media, in advertisements and in politicians' speeches. Education in this sense is no different from the wider world in which language and meaning are linked, but is a rich area to seek the ways in which it works. Here are some other examples:

- When teachers talk of children doing 'a comprehension' they have nominalised the verb 'to comprehend' and have chosen to conceive it as a name, a noun. But why does it make a difference to the meaning? Is it that 'a comprehension' is designed to keep children quiet in class whereas 'to comprehend' might involve much more noise and, heaven forbid, the exchange of genuinely different views?

- In recent years the British press have concerned themselves with the question of literacy standards and, indeed, we have the National Literacy Strategy (NLS) funded by the government. But what does it mean to be 'literate'? Consider how a definition of what a literate person is has changed across time. To be able to sign your name at your wedding or to read Latin were formerly signs of literacy in Britain. And how do definitions of literacy differ from culture to culture? Is knowing the Koran by heart a literate event for you? If the very term 'literacy' itself is loaded, contextual and disputable, so surely is the NLS.

- Why are teachers expected to develop children's use of standard English? Is it a form of classroom bullying in the sense that it penalises children from homes in localities where to say 'we was going' or 'I din do nuttin' is perfectly normal? And how then would you account for the Guyanese poet, John Agard (1983) who wrote a children's poetry book called *I Din Do Nuttin* in non-standard English? How could you understand why the black American academic Geneva Smitherman (1973/1980) has chosen to write some of her academic papers in what she calls 'standard Black English' with a grammar that is certainly not 'white British standard English'?

In these cases, in order to explain how language works, one would need to move outside a narrow focus of defining it just in terms of adjectives, verbs, words and sentences. For example, if you wanted to explain Smitherman's language choices you wouldn't find the answer in just the syntactical patterning of 'Black English':

> Ain nothin in a long time lit up the English teaching profession like the current hassle over Black English … And we black folks is not gon take all that weight, for no one has empirically demonstrated that linguistic/stylistic features of BE (Black English) impede educational progress in communication skills, or any other area of cognitive learning.
>
> (Smitherman, 1973: 158)

Her use of Black English is significant because not only is it used to construct and convey academic discourse but also because it acts simultaneously as a mechanism for *acculturation*, a vehicle for achieving group identity and as a protest against the power of standard English. Her decision, in essence, is political and her choices are not simply linguistic. One more example: if you were to look at advertisements to attract candidates into the teaching profession you might come across those for Fast Track applicants. They're aimed at people who already have a good degree, possibly working in another career but excited at the prospect of becoming a teacher. The key words, like 'ambition', 'rapid promotion' and 'extra incentives', that the adverts contain, link to the political climate that gave rise to the initiative. Its roots are in Margaret Thatcher's insistence that the state be rolled back to allow market forces into education and Tony Blair's plans to 'modernise' the teaching profession (see Chapter 7). In other words, these lexical items have had a very potent history in sociocultural practice and ideology.

LINGUISTIC THEORIES

Many theoretical models have grappled with the implications of these ideas and have aimed to expose the links between ideology and language. For example, the linguist Benjamin Whorf, in the Sapir–Whorf hypothesis, claimed that language embodied world views:

> ... thinking itself is in a language – in English, in Sanskrit, in Chinese. And every language is a vast pattern-system, different from others, in which are culturally ordained forms and categories by which the personality not only communicates, but also analyses nature, notices or neglects types of relationship and phenomena, channels his reasoning, and builds the house of his consciousness.
>
> (Whorf, 1956: 252)

By looking at Hopi, an American Indian language of Arizona, and by comparing the world views of these people with the dominant western view at the time, Whorf concluded with three propositions. First, the structure of the language one uses habitually influences the manner in which one understands the world; second, that the picture of the universe shifts from tongue to tongue; and third, that people with different languages, from different times and occupying different spaces, have different world views. Linguists since Whorf have developed the position and proposed that different world views exist *within* the same language. Theorists like Lakoff (1973), Spender (1980), Tannen (1990) and Cameron (2000) have been concerned with issues of language and gender and have suggested that we learn language as men or women and that this affects the way men and women see the world. Spender, for example, argued that women were subjugated by what she called *Man Made Language* (1980) – that 'chairman' rather than 'chair' for example, was indicative of sexism. Tannen (1990) developed a theory of difference that suggested that the two languages were neither better nor worse than the other, but in so doing may have minimised the issues of engendered power and the consequences of difference.

'Critical linguistics' was a term born in the 1970s and 1980s and associated with theorists like Gunter Kress (Kress and Tew, 1978; Kress 1985), Roger Fowler (1988) and Robert Hodge (Hodge and Kress, 1993). One of its legacies has been a linguistic toolbox of techniques for investigating language, such as 'passivisation', 'nominal-isation', 'transitivity', 'modality' and 'lexical selection'. *Passivisation* we've already touched on when I talked of the pen and of my choices of response. We've seen that it concerns the grammatical arrangement of a sentence, that it is a structure in which the affected participant or thing is brought to the important subject position in the sequence before the verb, and where the agent, relegated to the background, can be – optionally – deleted. In short, it's a device that allows a speaker or writer to emphasise their priorities.

Nominalisation   This was mentioned when I suggested teachers giving pupils comprehension work. It involves using a noun, or noun phrase, instead of a verb. So instead of saying that 'The child *was smacked* by teacher X' the nominalised form would be '*The smacking* of a child.' This representation of events has the effect of recasting the description of a process as a static condition, as a thing, a name, a noun. Although it is quite usual in certain types of genre to do this, as in a scientific text book or a newspaper report, nominalisation might also be seen as a device to obscure the times at which actions took place, the actors involved, as well as people's attitudes to them.

Transitivity   Also called 'transactivity' works like this: 'Sarah works hard at weekends, *marking* her pupils' books, *planning* next week's maths lessons, *writing* reports for the children, as well as looking after her own two children.' Here the process focuses clearly on the subject, Sarah, as the actor. The clauses contain processes done by her to something or somebody and involve the active voice. Thus our heroine, Sarah – the agent – is in the subject position of the sentence, followed by the processes undergone – the verbs – followed by the affected entities – the objects. In short, transitive verbs require an object upon which to be *active*. On the other hand intransitive verbs don't require this, as in 'an hour elapsed' or 'the boy sleeps'. In a passive sentence the transitive clause can be easily supplanted by an intransitive one, and so, again, we find the opportunity for the concealment of agency, time and place, e.g. 'Headteacher shot' rather than 'Enraged ex-pupil shoots headteacher in school playground.'

Modality   As we've already touched upon in the discussion of 'tu' and 'vous', this represents the interpersonal aspect of communication and, in this case, is signified by the choice of pronouns. Modality describes the way speakers or writers display their attitude towards themselves, their audience or their subject matter. For example, depending on the relationship you wish to strike with me, you might call me anything – 'Howard', 'Howie', 'Gibby', 'Mr G.', 'Dr Gibson', 'mate' – depending on the degree of formality, intimacy, friendliness, respect or dislike you may wish to convey. Here modality is established in the choice of noun, but it could equally be in the choice of verb phrase: 'It's *very likely that* the government will allow universities to extend their fees' or 'The government *must* extend the fee structure' or 'Universities *really ought* to think more clearly about fees.'

Lexical selection   This relates not to sentence grammar but to the particular words chosen. For example, in the last paragraph I could have referred to 'headmaster' or even 'headmistress' rather than 'headteacher'. Would this have been significant in terms of gender implications? Again, is a student finding difficulty with 'their' assignment – 'his' assignment? 'her' assignment? – best described as 'combating', 'fighting' or 'tussling' with the problem. If the overtones of militarism are too resonant for you, try and find your own word that isn't so ideologically loaded. Again, was the child 'patted', 'tapped', 'beaten', 'rapped', 'hit', 'knocked', 'banged', thumped', 'whacked', 'bopped', 'punched', 'slapped', 'struck', 'thrashed', 'clouted' or 'cuffed' by the teacher at break time? Your choice in this and other situations is significant. When assembling your thoughts about the children who took time out of school to protest against the war in Iraq (Bloom, 2003), consider that your 'militant teacher' may be someone else's 'unprofessional', just as their 'freedom fighter' might be your 'peaceful demonstrator' (see Chapter 4).

In the 1980s critical linguistics raised the idea that language choices encoded sociocultural or ideological imprints. But it wasn't that simple. There were theoretical limitations. Just as there can be no single reading of Shakespeare, it needed acknowledging that there could be no *one* reading of a newspaper or of a politician's speech. It became clear that texts were interpretable in different ways and linguistics lacked theoretical clarity in this respect. Social meanings were not transparent or obvious and some questioned the assumption that ideology could be interpreted from textual features alone. Because there were no rules for relating linguistic features to specific ideological functions, the term 'militant' used above, for example, could be employed in a pejorative sense by conservatives, but equally by others as a term of solidarity and endearment. Similarly, the use of modal auxiliary verbs was said to be ambiguous without details of the social or pragmatic context in which they are used. Consider, for example, all the possible readings of 'the lecturer *must be* in his office' – that could imply dereliction of duty, laziness or momentary vanishment. Only a theoretical concern for the social production, consumption and interpretation of texts outside their syntactical features could make these textual meanings understandable. Thus in the 1990s it became generally understood that critical linguistics needed to develop a more coherent social theory, and critical discourse analysis (CDA) attempted to do just this.

Critical discourse analysis

Fairclough's three-stage framework placed a spoken or written *text* at the centre, with what he called 'discourse practice' surrounding it, and 'social practice' surrounding the whole. Fairclough suggested that the surrounding social practice would leave traces or clues as to its potential meaning (Fairclough, 1995: 33). Thus a text, either written or spoken, might be analysed for such things as:

- aspects of *turn taking*, as in a college interview
- whether men use *tag questions* less than women in seminar groups
- who is using *passive sentences* in university tutorials
- who is controlling *the topics* of conversation in lecturer/student or teacher/pupil interactions
- the use of *archaic vocabulary* – like 'thine', 'wireless' or 'frock', 'particulars', 'stipendiary' or 'lodge'.

This descriptive stage pushes into the interpretative stage. Discourse practice is concerned with the mediation between those who produce and those who interpret a text. Think about the possibility that the same text can be written (or spoken) by one person with a certain intent, but read (or heard) quite differently by another. So, for example, the word 'bugger' shouted by a pupil at a teacher in a school corridor would need a quite different interpretation than the same word whispered by the same pupil at a punctured bicycle tyre. Indeed the word 'bugger' itself has a variety of meanings that depend upon a variety of discourse practices, on when, where and how the word is situated. History changes this, and those who hear, read or write texts constantly shift their judgement about the meaning that they ascribe to such textual features.

The explanation for this social, cultural and historical variability is the third part of Fairclough's framework. The broader sociocultural backdrop is concerned with the political significance of the discourse. So, to extend the example given above, the word 'bugger' shouted by a pupil at a teacher will probably be read as a linguistic infringement of the teacher's authority. On the other hand, the muttering of the same word to an inanimate tyre in the school's bike shed cannot share the same meaning, for institutional power is not being challenged. And if it seems *natural* that schools give weight to one interpretation – that it is always wrong to swear at teachers – then questions soon arise as to the *nature* of schooling and institutional power itself. For example, if a child swears at home without apparent condemnation, is the institution right to preference certain types of children with certain types of language? If the child actually uttered the word with good humour, would the teacher be wrong in choosing to read it as confrontational? Indeed, should teachers and schools be empowered to act upon these judgements at all? Schools like Summerhill, for instance, embrace alternative power structures and seem not to censure such language (see Chapter 12). In other words, there are political and moral choices being made here and Fairclough's model would urge us to enquire what they are and to investigate who controls them and why. Of course we won't necessarily agree about our judgements and interpretations, but this is different from pretending that existing sociocultural practices and power bases are *natural* and unchangeable.

CDA in educational contexts

To illustrate how CDA works in educational contexts there is a brief outline of three students' studies in this final section. Jane chose to develop an idea of Fairclough and did a CDA on the welcome pages of some very different university prospectuses. The idea was to see whether the institutions displayed any difference in the way they marketed their courses, or 'products', as she called them. She came to the conclusion that the 'elite institution' already had a positive image and that there was less need for it to employ the types of marketing approaches found in the other prospectuses, that instead of selling themselves their discourses seemed to involve highlighting their preferred applicant. This she linked with a discussion of the nature of advertisements for lecturers in the three institutions and how a spirit of self-promotion and competition – that would have been viewed as rather vulgar in former times – seemed naturalised in the two 'non-elite' universities. Her discussion also tried to account for the reason *why* universities today are required to market themselves competitively and positioned this historically as a change in ideology that was brought in by the move towards marketising education during the 1990s.

Simon looked at the way the National Literacy Strategy in primary schools had affected the way teachers talk to their pupils and so, having sought permission, tape-recorded some lessons. His texts showed the way teachers frequently employed the initiation-response-feedback communicative pattern outlined by Sinclair and Coulthard (1975) as the default mode of classroom exchange. He explained how teachers use questioning to establish what he argued was a power-base that inhibited more collaborative constructions of meaning, and then drew conclusions about the wider sociocultural significance of not making young learners more independent.

Nicky's study was called *A Critical Discourse Analysis of New Labour's Educational Philosophy* and took as one of its key texts Tony Blair's speech to the Labour Party Conference in 1997, the one where he famously talked of 'education, education, education'. Her analysis of it looked at the way modality was established through relational and expressive devices, how the speech used pronouns 'to assimilate Blair to his government' as she put it, and how 'the third way' was linked to the party's educational philosophy (see Chapter 7). As a linked text she then chose the *Additional Literacy Strategy [ALS] Handbook* (Department of Education and Employment [DfEE], 1999). The ALS was designed by the government to give resources to teachers to raise some pupils' attainment to the required national level. Having once been a classroom assistant employed to use the material before starting her degree, Nicky examined the reasons for the way the written text included a spoken, play-like script in order to teach the materials. She questioned such things as how conversation was mimicked, what types of interactions between teachers and pupils were deemed appropriate in such scripted teaching and, more importantly, who authored the material and whether teachers' professionalism was in question.

CONCLUSION

Wondering about the pen? No, I didn't go back to claim it. To be honest I got scared thinking about the language game I might need to play and decided it wasn't worth it. *Or here's another way …*

You may have wondered if I returned at a later date to reclaim that pen? The answer is 'no' for, upon reflection, I could never have considered it my rightful possession. (Two sentences, same propositional claims, different language, different intent.)

QUESTIONS FOR DISCUSSION

- In the *Times Educational Supplement*, find the headlines and make decisions about possible alternatives. Consider, for example, changing passive to active sentences, de-nominalising events, changing lexical preferences in order to highlight something different, altering the topic theme, and so on. What do your changes do?
- Have you been interviewed, possibly for a university place? Can you remember how the issue of (a) conversation and informality were assimilated with (b) the institutional power of the interviewer over you as interviewee, and how it

was resolved in the way you both used language? You might get permission to record a candidate at interview.

- A university tutor may pull you up for using an impersonal style in your assignment. Read Ivanic and Simpson (1992) and see if you agree with them that sometimes losing the identity of the person in academic writing can be economical but also dishonest, attributing personal views to the realm of timeless truths. Bringing back the 'I' in essays wouldn't be the same as a poor argument of course, but would you try it on principle? Are there benefits?

- Scan the *Times Higher Educational Supplement* for the way universities advertise (a) their courses and (b) for their staff. Are they all aggressively marketed and pitiably self-promotional, or does this depend on the school or faculty they represent? Does this depend on whether the university sees itself as an 'old' or 'new brick' establishment? Is there a history to this, and how is it all reflected in the language used? (see Chapter 3).

REFERENCES

Agard, J. (1983) *I Din Do Nuttin and Other Poems*, London: Methuen.

Bloom, A. (2003) 'Protests over war seen as truancy', *Times Educational Supplement*, 21 March, 2003.

Cameron, D. (2000) *Good to Talk? Living and Working in a Communication Culture*, London: Sage.

Department of Education and Employment [DfEE] (1999) *Additional Literacy Strategy Handbook*, London: DfEE.

Fairclough, N. (1995) *Critical Discourse Analysis: The Critical Study of Language*, London: Longman.

Fairclough, N. (2000a) *Language and Power*, 2nd edition, London: Longman.

Fairclough, N. (2000b) *New Labour, New Language?*, London: Routledge.

Fowler, R. (1988) 'Oral models in the press', in M. Maclure, T. Phillips and A. Wilkinson (eds) *Oracy Matters*, Milton Keynes: Open University Press.

Hodge, R. and Kress, G. (1993) *Language as Ideology*, 2nd edition, London: Routledge.

Ivanic, R. and Simpson, J. (1992) 'Who's who in academic writing', in N. Fairclough (ed.) *Critical Language Awareness*, London: Longman.

Kress, G. (1985) *Linguistic Processes in Sociocultural Practices*, Victoria, Australia: Deakin University Press.

Kress, G. and Trew, T. (1978) 'Ideological transformation of discourse; or how the *Sunday Times* got its message across', *Sociological Review*, 26(4): 755–6.

Lakoff, R. (1973) 'Language and women's place', *Language in Society*, 2: 45–80.

Sinclair, J.M. and Coulthard, R.M. (1975) *Towards an Analysis of Discourse: The English Used By Teachers and Pupils*, London: Oxford University Press.

Smitherman, G. (1973) *White English in Blackface, or Who Do I be?*, in L. Michaels and C. Ricks (eds) (1980) *The State of the Language*, Berkeley: University of California Press.

Spender, D. (1980) *Man Made Language*. London: Routledge and Kegan Paul.

Tannen, D. (1990) *You Just Don't Understand: Women and Men in Conversation*, New York: Ballantine Books.

Whorf, B.L. (1956) *Language, Thought and Reality: Selected Writings of Benjamin Lee Whorf*, (ed.) John B. Carroll, Cambridge, MA: The MIT Press.

RECOMMENDED READING

Cameron, D. (2000) *Good to Talk? Living and Working in a Communication Culture*, London: Sage.

Fairclough, N. (2000a) *Language and Power*, 2nd edition, London: Longman.

Fairclough, N. (2000b) *New Labour, New Language?*, London: Routledge.

Fowler, R. (1988) 'Oral models in the press', in M. Maclure, T. Phillips and A. Wilkinson (eds) *Oracy Matters*, Milton Keynes: Open University Press.

Fairclough's work isn't easy, but it's worth the effort. Start with the new introduction to his *Language and Power* and then look at *New Labour, New Language* if you're interested in politicians' rhetorical style. Look to Fowler 'Oral models in the press' for the still relevant explanation of why some tabloids seem to speak to us as their friend rather than 'simply' report the news. And if the links between gender and language interest you, look at Deborah Cameron's work, especially *Good to Talk*, for her chapter on 'Schooling spoken discourse'.

17 Knowledge and Learning in Art and Design

June Bianchi

> Artists … show us aspects of the world we had not noticed; they release us from the stupor of the familiar. The process they employ is called defamiliarization. In ethnography it's called making the familiar strange and the strange familiar.
>
> (Eisner, 2003: 53)

In this chapter we explore notions of what constitutes art and what kinds of meanings it holds, as well as discussing what kind of learning takes place within current art and design education. We will consider the significance of the cultural and social context within artistic production and consumption. We will also explore the role of art and design education in disseminating cultural and social values in education, celebrating both the diversity and the shared elements of human experience expressed through visual practice.

EXPLORING THE SIGNIFICANCE OF ART IN OUR LIVES

Consider a world without art

We start our exploration of the nature of learning in art and design with an activity specially designed for conspiracy theorists:

Imagine waking up in a world where aliens have landed. Unusually, they aren't interested in colonising the world or harvesting our vital organs. This is a species of intergalactic connoisseurs. All they want is our art, all of it! So what will we have to relinquish?

Initially you mentally take down treasured paintings from your walls, close the national galleries, remove all public sculpture from our cities and country parks. But what about the other artworks in our homes? The woven kelim brought back from holiday, the ceramic vase, the photographic print with stylish text advertising a recent arts festival, the poetry book selected for its illustrations. Where will the alien handover end? Consider other art forms you enjoy: jewellery, fashion and interior design, film, theatre design, digital graphics.

You are probably considering what we understand by the term 'art' and whether you would categorise all of the activities I have mentioned as art, or whether you would classify some of them under other headings: 'craft', or perhaps 'design'.

Make a list of activities you would include within the category of art. What additional activities would you include within the categories of craft and design? Consider what criteria you used to place an activity in one or other category. Were some activities difficult to categorise? Did some fit into more than one category?

As well as asking the vexed question 'What is art?' this activity was also designed to illustrate the significance of art and design in our lives. You may be a practising artist or a regular consumer of art through national, international and local venues or you may have no specific interest in art. But you are unlikely to get through one day without being affected by the work of an artist, craft-worker or designer. Surrounded by the products of visual practice of all kinds, you will have a high level of visual literacy and (assuming you have visual facility) you probably make regular choices based on your visual taste.

Your response to this activity would certainly be informed by a range of factors which have shaped your visual experience:

- perceptions and expectations of visual culture through your cultural and social background
- previous experience, breadth of access and attitude to visual art
- your art and design education.

ART, CRAFT AND DESIGN: CULTURE AND CONTEXTS

> Art is a method of opening up areas of feeling rather than merely an illustration of an object
>
> (Bacon, 1952: 620)

As the artist Francis Bacon suggests, art frequently extends beyond describing the physical universe. It also represents personal feelings and perspectives. While some type of artistic practice is prevalent in cultural experience across a diversity of time and place, we cannot necessarily ascribe equivalent meaning to art forms from different contexts; we rather need to examine it in relation to its setting. Art is not an entirely individualistic practice; rather, it functions within social structures and conceptual frameworks, presenting a viewpoint informed by socio-cultural value systems as well as those of the individual artist. 'If art contributes to, among other things, the way we view the world and shape social relations then it does matter whose image of the world it promotes and whose interest it serves' (Searle, 2000: 37).

The form the artwork takes will be an amalgam of factors. It will be a response to environmental conditions, availability of materials and lifestyle; the availability of technical expertise and the potential for future development; the impact of accepted means of representation within the cultural context, as well as the artist's potential for creative production through personal vision. John Dewey (1934) believed that art 'expresses the life of a community'. Changes in environmental, social and cultural conditions, attitudes, beliefs and power structures are all reflected in the visual art production of that community.

In a cultural comparison across a range of artistic contexts we could find difference as well as cohesion. We could question whether there can be any commonality in our understanding of art. In some cultures there is no generic term for art and the discrete generic western hierarchies of art, craft and design are irrelevant. 'There is no old word in most of the thousand or so languages still spoken in Africa that will translate the word "art"' (Appiah, 1995: 24).

However, anthropologist Richard Anderson studied art across 11 world cultures. He suggests that it holds a common purpose across a range of contexts in the way it acts as a sign for cultural meaning, defining art as having a 'culturally significant meaning skilfully encoded in an affective, sensuous medium' (Anderson 1990: 238).

All Our Futures: Creativity, Culture and Education (National Advisory Committee on Creative and Cultural Education [NACCCE], 1999) advocates four central roles for cultural education, enabling young people to:

a)   recognize and understand their own cultural assumptions and values
b)   celebrate cultural diversity through contact with the attitudes, values and traditions of other cultures
c)   relate contemporary values to the historical processes and events that have shaped them
d)   understand the evolutionary nature of culture and the processes and potential for change.

(NACCCE, 1999: 48)

Studying artworks with these considerations in mind yields a richer, deeper seam of information and knowledge than focusing alone on the formal elements of constituent parts, appearance and structure. Instead of asking only 'how does it look?' we can ask also, '*how* and *why* does it look like this?' Art can be a signifier of social transitions. In traditional Aboriginal art, nomadic tribal culture produced sacred community artworks, which were records and expressions of Aboriginal life and belief, produced for the benefit of the whole community. Recently, individual artists have begun to produce easel paintings for sale and for personal status. This is a western art paradigm since the early Renaissance and is part of the breakdown of the traditional Aboriginal way of life. There is now the *commodification* of Aboriginal art – the international art market directs the production and sale of artworks within the Aboriginal community. It would seem that the role of art and design is neither singular nor fixed; rather that it is shifting, evolutionary and dependent on its socio-cultural context.

The following is a short list of the potential functions of art and design across a range of cultural and historical contexts:

•   to describe and illustrate
•   to generate aesthetic qualities
•   to express emotions
•   to communicate concepts, ideas, beliefs and ideologies
•   to explore and innovate techniques and means of representation
•   to inspire and entertain
•   to challenge and provoke.

Of the roles listed, the first two are perhaps the most widely accepted. A reluctance to incorporate a wider range of visual creativity leads to a preference for predominantly decorative and illustrative art forms using established means of production. This can be seen in the popular media preference for traditional representation and a disdain for innovation and experiment. Contemporary western art is frequently regarded as problematic and difficult, characterised by ceaseless innovation leading to unfamiliar forms which challenge perceptions of beauty. Whether or not all contemporary art appeals to your own taste and sensibilities, it deals with a wide spectrum of artistic roles. It addresses artistic, philosophical and cultural issues: formal and aesthetic elements, social and political concerns, notions of identity, our relationship with the environment, issues of equity and justice.

Comparing portraits across cultural and historical contexts

Make a selection of portraits from a range of cultural and historical contexts and consider in each case what you think the artist's intentions were in creating the image. To what extent was the artist fulfilling any of the roles outlined?

Here are some suggestions for artworks and artists you could study, although you can make your own selection:

- A range of portraits from diverse cultural sources: Hellenistic or Roman; medieval depictions of Christ; fifteenth- and sixteenth-century Renaissance portraitists such as Leonardo da Vinci and Raphael; seventeenth-century Mughal painting; eighteenth-century Japanese woodblock prints; nineteenth-century Impressionists such as Berthe Morisot or Mary Cassatt; twentieth-century portraits by artists such as Gwen John and David Hockney.
- Self-portraits from historical periods: seventeenth century (Rembrandt); nineteenth-century Post-Impressionists (Van Gogh); twentieth century (Frida Kahlo, Cindy Sherman, Antony Gormley and Tracey Emin).
- Court and society portraits: ancient Egyptian pharaonic portraits; sixteenth-century Benin bronzes, seventeenth century (Holbein); eighteenth century (Gainsborough and Rosalba Carriera); twentieth century (Andy Warhol).
- Genre images of everyday life: sixteenth century (Pieter Bruegel); seventeenth century (Frans Hals); eighteenth century (Hogarth); eighteenth and nineteenth century (Japanese *ukiyo-e*); nineteenth century (Toulouse Lautrec); twentieth century (George Grosz).

READING THE SIGNS: MAKING SENSE OF ART

Having looked at a range of artwork from different cultural and historical contexts you may have an appreciation and understanding of some pieces while others may seem alienating or even incomprehensible to your personal aesthetic. So does access to works of art, craft and design depend entirely on taste informed by familiarity of design, concept and purpose? Or is it possible to appreciate artworks despite the challenge of their *iconography*, or means of representation, and their sometimes abstruse meaning? Gaining a deeper understanding of 'what makes an artwork tick' may still result in the conclusion, 'It's not for me,' but this can be a more informed decision based on awareness of its meaning and the intentions of the artist within a specific social setting.

Art invariably tells a number of explicit and implicit stories informed by its context:

- the declared subject of the work
- its means of representation – media, technique, style
- the ideas and attitudes it conveys both implicitly and explicitly – culture and ethnicity, social class, hierarchies, attitudes to gender.

Just as the artist creates from within a socio-cultural context, so the audience views from one. The 'innocent eye' does not exist and all our judgements as creators or viewers of art are an interaction between the social milieu and our own inner vision and perception. A number of critical approaches have been developed to facilitate a deeper access to artwork beyond the initial 'What does it look like?' and 'Is this to our taste?' Different approaches will ask different questions or evoke a range of responses and information from the same artwork.

Rod Taylor's critical approach to art has become a key methodology within art education for generating discussion and extending knowledge (Thistlewood, 1990). It is based on an exploration of four key elements in artistic production: content, form, process and mood.

Taylor's method of analysis

1   Content: What is the work about? Does it have a narrative or theme? Was the subject matter observed, remembered or imagined?
2   Form: How has the work been arranged? How are shapes, lines, colour, texture and forms used?
3   Process: What materials, tools, processes, and techniques were used? How was the work made?
4   Mood: Does the work affect you emotionally? How does it evoke or express a mood?

Despite its popularity as a means of extending understanding of art, Taylor's approach has been criticized as reductionist in its visual emphasis with inadequate attention paid to exploring the socio-cultural context of the piece. Alison Bancroft (1995) suggests an approach to critical studies based on three levels of understanding:

1   Level One: Explore personal response to the artwork.
2   Level Two: Research information on the artist, school of art, style, techniques used.
3   Level Three: Extend understanding of historical and socio-cultural context of the work as well as studying various critical approaches to it.

We only have to study news coverage of a prominent or controversial exhibition in order to realise that critical response to artworks carries its own agenda and orientation. The now traditional media furore over the latest 'Turner Prize Shocker' will be exacerbated or mitigated by the particular political and cultural slant of the writer and publication. Certainly reviews in *Modern Painters*, *The Times*, *The Guardian* or *The Sun* are likely to be different and their editorial will be as much about the values they ascribe to contemporary art as about the visual qualities of the work.

Just as a work of art is produced within the context of its social environment, so does its critical reception present a particular viewpoint informed by art historical approaches, which have their roots in philosophical ideas. Neither art's production nor its interpretation occupy neutral territory and it would be erroneous to think that any critical approach could be free of value judgements or ideological content.

The methods of understand and interpreting art all make assumptions and have underlying ideological perspectives. For example, the Eurocentric viewpoint of art historians such as E.H. Gombrich (1989) views art as *western* art, establishing a sequence of artistic innovation and development, and primarily viewing non-western art only in terms of its impact on western art movements. Conversely an internationalist or post-colonialist approach reappraises the artistic canon (the set of accepted works) to include work of a wider ethnic and cultural sensibility, recognising the ethnocentricity of much art theory. Modernist critic Clement Greenberg (1961) considered the main content of art to be its formal elements, such as colour, line, structure, form and composition. Other writers have focused on its social historical context – the social or political conditions of production and consumption – or on the relevance of gender issues on the artist and viewer.

So an awareness of the various possible interfaces which occur between artwork and viewer is useful in your own responses to both works of art and critical writing on art. This would *not* be in order to obtain a definitive, objective reading of the work of art, but rather to access particular aspects of interest with an understanding that the critical approach adopted will inform your view.

Applying a critical approach to analysis of an artwork

Select one of the portraits you have already studied and reconsider it in the light of either Taylor's or Bancroft's methodology of analysis.

Consider how the artwork could be discussed from the standpoint of one of the critical perspectives mentioned. Focus on either a formal element of the work or on a particular approach to its production.

- How did the critical approach you applied affect your reading of the artwork?
- Was some information more easily accessed through that approach?
- Would you vary the critical approach you used to analyse specific artworks, and what would inform your choice?

THE ROLE OF ART, CRAFT AND DESIGN IN EDUCATION

Visual art is pivotal in offering opportunities for creative development and facilitating an enquiring approach to the world. The NACCCE (1999) report recommends that art and design should be given parity with other subjects within an 'arts education' discipline area of the curriculum. The report advocates a far greater emphasis on creative and cultural education for Curriculum 2000 and beyond, regarding it as instrumental in evolving an educational approach to future living: '… creative activity can itself be regarded as a form of learning particularly suited to the testing and complex conditions which will face us all in the twenty-first century' (NACCCE, 1999: 92).

While everyone may not continue to produce artwork throughout their entire life, we will all participate in visual practice through the various avenues we have already discussed. So an art education needs to encompass critical as well as practical processes. As psychologist and art educationalist Eliot Eisner (1989: 17), states 'There are four major things that people do with art. They make it. They look at it. They understand its place in culture over time. They make judgements about its quality.'

Provision for these aspects of art practice has been addressed within the National Curriculum Order for art and design for pupils from Key Stage 1 to Key Stage 3. The Attainment Target, 'Knowledge, skills and understanding' requires critical investigation and an exploration of media and techniques. The single Attainment Target seeks to establish good practice as the integration of knowing and experiencing, emerging from a process of investigation, research, experimentation, evaluation and development. Frequently the practical aspect of art education will emerge from an experience of art, craft and design gained from seeing primary source material (original art works) and secondary source material (reproductions). This integration of critical and practical skills, knowledge and understanding is a feature of good practice.

The National Curriculum for Art and Design (Department of Education and Employment [DfEE], 2000) provides a blueprint for a model of process-based investigation with the range of materials and techniques to be taught at all key stages. Suggested processes are: painting, collage, print-making, digital media, textiles, ceramics, sculpture. No individual artists are specified for study, but there is a recommendation that pupils at all key stages be taught about a range of artists, craftspeople and designers from different times and cultures. Although this educational model appears far less restrictive than that of many other subject areas, its inception in 2000 was greeted as contentious by the main representative body for art education, The National Society for Education in Art and Design. Writing in its *Journal of Art and Design Education (JADE)*, Swift and Steers (1997: 7) criticise its incipient uniformity and call for: 'a postmodern view of art in education with an emphasis on difference, plurality and independence of mind ... for more decision-making and autonomy for teachers and learners within a climate that emphasises and expects enquiry, experiment and creative opportunity.'

Continuing the debate after three years of implementation of the revised Order for art, Steers (2003) challenges the whole notion of a National Curriculum:

> While I believe that art and design should be a statutory *entitlement* for all pupils during their years of compulsory schooling, I am by no means convinced that the subject is best served by a statutory order; one prescribed curriculum restricts choice.
>
> (Steers, 2003: 23)

The Curriculum Orders could be viewed as expansive enough to encompass diversity of response, and examples of highly innovative artwork can be seen in many educational settings. Yet the limitations of a standardised, orthodox approach to art education criticized by Swift and Steers can also be observed in some schools. The National Curriculum's process-based structure can provide a starting point for creative and imaginative possibilities, but can become a didactic route towards predictable and repetitive outcomes. The decisive factor is the quality and vision of the teacher interpreting the Order's requirements: the department which encourages creativity and innovation; the school which recognises the centrality of art and design within a holistic education.

The emphasis given to the core subjects in the curriculum has had a detrimental impact upon allocation of time and resources on the arts within the timetables of both primary and secondary schools. Art and design is also designated as a means to extend learning across other areas including interpersonal and intrapersonal aspects, social, moral, cultural and spiritual development, key skills (such as numeracy, literacy, information and communications technology, problem solving) and other aspects of knowledge (such as thinking skills, sustainable development, enterprise). This should be welcomed as addressing holistic educational development with art practice. Conversely it can be viewed as another distraction from the limited time and significance awarded to visual art within the curriculum provision. Likewise, the imperative to develop an inclusive curriculum which addresses all pupils' needs could be regarded either as utopianism or as a vital impetus to communicate an essential subject in a form accessible to each child.

Evaluating the National Curriculum Orders for art and design

Find out as much as you can about the Orders for art and design. You can access the Orders for art and design on the National Curriculum website (www.qca.org.uk).

Research the implementation of the Orders for art and design by studying children's art in a range of educational settings and through art educational Internet sites.

Focus on a Key Stage that interests you: Key Stage 1 (5–7 years); Key Stage 2 (7–11 years); Key Stage 3 (11–14 years).

- Do you think the orders provide a creative structure for art education or can they promote a narrow orthodoxy?
- Do you feel that using art to address the core curriculum is an asset or a distraction in provision for art and design in the curriculum?

Ways of seeing, ways of knowing: widening access to visual art education

An inclusive art and design curriculum which addresses all pupils' needs within the full spectrum of age and ability requires an awareness of the specific stages of children's development. Viktor Lowenfeld's (1947) theory of artistic stages of development remains highly influential in establishing expectations of children's artistic processes, albeit within a western context. Lowenfeld outlines suggested parameters of ages characterised by specific types of artistic practice:

- Scribbling stage 2–4 years: beginnings of self expression
- Preschematic stage 4–7 years: first representational attempts
- Schematic stage 7–9 years: the achievement of a form concept
- Stage of dawning realism /gang stage 9–12 years: the development of realism
- Pseudonaturalistic stage 12–14 years: the age of reasoning
- Adolescent stage 14–17 years: the period of decision.

From early adolescence Lowenfeld suggests that the child would orientate towards a predominantly either *visual* or *haptic* approach to artistic expression. A visually orientated child would focus on observation and analysis in both artistic perception and production, while the haptic child would respond through touch – tactile and kinaesthetic stimuli. An inclusive curriculum would provide opportunities for working in both modes, giving weight to the developing artist's wish to produce and appreciate artwork which is both expressive and affective as well as descriptive and representational.

Inclusion welcomes diversity and we should not privilege certain types of learning over others. The emphasis on developing logical, deductive and sequential thinking over intuitive, expressive response has been characterised as the dominance of left brain over right brain functioning. In *Drawing on the Right Side of the Brain*, Betty Edwards (1986) argues that the left/right brain hierarchy works against full access to the fluid, spontaneous, creative expressivity which we are all capable of. She suggests a series of artistic exercises to stimulate right brain processing.

If an inclusive curriculum is to be more than political rhetoric it should recognise and incorporate provision for a diversity of learning needs: social and cultural environmental considerations; cognitive, motor, neurological factors; emotional needs; preferred learning styles. In facilitating inclusive approaches to art education, projects can be set up which establish creative partnerships between diverse participants:

- the spectrum of educational providers from early years to higher education
- galleries and artists
- arts and cultural agencies.

The following case study gives an example of such a pluralist approach which addresses a diverse catchment of age, ability and need.

Case study: *House of Cards* sculpture trail 2002

The project was based around an exhibition 'House of Cards' by the women paper-artists' collective PaperWeight, held at the Michael Tippet Centre Gallery, Bath Spa University College in October–November 2002. The sculpture trail was planned as an exhibition which presented paper as a creative medium exploring the theme 'House of Cards' in both two- and three-dimensional formats. PaperWeight artists produced sculptures and reliefs which interpreted the playing card imagery with humour, drama and a range of cultural references. The project developed through the following stages:

1   Secondary Postgraduate Certificate in Education (PGCE) art and design trainee-teachers visited the exhibition, researched the cultural uses and iconography of cards and produced their own sculptures on the 'House of Cards' theme, using materials suitable for outdoor installation – wire, withies, plaster, textiles, plastic, etc. as well as organic materials available from the site. The trainees also worked with General Certificate in Secondary Education (GCSE) and post-16 pupils in their schools to present the project's theme and initiate research and preparation for the second stage of the project.

2   GCSE and post-16 pupils from local schools and colleges spent a day visiting the exhibition and the sculpture trail and, supported by the trainee teachers,

producing their own three-dimensional pieces which were also installed on the sculpture trail.

3   Primary-aged children with autistic spectrum disorders from a local specialist school spent a day with the trainee teachers exploring the exhibition and sculpture trail and producing artwork as part of the trail.

4   The sculpture trail featured in the local press and was open to the public.

The project was conceived as educationally inclusive, providing opportunities for generating wider access to both the experience of gallery-visiting and potential for artistic response across a diverse educational span. Both the positive verbal feedback and the exciting outcomes created by participants demonstrated that an exhibition can be viewed and responded to at a level appropriate to viewers' age, ability and experience, providing a focus for developing visual literacy in relation to concepts, ideas and technical approaches.

CONCLUSION

An inclusive art and design curriculum will be a pluralist one with opportunities for synthesis between the critical and practical domains, providing for all pupils:

* provision of a range of artistic media and techniques
* experience of a broad visual, cultural and conceptual framework
* exposure to 'cultural capital' across age, ability and socio-cultural catchment.

Access to original artwork, to the diverse cultural settings where it can be experienced, and to the materials and ideas that generate new visual forms, are the entitlement of all within an inclusive art educational practice.

REFERENCES

Anderson, R. (1990) *Calliope's Sisters: A Comparative Study of Philosophies of Art*, Englewood Cliffs, NJ: Prentice Hall.

Appiah, K.A. (1995) 'Why Africa, why art?', in T. Phillips (ed.) *Africa: The Art of a Continent*, London: Royal Academy.

Bacon, F. (1952) 'Statements, *Time* Magazine New York', in H.B. Chipp (ed.) (1968) *Theories of Modern Art*, Berkely, CA: University of California Press.

Bancroft, A. (1995) 'What do dragons think about?' *Journal of Art and Design Education*, 41(1): 21–31.

Dewey, J. (1934) 'Art as experience', in C. Freeland (ed.) (2001) *But is it Art?* Oxford: Oxford University Press.

DfEE (2000) *National Curriculum for Art and Design*, London: DfEE.

Edwards, B. (1986) *Drawing on the Right Side of the Brain*, Glasgow: Fontana/Collins.

Eisner, E. (1989) 'Structure and magic in discipline-based art education', in D. Thistlewood (ed.) *Critical Studies in Art and Design Education*, London: Longman.

Eisner, E. (2003) 'Concerns and aspirations for qualitative research in the new millennium', in N. Addison and L. Burgess (eds) *Issues in Art and Design Education*, London: RoutledgeFalmer.

Gombrich. E.H. (1989) *The Story of Art*, London: Phaidon Press.

Greenberg. C. (1961) *Art and Culture: Critical Essays*, Boston: Beacon Press.

Lowenfeld, V. (1947) *Creative and Mental Growth*, New York: Collier-Macmillan.

NACCCE (1999) *All our Futures: Creativity, Culture and Education*, London: DfEE Publications.

Searle, A. (2000) 'Art Guardian weekend', in R. Hickman (ed.) *Art Education 11–18*, London: Continuum.

Steers, J. (2003) 'Art and design in the UK: the theory gap', in N. Addison and L. Burgess (eds) *Issues in Art and Design Education*, London: RoutledgeFalmer.

Swift, J. and Steers, J. (1999) 'A manifesto for art in schools', *Journal of Art and Design Education (JADE)*, 18(1): 7–13.

Thistlewood, D. (1990) *Issues in Design Education*, London: Longman.

RECOMMENDED READING

Addison, N. and Burgess, L. (eds) *Issues in Art and Design Education*, London: RoutledgeFalmer. A good introduction to the current issues in Art Education.

Lowenfeld, V. (1947) *Creative and Mental Growth*, New York: Collier-Macmillan. This is old, but still the standard text on developmental growth in children's art.

NACCCE (1999) *All our Futures: Creativity, Culture and Education*, London: DfEE Publications. This report, commissioned by the government, gives a strong account of the possibilities for creativity in education.

18 The Humanities in Education

Meg Gomersall

The main points in this chapter are:
*   definitions of 'the humanities'
*   the contested nature of knowledge in history and geography
*   education for the future.

WHAT DO WE MEAN BY THE HUMANITIES?

Mind mapping of students' thoughts about the humanities reveals a diversity of ideas that generally are linked by a common conceptual framework. These present a view of the humanities that is based on subject areas such as history, geography, religious education, psychology and sociology; that is, subjects that are concerned with various aspects of human existence and experience. While all these subjects address human experience in different ways, this chapter concentrates on the contributions which history and geography can make to the humanities curriculum.

Beddis (1995) defines the humanities in terms of developing understanding, knowledge, skills and values in the context of learning about 'human beliefs, experiences and behaviour, and the expression of these'. In his definition, humanities education is concerned with the following:

> It is about the past – as things were; the present – as things are; the future – what things are likely to be and what they might/ought to be. It is about individual experience, about groups and nations and the whole human experience. It is concerned with the immediate and local, and with the distant and global. It is concerned with the relationships between people, between people and the environment and the relationship of people to their spiritual worlds.

> (Beddis, 1995: Frontispiece)

Not 'subjects' as such then, rather disciplines, and the models of thinking they offer in seeking to understand human experiences in the past and present and in attempts to project such understanding into the future. Humanities should not be teaching about the past (history) and people and places in the present (geography) as bodies of knowledge to be ingested and remembered. Instead, our first purpose is to develop understanding of the nature of the subjects and the investigative and critical thinking skills at the heart of the two disciplines. While not explicitly including other contributory disciplines such as religious education, the methodological concepts common to both disciplines enable an engagement with cause, motivation and consequence, including the significance of spiritual concerns, values and beliefs within human experiences in the past and present.

Our second purpose is to support the development of *metacognitive* skills; that is, being able to reflect on one's own learning through analysis and evaluation of the learning processes of the work undertaken. This also enables students to recognise the rich opportunities for learning offered by the humanities to any learner, whatever their age, and to be able critically to analyse the society they are living in.

We are at odds here with many across and within different countries and cultures, and governments often want to control the curriculum to affirm their political ideals. Nikita Khrushchev, Premier of the Communist Soviet Union (1958–64) once said, 'Historians are dangerous people. They are capable of upsetting everything' (DES, 1985: 1). Though this fear of potential subversion may be missing from the 'traditional' British view of history as a subject to be taught in schools, both geography and history frequently are perceived as subjects primarily concerned with the transmission of factual content.

HISTORY TEACHING AND LEARNING

With regard to history as it traditionally was taught in this country, there was no fear of any undermining of the social and political status quo and, unlike the case in many other countries, British governments did not seek to interfere with the history curriculum (see Chapter 7). On the contrary, there was a 'great tradition' (Sylvester, 1994: 1) or 'inherited consensus' that meant that the history taught was 'accepted' and non-controversial. Slater (2000) illustrated this in the following parody:

> Content was largely British, or rather Southern English; Celts looked in to starve, emigrate or rebel; the North to invent looms or work in the mills; abroad was of interest once it was part of the Empire; foreigners were either, sensibly allies, or rightly defeated. Skills – did we even use the word? – were mainly those of recalling accepted facts about famous dead Englishmen, and communicated in a very eccentric literary form, the examination length essay.
> (Slater, 2000: 1)

This may be a parody but it makes two essential points about the nature and purpose of history teaching and learning in Britain through much of the twentieth century. History was essentially non-controversial because it reflected and perpetuated an apparent homogeneity of class structure and patriarchy. It was Anglocentric and male dominated, with an axiomatic dismissal of anything beyond such parameters as being insignificant. Learning in history was, therefore, simply an exercise in the acquisition of the sort of 'knowledge' that was seen to be significant by dominant social groups.

My thinking about the nature of history in education began with my early experiences teaching Year 5 children in an inner-London primary school in the 1970s. In those pre-National Curriculum days, the history aspects of my 'topic' on Guy Fawkes and the gunpowder plot singularly failed to capture children's interest and I began to question why I was teaching it at all. My class was misbehaving because they did not enjoy history, so why was I teaching it? More seriously, what relevance did knowledge about a plot to overturn the English government in 1605 have to this group of children whose family origins lay in many different countries around the world? I was also uncomfortably conscious that, in trying to make the events accessible to children, I was oversimplifying causes and consequences and was thereby being intellectually dishonest. My class deserved better than this.

The history curriculum as 'inherited consensus' began to be challenged and 'new history' began to emerge in the 1970s. Influenced by the theories of educationalists such as Jerome Bruner, 'new' history sought to engage pupils with the skills and concepts at the heart of the discipline of history. They should be 'history detectives' actively investigating the past and the causes and consequences of changes, events and developments. Knowledge about the past remained important; the relationship between knowledge, understanding and skills is a symbiotic one, but learning through history was equally as important as learning about the past.

The content of the history curriculum also changed, influenced by the growth of multicultural communities and by an upsurge of interest in 'history from below' – the history of the working classes from their own perspectives – and in women's history. So, in my classroom, for example, we studied the events of World War II largely through oral witness. The school secretary's mother recounted her experiences of living through the blitz and Kavneet, one of my pupils, took great pride in inviting his grandfather into the classroom to tell us about his experiences of war in India. A genuine enthusiasm for history was generated and, most importantly, the children were developing knowledge, understanding and skills that were worth learning; asking and seeking answers to questions, debating, discussing, developing a respect for evidence and the sort of healthy scepticism that meant they did not always accept what they read or heard as being the truth – even when I said it!

Such approaches were not without their critics, particularly from the New Right. British (more accurately English) history had been abandoned in favour of 'multi-cultural' history, it was claimed; there was an obsession with skills, concepts and attitudes such as *empathy* and nothing of any worth was being taught in history class-rooms (Arthur and Phillips, 2000). The issues came to a head in the long and frequently heated debate that surrounded the development of the National Curriculum for History, with the History Working Party coming under pressure from Tory politicians to return to the 'inherited consensus' with its emphasis on English history and on knowledge acquisition. Prime Minister Margaret Thatcher, for example, was parti-cularly disapproving of what she saw as insufficient attention to British history, the failure to include assessment of historical knowledge and the inclusion of 'interpreta-tions' as a learning objective. Encouraging children to look for the points of view behind what is said or written about the past was not worth learning, in her view.

David Coulby (Chapter 4) refers to 'the nationalist versions of history and culture promoted by European curricular systems' with their associated 'triumphalistic' tones. That the history curriculum frequently has been, and may still be seen as, a means of promoting a shared sense of jingoistic nationhood is clear. Herein lies the vulnerability of history. The non-statutory guidelines to the first version of the National Curriculum for History made explicit that one of the purposes of teaching pupils to recognise different interpretations of the past was to further their understanding that history can be exploited for social and political purposes (DES, 1991). One might have laughed at John Major's 'back to basics' campaign in the early 1990s which invoked images of a 'golden age' when spinsters cycled to church and cricketers drank warm beer on the village green. But there is nothing to laugh about in the account of the battle of Vegkop, 1836, given in the official South African primary history text book published in 1980:

> The trekkers hurried into the laager … All around were the Matabele hordes, sharpening their assegais, killing animals and drinking the raw blood. Sarel Celliers offered up a prayer … After a fierce battle, the Matabele fled with their tails between their legs. The voortrekkers gave thanks to God for their deliverance.
>
> (cited in Wray and Lewis, 1997: 106)

Fed with a diet of such historical 'knowledge' – that the 'Matabele', more properly Ndebele, people were like savage animals, but the Afrikaaners were God fearing and brave – the children in South African schools were being groomed as citizens of an apartheid state, with the depiction of native peoples serving to justify the inequalities of oppression. What might have been the 'knowledge' about, for example, the history of trade unionism that would have been taught and assessed as being right or wrong in the English history curriculum if Margaret Thatcher had got her way? And to take this question wider: what content is *significant* in the history curriculum? Who should decide?

KNOWLEDGE IN GEOGRAPHY

Geography was also traditionally seen as being unproblematic and uncontroversial. The purpose of learning geography was to learn 'information about the world', as a set of immutable facts. But geographical 'facts', like historical 'facts', are vulnerable to distortion. There is, firstly, the danger of stereotyping through the presentation of inaccurate and over-generalised images of peoples and places through what Bale describes as a 'hunters of the frozen north' approach (Bale, 1987: 95). More seriously, sometimes explicitly and sometimes by default, place-creation by the state or by nationalist groups often involves creating positive images of 'our people' and 'our place' and negative views of others. This is most sharply evident at times of international and intra-national tensions: the images of the Soviet Union promoted by the *Reader's Digest* magazine in the era of the Cold War, for example, and those promoted by antagonistic factions in the segregated city of Belfast (Johnson, 1996). Even the supposedly objective information presented in world maps has its subjectivities, with subtle messages about the relative importance of my place as opposed to yours. Picture the map of the world that you are most familiar with. Where is Europe located in relation to the rest of the world? What subtle messages about the significance of Europe on the world stage are thereby conveyed? Now visualise a map that puts the African continent at centre stage. Where is Europe now in geographical position and in terms of implied global importance?

Images of the world are also constructed by popular media. I have encountered primary age pupils whose concepts of Germany in the 1980s were informed by their 'knowledge' that Hitler and his Nazi henchmen were still alive and in power. They knew this was true, because they saw this on television and read about it in comics. More seriously, analysis of the language employed by the British press during the first Gulf War shows the pervasive use of subtle persuasion to inform negative images of the Iraqi nation. 'Our' soldiers were 'boys, lads, cautious, confident, loyal and brave', while Iraqi soldiers were 'troops, hordes, cowardly, desperate, blindly obedient and fanatical' (Wray and Lewis, 1997: 106). One wonders what subliminal images of Iraq and of Moslems have been absorbed in the context of current conflicts. 'Knowledge is power' was the slogan of a radical working-class group in the nineteenth century, but power for what purpose? To manipulate? Or, to inform about commonalities of experience and *critically* to consider the causes and consequences of the events and developments that have shaped people's lives?

These and other issues prompted a number of developments in thinking about the nature of learning in geography in the 1970s and 1980s. Again, the work of Jerome Bruner was an important influence on changes in thinking, with the opportunities for progression in conceptual understanding and skill development offered in geography. Bruner was associated with the project 'Man: A Course of Study' and he highlighted the dimension of *values*. He argued that the intention goes beyond helping pupils to learn about human life as it is but in thinking also about improving society. As Bruner put it, 'What makes man human? And can he become more so?' (Campbell and Little, 1989: 3).

In the United Kingdom the Schools Council Curriculum Project on *Place, Time and Society, 8–13* (Blyth et al., 1976) integrated geography and history through a focus on their common methodological concepts (similarities and differences, change and causation) and identified the key concepts of communication, power, values and beliefs and conflict/consensus as ways of developing children's understanding of human society. Importance was also given to the development of attitudes and values in what Blyth (1990: 23) describes as an 'enabling curriculum'. Objectives for learning included attitudes such as respect for evidence combined with a healthy scepticism and open-mindedness and empathy. Blyth defines 'empathy' as 'the cognitive and emotional capacity to identify with someone else and to understand their position as it were from the inside, without adopting or supporting their point of view' (Blyth, 1984, cited in Campbell and Little, 1989: 3). In short, this was a curriculum programme designed from the humanities perspective.

Innovative curriculum programmes such as these did not inform the National Curriculum for Geography. Instead it was based on the traditional concept of geography as uncontroversial knowledge about the world. The new approaches to geography as 'people-environment' and enquiry-based teaching and learning were associated with so-called 'progressive' methods. These were an anathema to the Conservative New Right political intentions for the National Curriculum (see Chapter 7) and so they had no place in the new educational order (Davidson and Catling, 2000: 272).

The process learning model that was informing innovation in history and geography as humanities subjects was gradually being eroded. Pressure to 'deliver' heavy programmes of subject content, the ever-declining importance given to non-core subject areas and the publication of 'ready-made' and frequently dreary curriculum plans by the Qualifications and Curriculum Authority (DfEE/QCA, 2000) all threatened to re-establish an 'inherited consensus' for geography and history. Thus, though some lively work continues, Davidson and Catling, 2000, cite many criticisms of geographical teaching and learning including those of Leat (1997) which suggest that:

> Essentially, there is too much concern with teaching and not enough with learning; reports frequently refer to weaknesses in investigative learning in history and too much emphasis on substantive aspects of geography and not enough on the intellectual development of pupils.
>
> (Leat, 1994: 143)

CONCLUSION

Yet there are grounds for optimism. Integrated 'topic' work might still be an outmoded term, but such thinking is re-emerging in the guise of transferable learning and the teaching of 'key skills'. Thinking skills across the curriculum is even recommended in the current version of the National Curriculum (DfEE/QCA, 1999: 20). Environmental concerns and issues of globalisation are also exerting powerful pressures on ideas about geography's contribution to preparing young people for adult life, and there is considerable scope for recognition of the continuing value of the humanities curriculum. If we are effectively to educate pupils for the future – and this is a stated purpose of the National Curriculum – the learning opportunities offered by the disciplines of history and geography offer us very powerful tools for seeking critically to understand ways in which humans live and relate to each other now and in the future.

A note of caution is necessary. The humanities curriculum is not about teaching young people to think *correctly* or imposing our values, no matter how strongly we may feel about things. This was the kind of thinking that informed the writing of the South African history textbook referred to earlier. As Lambert and Balderstone (2000: 372) argue in their discussion of education for sustainability, there can be a tendency to suggest that 'we know what a "more sustainable society" is – and that the mission of teachers is to guide the new generation to the same wisdom'. But the concept of sustainability is contested and it is vital to establish 'a culture of argument' in which pupils take an active part in reaching their own individual and community conclusions (see Chapter 3). This may raise tensions and bring the curriculum to the direct attention of politicians and others who wish to subdue anti-capitalist movements (see Chapter 5). There may be pressure to confine education for sustainable development to 'safe' issues such as recycling. But the words of Douglas Barnes nearly 30 years ago are even more relevant to the rapidly changing and complex world of the twenty-first century: 'We educate children in order to change their behaviour by changing their view of the world … not so they will carry out our purposes, but so they can formulate their own purposes and estimate their value' (Campbell and Little, 1989: 2).

QUESTIONS FOR DISCUSSION

- What historical or geographical content should be specified in the National Curriculum? Why is this significant to you?
- Who should decide what the humanities curriculum should be?
- To what extent should the school curriculum be informed by issues such as equality and sustainability?

REFERENCES

Arthur, J. and Phillips, R. (2000) *Issues in History Teaching*, London: RoutledgeFalmer.

Bale, J. (1987) *Geography in the Primary School*, London: Routledge and Kegan Paul.

Beddis, R. (1995) 'Frontispiece', in D. Kimber, N. Clough, M. Forrest, P. Harnett, I. Menter and E. Newman (eds) *Humanities in Primary Education*, London: David Fulton.

Blyth, A. (1990) *Making the Grade in Primary Humanities*, Buckingham: Open University.

Blyth, A. *et al.* (1976) *Place, Time and Society 8–13: Curriculum Planning in History, Geography and Social Science*, Bristol: Collins/ESL, Bristol for the Schools' Council.

Campbell, J. and Little, V.J. (1989) *Humanities in the Primary School*, Lewes: Falmer Press.

Davidson, G. and Catling, S. (2000) 'Towards the question-led curriculum', in C. Fisher and T. Binns (eds) *Issues in Geography Teaching*, London: RoutledgeFalmer.

DES (1985) *History in the Primary and Secondary Years: An HMI view*, London: HMSO.

DES (1991) *History in the National Curriculum: Non-statutory Guidance*, London: HMSO.

DfEE/QCA (1998) *Scheme of Work for History*, London: DfEE.

DfEE/QCA (1999) *The National Curriculum: Handbook for Primary Teachers*, London: DfEE.

DfEE/QCA (2000) *Scheme of Work for Geography*, London: DfEE.

Fisher, C and Binns, T. (2000) *Issues in Geography Teaching*, London: RoutledgeFalmer.

Lambert, D. and Balderstone, D. (2000) *Learning to Teach Geography in the Secondary School*, London: RoutledgeFalmer.

Leat, D. (1997) 'Cognitive acceleration in geography education', in D. Tilbury and M. Williams (eds) *Teaching and Learning in Geography*, London: Routledge.

Johnson, R.J. (1996) 'A place in geography', in E. Rawlings and R. Daugherty (eds) *Geography into the Twenty-first Century*, London: John Wiley and Sons.

Slater, J. (2000) 'The politics of history teaching', in J. Arthur and R. Phillips (eds) *Issues in History Teaching*, London: RoutledgeFalmer.

Sylvester, D. (1994) 'Change and Continuity in history teaching 1900–1993', in H. Bourdillon (ed.) *Teaching History*, London: Routledge.

Wray, D. and Lewis, M. (1997) *Extending Literacy*, London: Routledge.

RECOMMENDED READING

Arthur, J. and Phillips, R. (2000) *Issues in History Teaching*, London: RoutledgeFalmer.

Index